The Rose &
The Sword

How to Balance Your Feminine
and Masculine Energies

Judith Bach, Ph.D.
&
Nanette Hucknall

For information, contact:

MSI Press
1760-F Airline Highway, 203
Hollister, CA 95023
Orders@MSIPress.com
Telephone/Fax: 831-886-2486

Library of Congress Control Number 2013949832

ISBN 978-1-933455-36-5

Cover design by Carl Leaver

To Helena Roerich who inspired this book
and is an example of someone who has achieved
the balance of feminine and masculine energies

Contents

Judith Bach, Ph.D. & Nanette Hucknall

Acknowledgements

Our thanks go to:

- First and most important, Betty Leaver, the managing editor, who was most helpful at all times and a very nice person to work with;

- To our copy editor, Mary Ann Raemisch, who not only did an excellent job but also had a very tight deadline to meet;

- To Olga Denisko, who edited the material as it was developed and gave us insightful suggestions around some of the content;

- To Dr. Maureen Sinclair whose editing of the psychological content was most helpful;

- To Kristian Williams, our contract consultant;

- To Kathy Crowe, a great computer lady, who always solved our computer glitches;

- And to Carl Leaver for designing the beautiful cover.

Last, we want to acknowledge the people who attended our workshops and kept asking us to write a book on the subject. Their encouragement made this happen.

Judith Bach, Ph.D. & Nanette Hucknall

Introduction

The popular ideal of finding one's "soul mate" in a partner stems from the relationship between the two basic energies that exist, beyond gender and sexual identity, in each of us. We all possess a mix of these energies. When the inner feminine energy is weak and the inner masculine energy is dominant, a person loses his or her inner direction, for feminine energy is like a guiding system; without its guidance, actions can lead to unchecked aggression. When the inner masculine energy is undeveloped and the inner feminine energy is strong, swirls of inspired thought dissolve like mist, ungrounded in the action needed for manifestation. When these two energies are equally developed, the individual is richly endowed with inspiration and intuition (the feminine) as well as the ability to express these riches in the world (the masculine).

In *The Rose and the Sword: How to Balance Your Feminine and Masculine Energies*, we invite our readers to enter a realm of both contemporary and fantasy tales that will stimulate both their minds and their emotions. Each tale addresses different aspects of the feminine and masculine energies. Four archetypal characters will appear throughout the book: Sophia and William represent the positive feminine and masculine energies; Lillith and Ruel represent the negative feminine and masculine energies. Our heroines and heroes will face bright visions of dazzling beauty and dark views of the abyss while discovering other worlds that overlay the mundane.

There is a psychological commentary at the end of each story, which provides readers with a deeper understanding of the chapter's subject, and an exercise, inviting readers, at their discretion, to begin the process of integrating the energies highlighted in the chapter into their own lives.

Judith Bach, Ph.D. & Nanette Hucknall

Part One: The Inner Feminine

Judith Bach, Ph.D. & Nanette Hucknall

.

1
Tend the Light

One of the positive qualities of the feminine energy is beauty—beauty in all its forms. The experience of beauty opens one's heart, and also changes relationships.

People often think of beauty in a superficial way and fail to appreciate its impact on their lives. The sheer number of people who frequent art museums is always striking: although some may be drawn to one particular artist, or are knowledgeable about art in an intellectual sense, it is essentially the beauty that draws them in; beauty is the magnet.

A similar experience can occur through all arts: listening to a concert, watching a dance, absorbing a great piece of writing—all forms of artistic beauty can touch our hearts, as can nature. Why are we so drawn to beautiful sunsets and sunrises? When nature paints glorious images on the canvas of the sky, are we not reborn in some way?

The following tale illustrates the transformative power of beauty:

Robert sat at his desk with the bile of anger rising in him. He fantasized about charging into his boss's office in the executive wing, slamming his resignation down on the desk and yelling, "I quit!" at that bland, expressionless face. Ah, that would get a rise out of him, wouldn't it?

He sighed, and stared down at the shoppers going in and out of the store. Viewed from the top floor they looked like little robots dodging toy cars in the street. It was drizzling. Spring was refusing to come this year; maybe he'd feel better when it warmed up. He shivered, and tried to shake off his bleak mood.

Lately, he always felt either angry or listless. At least when he was angry he had some energy. Every morning the corridor leading to his corner office seemed to stretch endlessly into a gray void. He recalled earlier days, bouncing down that corridor full of life and enthusiasm.

Robert was a manager at Sykes Department Store. He'd started working there at the age of twenty-four. How ambitious he'd been back then, hoping eventually to take over a whole floor, or, who knows, even become a vice-president! He was a good salesman and had achieved his present position fairly quickly, but then everything stopped. He was aware of the "glass ceiling" in the corporate world, which keeps women from being promoted to top positions, and he realized he'd bumped into his own. For the last ten years he had felt stalled in his life.

Oh, well, he comforted himself yet again. At least if I stay long enough I'll have a pension and there will be enough money for the family to live comfortably. The store was very solid and offered great stock bonuses. When he retired he and Arlene would be well off enough to travel as much as they wanted. He grinned as he heard his grandson Johnny's voice chant out, "Bo-ring!" It was the boy's current refrain about the state of his adolescent world. He hoped Johnny would never end up like him. Now there's a depressing thought!

Robert managed the household goods department. In the early days, all department managers reported directly to the president, but since the store had grown, with branches all over the country, a layer of vice-presidents was created, and all managers now reported to them. So, although he'd started as a sales clerk and worked his way up to manager, he now felt he was moving down in the hierarchy. He hardly saw the president on a day-to-day basis anymore. His job had become lackluster. What made things worse, he thought, pounding his fist tiredly on his desk, was that whenever a vacancy for vice-president came up, everyone around him was promoted, not him. It seemed as if a stream of younger and less experienced people was passing him by. Let's face it. I'm thoroughly stuck! It wasn't that he hadn't said anything. He'd asked the big boss about it several times, but he always got the same answer: a big wink, a smile, a pat on the back, and a "Your department is doing so well that we can't afford to take a chance on someone else!"

At first he was flattered, but then he wondered what was really going on. Some years back he even went on a job search. His resume was excellent, but no company could pay him what he was making at Sykes with the raises and bonuses that had built up over the years.

He began to think about his young assistant, Ruel. Ambitious, energetic and, let's face it, pushy. He knew the younger man was after his job. He sighed wearily. Well, that was me, too. I used to have that kind of energy. All I thought about was getting ahead, and look at me now! I'm getting nowhere. For all I know, he'll end up with my job, and I'll be out on the street.

He plunged into his work, checking inventory, meeting with the sales staff, his usual routine. By 11 o'clock he was already thinking about lunch and watching the infuriatingly slow minutes crawl by. He recalled how he used to feel at school watching the clock. It felt the same way. Has nothing changed? Is this what life is all about? For the first time he understood why people killed themselves. Not that I would ever do that. He believed there must be something he could do to make life more interesting, more challenging! I can do this job with my eyes closed, he thought dismally.

At noon, he heaved a sigh and arranged his sandwich and newspaper on his desk. The street below was packed with cars that were barely moving. It was much too rainy to eat in the park today. Sometimes a colleague would join him down there, and they would talk about everything except work. That was a rule they'd set up many years ago, to have the freedom of the hour to relax.

Today, he read the paper with little energy. After a few minutes he put it down. Josie needs talking to. What a bother. She gets defensive every time I try to tell her something. Why can't Arlene do it for a change?

Josie was their late-life surprise. The other children were all married, but she was only sixteen, and a handful, wanting her own way and not listening to sensible advice. He sighed. I guess I should be happy. At least she's not on drugs.

As he was munching his sandwich there was a knock on the door. Before he could respond, his assistant, Ruel, rushed in, shouting, "Come on, hurry! We just caught someone shoplifting."

Not again, he thought, annoyed at the intrusion and Ruel's attitude of self-importance. Good-looking and full of himself too. If he didn't watch out, he'd walk in one day and find Ruel at his desk. He stood up wearily to deal with the thief. His department had been hit more than usual recently after putting in some expensive knickknack items and toiletries. Kids, it's always kids! He followed the younger man to the security office, where the guard was hovering over a well-dressed elderly woman who was sitting very upright in her chair.

"What's going on?" Robert asked the guard. He then turned to Ruel and said, "Alright, you can go. I'll take care of this."

The younger man frowned and started to protest but then left reluctantly.

"Caught her red-handed putting this in her purse." The guard held up a 10-inch tall statue of a woman reclining on a bed made out of a shell.

Robert sat down opposite the woman. She was wearing an expensive-looking grey silk suit and a pearl necklace that gave her a final touch of elegance. Her white hair was pulled back into a French knot, and she was holding a large black shopping bag tightly in her hands. She looked very poised and calm. Only the twitching of her hands on the clasp of her bag betrayed her anxiety.

"Did you call the police?" he asked the guard.

"Right away. They'll be here shortly."

Tears slipped down the woman's cheeks from her glistening blue eyes. She looked downward, as if resigned to the outcome.

As he pulled a chair to sit opposite her, he dismissed the guard. "Why did you do it? You don't have the appearance of a shoplifter." As he spoke, he was thinking that this was just another case of kleptomania. She looked so pathetic that he wanted to pat her on the head. He stifled the impulse and repeated his question.

"I had to have that statue." Her voice was soft and low. "I know it was wrong to do, but I needed that statue."

She then looked up at him. Her gaze was strong and unwavering. "I have never done this before. Believe me!"

How many times had he heard that?

"There's always a first time for stealing," Robert said. He picked up a pad from the desk and started writing up the incident report required by the store.

Once the particulars were addressed, he turned to her and said, "Who you are doesn't matter to me. What you just did, does. I need a statement from you for my report."

"Who I am does matter to me, and certainly needs to be part of your report!" She glared sternly at him. "I did not steal this statue. It belongs to me. My name is Roselyn Hastings."

She paused, as if waiting for him to acknowledge her. When he didn't, she continued, "I'm certain you have heard of the Hastings family. I have owned this statue since I was eight. It was stolen from me five years ago. A new handyman came into my house to do some repairs, and I found it was missing, along with some other pieces, soon afterward. It is a very valuable piece. Obviously you were not aware of its true value, as the marked price was very low."

"But, why didn't you tell the store, or just buy it?" Robert interrupted.

"I know I should have, but I was terrified that something would happen and I wouldn't get it back if I told the store; and frankly, I couldn't afford to buy it even at this low price. Also, perhaps I wouldn't have been believed if I told the truth. My reaction when I saw it was to just take it."

Robert picked up the statue, which had been placed on the table. Looking at it closely, he saw that it was made of bronze and was exquisitely crafted: smooth in some areas, textured in others. The shell cupped the woman's body as if she had been sleeping in its depth and was now being born anew. He recalled having bought it in an assortment of less valuable pieces. He hadn't examined it carefully but had just assumed it was of the same quality as the others.

"Well, what you did was wrong, but under the circumstances, we won't press charges. But, we do need proof from you that you owned this piece and that it was stolen."

"I have proof. A police report was filed at the time; and since this piece is worth a half million dollars, I assure you it was well described."

"A half million dollars?" Robert was shocked.

"It's an original Rodin." She smiled for the first time, and Robert saw the beauty of her face.

"A Rodin!" Robert looked at the piece again and realized that it could indeed be a Rodin.

"I bought it at an auction with a lot of inexpensive things. It never dawned on me that it could be that valuable. It must have gone through the hands of quite a few people who never questioned it either."

She continued, "You can imagine how surprised I was to see it sitting here in the store. I thought it must be a copy of mine, but when I examined it, I saw a mark in the bronze that has always been there, and I knew it had to be mine."

At that moment, the police arrived. When everything was explained, the police said they would hold on to the statue until they received verification that it belonged to Roselyn. Robert saw fear in her eyes as they reached for the statue.

"No," he said. "This is still the property of the store, until it's proven otherwise. I'll take care of it personally and keep it safely locked up." Robert smiled at Roselyn. "It shouldn't take long to verify that it belongs to you. I promise to take good care of it." She thanked him with a grateful smile.

When Robert returned to his office, he put the statue on his desk. Just for now. I'll put it in the store vault later.

But he couldn't get back to work. In spite of the pile of inventory he needed to go through, he found himself just gazing at the statue. He had never been big on art, particularly sculptures, but this piece was different. The woman's body was full and voluptuous, her curves accentuated by the contour of the shell. Robert was mesmerized. He even picked the statue up a few times and turned it in the sunlight that was streaming through the window so he could see all the details. The piece was so alive that at any moment he expected the woman to reach out to him for help stepping out of the shell.

A strange feeling crept into his heart, a kind of warmth. What was it? He felt happy. Maybe that was it, but it was more than that. It was not happy like 'fun happy'; it was a happiness that filled his whole body, as if his heart was simply content with life. How could that be? He looked around his boring office, at the work that he hated piled up on the table, but now everything felt exciting and challenging. Nothing would be boring again, not with the statue there. She made life beautiful. That's it! She's the cause of my euphoria.

Then he began working. In less than two hours he went through the tedious task of checking the inventory, noting what he needed to reorder, and recording the income received and spent by the store; his heart was happy the entire time.

The phone rang. It was his wife, complaining, yet again, about Josie. At least every other day he would receive such a call, and he would half listen, and say, "yes, yes," not bothering to comment to any real extent as it was usually the same complaints. This time, however, he listened fully, and instead of agreeing, he said, "How do you feel when she doesn't listen to your advice?"

The silence was long. "What do you mean, how do I feel?"

"Just what I said. When she acts up around you, how does that make you feel?"

"I guess I feel frustrated."

"Anything else?"

"Maybe scared that she won't turn out okay?"

"So it sounds like you worry about her."

"Of course I worry."

"You know, Arlene, worrying isn't going to help her. Maybe it would be better just to love her and believe in her."

When Robert hung up the phone, he sat in silence. The words had come out of his mouth from nowhere. What was happening to him?

Again he looked at the statue, and he knew that it was changing him, making him softer. Like the curves that flowed from the shell to the figure, everything he did now flowed with a gentle movement. It was feminine, but not in a way that he would normally attribute to femininity; it was a more internal way of being. He still felt masculine, but even his masculine energy was now softer and not as demanding.

I can't let this happen to me. Robert experienced a shot of fear. He didn't want to become feminine. That's the last thing he wanted.

Just then, Ruel showed up. Robert felt embarrassed about the fact that the statue was still sitting on his desk. Ruel looked like he was smirking—or was it his imagination? Suddenly uncomfortable that he had spent so much time gazing at the voluptuous figure, and wondering what Ruel was thinking, Robert abruptly told him to find a box for the piece. When the younger man returned with the box, Robert sent him on his way.

Before placing the statue in the box, Robert sat and gazed at it one last time. His earlier embarrassment vanished as the outlines of the statue seemed to pulsate and an essence of some kind radiated from it and touched his heart with a gentle joy. No, he thought, no young idiot who doesn't understand anything is going to get to me. At that moment he decided he was going to learn more about art. It would be a great thing to share with Arlene, and Josie too.

As he placed the statue inside the box, he had difficulty closing the lid. It wasn't because of the fit – there was plenty of room. It was his hands. They seemed to have a life of their own, and they were reluctant to close him off from the figure that had brought him so much happiness.

He finally carefully sealed the box, wrote his name on it and took it to Security to be placed in the vault. Returning to his office, he sat at his desk and sighed. Everything was back to normal again.

That evening things were quiet at home. Even Josie and Arlene were calm. There were no fights. He was still feeling serene, but he was certain the effect of the statue would wear off and he would soon be his old self again.

The next day at work, Robert had a staff meeting with the buyers. It was a weekly meeting, during which he routinely discussed what new goods needed to be acquired and then gave instructions to be carried out. Even though he had several buyers working for him, Robert still insisted on doing most of the work himself. The result was that the buyers had very little input; they simply followed his directions. The buyers often left his department because of this, but Robert didn't care. Selecting new goods was his favorite part of the job, and his only creative outlet.

Today, the meeting was droning along as usual, until he found himself saying to his oldest buyer, "Pauline, I need you to determine the new line. There's some beautiful bed linen coming out that I'd like you to look at. I'm going to leave the decision up to you."

Robert then gave similar instructions to the other two buyers, who glanced at each other, excited and utterly flabbergasted. There was a very different energy in the room, a quality of lightness that seemed to replace the tired, humdrum feeling that usually permeated these meetings.

When they left, Robert again felt very happy, almost joyful. He looked at his desk, expecting to see the statue sitting there, but no, there was only the usual picture of his wife and kids.

After several days, he was still acting in this new, strange way. By now everyone had noticed. His wife and daughter were getting along so well that home was a loving place for the first time in years. He no longer had to work such long hours in order to finish everything because he delegated work to the staff, and they all seemed much happier too. His friends asked if everything was all right: Was he on some kind of medication?

One day several months later, Robert's boss, Frank, called him into his office and informed him that the Executive Board members were very pleased with his new policies, and they had decided to give him the new vice-president position.

When Robert returned to his office and pondered these recent events, he suddenly recalled the statue. It was the statue that had caused his transformation! Yes, that must be it! Everything had changed since then. He didn't understand how it had happened. Now he wondered why he hadn't ever received a notice to return the statue to the woman. Immediately, he phoned the police and inquired about the event.

After a long moment, the desk officer reported, "I'm looking at the records of the dispatch unit for that day. There's no record of your store calling us and no report was filed. Are you sure you have the right day?"

"Of course," he replied. "I made out the report myself, and I am holding the statue for verification."

"Let me do a search on the Roselyn Hastings robbery and get back to you."

Later that day the policeman called. "Mr. Burns? This is Adam Ferguson, the policeman you spoke to earlier."

"Yes? What have you found out?"

"We've investigated the supposed robbery of five years ago. We even went as far back as ten years." Adam paused. "We found no record of any robbery. So, I called the Hastings home and was told by the maid that there was a Roselyn Hastings, but she's been dead for five years."

"But, that's impossible. I saw her! Several people saw her."

"Well, I asked the maid to describe her, and it fits the description you gave me earlier today."

"That's not possible!" Robert was speechless.

"I also asked about the statue," Adam continued, "and the maid said that yes, there was a Rodin statue that belonged to Roselyn, and it now belongs to her son, Robert."

After he hung up, Robert slumped down in his chair. His stomach was churning and his head spinning. He took some time to calm down, and then he stood up, headed for the Security office and asked the guard for the box. When the guard handed it over, Robert realized it was much too light. Upon returning to his office, he opened the box with shaking hands. It was empty.

Commentary

In this story, Robert's heart is awakened through the experience of beauty. Just as the statue affected Robert, we are affected and changed when we relate to the work of an artist who has conveyed different realms of beauty through canvas, clay or any other medium. When we leave a gallery or a museum where such beauty exists, we leave with a more open heart and uplifted spirit.

Robert's experience brings him a new sense of understanding as the exquisite statue awakens his inner feminine energy. One of the qualities deepened by the feminine is the ability to relate to others; Robert therefore finds himself communicating with his staff and his family with greater ease and understanding. He no longer needs to control them—an aspect of the negative masculine energy. His young assistant, Ruel, who carries echoes of a younger Robert, embodies other aspects of the negative masculine: ambition and single-mindedness, without a shred of understanding or compassion.

As Robert grows to accept the qualities of the feminine, he is able to approach his job with renewed vitality, creativity and interest, and he finds a deepening sense of peace and joy in his life. His journey provides a map for readers to use on their own inner quests.

Neither the masculine nor the feminine can stand alone. If we are predominately one or the other, then we are literally living half a life: either an inner one that we cannot express in the world, or an outer one, like Robert's, that is lacking in inspiration and compassion. It is only when we strive to achieve balance that we can fully enjoy the richness of life that is our birthright.

The following exercise invites you to experience the effects of beauty:

Find something that you feel is really beautiful. It can be a painting, a flower, a piece of music, et cetera.

Find a place to sit comfortably and just be with what you have chosen. Try to see or hear it as much as you can. For example, if it is a painting, look closely at the colors and see how they blend together. If it's a piece of music, listen to it several times, exploring the nuances of its tones. Let yourself absorb the beauty as deeply as you can.

When you are ready, imagine bringing the experience into your heart, and feeling it. Breathe it in, and feel its energy. Keep doing this for a few moments, and then close your eyes and continue feeling and experiencing the beauty within your whole being.

As you open your eyes and come back to the room you're in, take time to notice the effects this experience had on you.

Judith Bach, Ph.D. & Nanette Hucknall

2
A Walk in the Shadows

Life invariably offers us choices that either bring us rewards, such as love and joy, or take us down paths to self-destruction. This freedom to choose is called free will. In the following tale, Emily, the heroine, is caught in the middle of an archetypal battle for her soul between the positive masculine and feminine energies (Will and Sophia) and the negative masculine and feminine energies (Ruel and Lillith).

Her story is a metaphor for the struggle that we all face on our journey through life:

Emily glimpsed a shadow off to the left of the park bench she was sitting on. Cold fear shot through her body. Her heart thudding, she sat up straight. Whatever it was had vanished, or maybe it had been nothing, just a stray dog or something. She thought, I'd better get home before I really lose it!

She stood up. Again, she glimpsed something moving out of the corner of her eye. There was a man lurking in the shadows. As she began to move, he suddenly appeared in front of her. She moaned, "Oh, no!"

He put up his hand. "Whoa, whoa, sorry! I didn't mean to frighten you. I'm just here to get a bus." He pointed to the bus sign.

"Oh, my god," said Emily, gasping. "I forgot this is a bus stop. You really scared me."

"Come back and sit down. You look pale."

As they walked back to the bench, Emily was hot with embarrassment. "I'm the one who should apologize. I guess I'm just jumpy."

"Mind if I sit?" he asked.

"Oh, no. Please." She moved over to the edge of the bench. "Here, there's plenty of room."

"Now, just take a couple of deep breaths," he said, grinning at her. "I promise, I don't bite."

"Wow," she smiled. "You look pretty normal."

Well, better than normal, she thought. He was really good looking in a tough, masculine way, with slick black hair and black eyes. And what a build! Hard to say how old he was.

"So, what bus are you taking?" he asked.

"Oh, I'm walking. I live near here. It's so nice out, I decided to sit in the moonlight for a while."

"My name's Ruel. What's yours?"

"Emily," she replied. She was surprised to discover that she was attracted to him. It was something about his manner: a kind of macho presence. She'd always been attracted to this kind of man, but she hadn't met anyone she even remotely liked since her divorce. What with work and taking care of the boys, who had time to even think about that?

"What kind of a name is Ruel?" She asked. "It's interesting." It felt good sitting in the moonlight with an attractive man.

"Who knows?" he laughed. "My mother came up with it—something original."

"I like it. It's nice," said Emily.

He grinned at her again.

Suddenly, the bus was in view. She was surprised at her disappointment. Lord, I've only just met him! He could be an axe murderer for all I know. Or worse yet, married!

He stood up, looking very tall in the moonlight. As the bus pulled up, brakes squealing, he smiled and handed her a card. "I'd like to have coffee with you sometime. My number's there if you want to call me."

"Oh," she said, pleased. "Maybe I'll do that!"

As he entered the bus, he turned toward her and fixed his eyes on hers. "Bye, Emily," he said as the doors closed.

She watched the bus wheeze away, then she opened her purse, pulled out a mirror and studied her face, illuminated by the full moon. Not too bad, she thought as she smoothed back stray strands of her long hair. It's a good face. Not pretty, but interesting because of my blue eyes and almost black hair. With some eye shadow and lipstick I could pass for ... well, late twenties. Lord, I'm still young, just thirty-five. I've got to get out more! I'd better get some sleep. Time to go home.

The apartment was dark and still. It always felt so empty when the kids were away. Later, lying in bed, she smiled as she went over her meeting with Ruel. Who knows? He seemed to like her. Maybe I'll call him, she thought. But who has time for a social life? She argued with herself, her mood darkening. Between the kids and work, I have no life. If I could only get a better job! But I'd have to go back to school, and what would I do, anyway? God, it never ends. I feel so trapped!

Her life felt like a patchwork quilt—things just happened to her; it was as if she didn't have a hand in anything that took place. Actually, she liked it that way; it seemed more adventuresome. She half admired women who had goals and worked toward them, but she never wanted that for herself. That lifestyle seemed so out of reach, Emily couldn't even imagine it. Actually, she thought it amazing that she had managed to get through two years of college. She had had to quit because of marriage, children and the need to work. With that kind of track record, I'll be eighty before I have a job I like. She sighed, feeling a little depressed.

Recently she'd found work as an office manager at the Jazz Café—a fancy title for a menial job: taking reservations, paying bills, and handling food and liquor orders that came in during the day. The pay was low, but it helped. Her big problem with the job was being confined to a desk and doing detail work, which she never was good at.

Emily finally fell asleep and began to dream about a beautiful woman wearing a long white gossamer dress that shimmered with iridescent colors. Her shining blond hair fell down her back, almost to the floor, like a golden fur cloak. She had green eyes, a petite nose and small, full lips colored a rosy pink. The woman smiled at her and said, "Hello, Emily."

The vision was so real that it woke her. To her shock, when she opened her eyes the woman was still there, standing by her bed! Emily sat up and gasped, "Who are you? What are you doing here?"

"Shh, don't be afraid." The woman's voice was low, almost cooing.

"But I'm dreaming, right?"

"Yes and no."

"What do you mean?" I'm dreaming. I'm dreaming, she told herself, panic flooding her body as she fought to understand what was happening.

"Well, that's true, you are!" the woman said. "The boundary between worlds is very thin. It really doesn't matter, does it? You can just believe it's a dream."

"Can you read my mind?"

"Yes, I can, and that's why I came. I'm here because you need me."

"What are you talking about? I don't even know you."

The woman sat on the edge of the bed. Oddly, the mattress didn't sink; the woman was weightless. Emily felt a sudden chill and pulled the blanket tighter around herself.

"My name is Lillith, Emily. Why don't you think of me as your guardian angel? I heard your thoughts, and I'm here to protect and help you."

"Really?" Emily asked, suddenly feeling small. She had an uneasy feeling that something unclean lurked at the edge of her awareness. Before she could fully register this impression, Lillith continued, "I've been with you for years. I know everything about you, and I've been watching over you. Now I'm here to help you."

Emily's eyes filled with tears. Whoa, she thought to herself. What's going on? Why am I crying? "Really? You really mean it? I feel so stuck! Can you help me get out of this rut I'm in?" she exclaimed in a childish voice as she struggled to control herself. The tears streamed down her face.

"Shhh! It's all right. You can trust me. Now you need your sleep. Lie down and we'll talk about your future another time. Everything will be just fine."

At the sound of Lillith's hypnotic voice, Emily lay back and closed her eyes. The last thing she remembered as she fell asleep was the sensation of cool hands flowing over her body.

The next day was a real killer. Emily had to work late because it was the weekend and a new band was coming in. Reservations were flooding in all day. When she left at 9:30, she was exhausted.

As she walked past the park the atmosphere felt both inviting and disquieting. The night was misty, and the moon was just starting to rise. Once more, she sat on the bench. She felt like a teenager as she realized that she had hoped Ruel would show up again. Remembering his handsome face and muscular body, she closed her eyes and began to fantasize that she was naked in bed with him and he was kissing her passionately.

At that moment, she felt a strong, almost electric presence near her. Opening her eyes, she was shaken to see someone standing a few feet away from her, staring at her. The creature had wolf-like features. Its large canine head was covered with thick brown fur. The eyes were deep pools of black liquid that peered over a long snout, which framed thick, red-painted lips. The body was curvaceous, with large breasts, slim hips and long elegant legs. It–or she–wore tight leotard pants, high boots and a long-sleeved turtleneck, all in black. Emily stood up and began to edge backwards, away from this freaky creature.

"So, you finally called me." The creature smiled cunningly, her sharp white teeth glistened in the moonlight. A sudden wind flattened her fur against her head.

"What?" Emily said, startled. "What are you talking about? I didn't call you."

"Yes, you did, when you were fantasizing about Ruel." Her eyes glowed as she growled, "I love Ruel."

"You do?" Emily felt embarrassed, confused, and even a little jealous.

"Well, you're finally listening to me."

"What do you mean I'm listening to you? Who are you, anyway?"

"Who do I look like?" she asked. "Just call me the Woman of the Wolves."

As Emily stared at her, the woman's strong feral emanations sickened and almost overwhelmed her. At the same time, scenes of herself having sex with all kinds of men began to flash in front of her eyes. She felt on fire. Rage exploded within her, and she thought, why didn't Steve ever make me feel like this?

"Because he was wrong for you, but now you can have it all with anybody you want!"

Emily's head was spinning. Now she's reading my thoughts! Or did I say it out loud? I'm going nuts!

At that moment, the Wolf Woman threw her head back, howled in delight, and vanished into the shadows. Another howl echoed in the distance and the moon seemed to become brighter.

What's happening to me? I've got to get out of here. Emily turned to hurry home.

Suddenly, Lillith appeared under the streetlight in a silvery gown, as if she had sprung from the moon. Emily again felt an edge of disquiet, like a wrongly tilted wall. She shook her head slightly, dismissed her uneasiness and greeted Lillith like an old friend.

"Thank God you're here." Emily sighed in relief. Then she noticed that the spring-green grass Lillith was standing on was beginning to wither and turn yellow under her feet. Emily pointed and said, "What's happening?"

"Nothing can withstand my powerful energy," Lillith replied sharply. "Watch!" She suddenly disappeared, and in her place was the Wolf Woman. Before Emily could utter a sound, Lillith was back, smiling prettily at her.

Emily gasped, "What's happening?"

"Don't be afraid, my dear. That was just to show you my magic!" She leaned close to Emily and said in a low voice, "I can teach you special tricks that will bring you what you want. And," she whispered, "I could show you things: how to get Ruel, and how to make wonderful things happen in your life."

Suddenly, the moon disappeared behind swirling black clouds, and the air became cold. Shivering, with her stomach in knots, Emily backed away from Lillith.

"I don't understand all this. What's happening to me?" Lillith then reached out to her, and Emily screamed. "Help! Help!"

At that moment, a whirling, cone-like shape appeared and transformed into a knight that galloped toward them on a great white horse. He came to a halt next to Emily, the horse snorting and stamping. Lillith, her face twisted in fury, backed away.

The knight dismounted and removed his helmet, revealing strong, craggy features and cobalt blue eyes. His blond hair fell onto broad shoulders. His silver armor was embossed with symbols and decorative rosettes. A spiraling snake holding an egg in its mouth adorned the chest, and surrounding the snake were rays of sunlight. The armor appeared to glow from an inner source of light.

The knight waved his hand and his horse trotted off into the park and began to munch on the grass. Turning to Lillith, the knight declared, "Get back to your hole in the ground and leave this woman alone!"

Lillith backed off, almost hissing.

"Who are you? What's going on?" Emily cried.

"My name is Will," he said, turning to Emily. "You don't want to get involved with this woman. Let me take you home. Come, ride with me. You'll be safe."

Lillith, her eyes narrowed into green slits, moved slowly towards Emily. "Have you forgotten me? Remember what I told you. I will help you in ways that nobody else can. I can give you power over others. You can have whatever you want—money, security, a comfortable life. You won't have to work so hard." She stared intently at Emily.

"How ... how can do you that? How do I know I can believe you?"

"Emily," she whispered harshly, "I want you to succeed. We women must stick together! We'll show them. Why should you trust a man? What have men done for you?"

Emily felt her energy drain out of her as if someone had pulled a plug. "Oh, I'm so tired. I feel like I could sleep forever. Maybe you're right. Life's too hard."

She slumped down on the bench, wailing, "I need money. I want security. I'm tired of working so hard."

Like a defiant child, she challenged Will, "Can you do that for me? Can you?"

"Answer her!" Lillith demanded. "You heard what she wants. Can you give her those things?" Her lips curled in a triumphant smile that failed to reach her cold eyes.

Quietly, Will said to Emily, "Don't listen to her. I can give you the ability to make the most of your life, the spirit of the best person you can be, and the joy of fulfilling your real purpose in life."

Paralyzed with fear and indecision, Emily felt as if a line had been drawn down the center of her body and she had to make a choice that she didn't understand.

Suddenly, Lillith became the Wolf Woman again. She undulated her thin body from side to side. "Just see what I can give you! Remember how alive you felt before? The excitement? The energy? I can give you the power of your rage. Nothing can stand in the way of that!" She moved closer to Emily and said, "Feel it? Can you feel it?"

As a wave of hot red rage exploded in Emily's solar plexus, she thought, where did this come from? I feel I can conquer the world!

Lillith, very close to her now, whispered in her ear, "Yes, and this is what the world needs. You can make a difference in the world with this kind of power."

A difference. A difference, she thought. Yes, that's right. I always wanted to make a difference. I feel like I could do anything, anything! There was a loud roaring in her ears. It was as if only she and Lillith existed. She saw visions of herself that flicked by so fast she couldn't hold onto them. In all of them, she was in charge, in full command, and fueled by a rage that could catapult her around the world. Her heart was pounding and her body was hot, yet her mind felt clear, almost cold.

Will raised his sword and pointed it at Lillith. A stream of golden light poured from its tip, bathing her in its rays.

"Stop it," she screamed, as she changed into a dark witch-like crone. She now had long, gray and scraggly hair that came to her waist, and the harsh features of her wrinkled face and crooked nose were the backdrop for the most evil, intense eyes Emily had ever seen.

"What happened to you?" Emily cried. "You were so beautiful."

As Will held the light steadily on the crone, she grew smaller and smaller, until she turned into a toad. Grabbing it and holding it tightly in front of him, he said, "Look at you!" He tossed the toad on the ground. "You're an insult to the toad family. Come back to your true nature," he commanded.

The toad turned back into the crone, glaring icily at the knight. He resumed shining the light from his sword on her. It was as if she were pinned in place. She croaked out to Emily, "It's a trick! His magic light makes me look evil. I'm a crone. Crones are old and wise. I only make myself beautiful because people expect me to appear that way. My wisdom is ancient, and old, and far more powerful than his. I have the ultimate power, and that's all that counts."

"Is that true?" Emily asked Will.

"Well, look at her! Is that what you really want? Power is power. It can be used for good or evil."

He then lowered his sword. Lillith's eyes were gleaming through the gloom, riveted on Emily.

"I want you to understand," he continued, "that as long as I'm with you, she can't hurt you, but it's your choice. She comes from the dark side and whispers to you. Each time you listen to her, you become more helpless."

"What do you mean?" Emily cried. "I just met her!"

"She's been with you for a very long time. Remember how she told you that?"

"Yes, she did. You're right."

"And do you remember when your friends were encouraging you to go back to school? What happened?"

Emily was silent for a moment. She recalled the previous year when she was talking to her friend, Amy, about her school plans. Amy was very encouraging and suggested that Emily join a support group for women who were starting new careers. Emily excitedly wrote down all the information. However, as soon as she hung up, she recalled, harsh, nagging thoughts had come in. She remembered how they were phrased: "You could never do that. You'd make a fool of yourself. These women are much more worldly than you, and besides, who do you think you are? The voice had kept on and on. "How can you possibly even think about going back to college? You'll fail, and then everybody will laugh at you!" Crushed by the harshness, Emily had thrown the number away and dropped any notions of going to school.

She whipped around and confronted Lillith, who was slowly moving closer. "Was that you? You said all that to me? I thought it was coming from me!"

"No," she retorted. "He's lying to you. You can't trust any man. Don't you know that by now?" Then, in a wheedling voice, she said, "Look at him. Look what he's doing now. He's no different from any other man, always needing to be in control! I want you to be powerful, don't you see? I've told you, with my help you can have anything you want. You don't have to go to school to get that. You'll have money, riches, and fame."

Torn, Emily looked from one to the other.

Lillith rushed forward and stood behind Emily, who at once felt her simmering anger turning into rage again.

"Watch out," warned the knight. "She's taking you over!"

"But I need her. I'm full of anger, years and years of anger," Emily protested.

She flashed back to a moment when Steve had been yelling at her, but now, instead of just standing there and taking it, she was screaming back at him. Her anger became so intense that it stopped him completely. He looked totally defeated.

Lillith rasped, "See what I can do for you?"

The night was growing darker, its shadows stretching into unseen dimensions. "Now do you feel my energy? You don't have to feel all that pain. Try me. Don't fight me."

"Alright. Yes!" Emily closed her eyes as Lillith entered her body.

Oh, what power! I can't believe this! I feel like I could conquer the world!

She heard Will speak, his voice echoing as if down a long tunnel. "Emily, this is not good. It's the wrong kind of power. There is no love in it."

"What's wrong with it? It feels great. This is what I need. I can do anything I want!"

As she opened her eyes, she heard Lillith whisper sibilantly, "That's right. This is my gift to you."

Defiantly, Emily turned to Will, who was standing quietly and watching her. "How do I know if you're right or not? I really loved the experience with Lillith, and I don't see what's wrong with being strong. I've been so … nothing all my life. I need a change. There's so much I want! I'm just tired!"

Like a stubborn child, she felt a rebellious anger rise inside her. She declared, "Besides, men have given me nothing but heartache. She's a strong woman. I want to be like her. She's offering me a way out."

"There's another way," said Will, moving closer to her. Lillith retreated angrily as he intruded on her space.

"Calm yourself now," he said quietly to Emily.

Then, to her surprise, he handed her his sword. "Hold this, and you will know what I can offer you."

Grasping the sword, Emily was surprised at its lightness. She immediately felt her heart expand with warmth, and a surge of energy spread throughout her body. For a moment, she felt strong and courageous, but she soon succumbed to old feelings of self-doubt.

"I have never felt this way before. It's scary."

"That's because you haven't developed this energy in yourself yet."

He gestured to Lillith, raging in the shadows, and said, "All she can do is influence you and control you in negative ways. If you let go of her, I can help you open up your own inner power, which will help you create the life you want for yourself. Then you will be able to embrace your true feminine nature."

"Now," he said, taking back the sword and standing directly in front of her, "close your eyes and open your heart."

With her eyes closed, Emily felt a warmth in the center of her chest and could almost sense a ray of light coming from his heart to hers. Suddenly, an image of Steve formed in her mind. He looked sad, even desperate. His eyes seemed to carry years of suffering and exhaustion. Emily's eyes began to sting with tears, and she felt an overwhelming pity for him and for their life together.

"See?" she heard the knight murmur in a low voice. "It's not anger you need to feel. Your heart knows the truth. Now, open your eyes and see."

He pointed his sword upward and shot a beam of light into the sky. The light penetrated the mist and became a shimmering oval in which the figure of a seated woman in cobalt blue robes appeared.

The woman's strong, compassionate gaze transfixed Emily, whose pain turned to wonder.

"Who is she?" she whispered. "She's so beautiful."

"She is Sophia, the positive feminine. She is all you can learn to be—strong and loving, wise and inspired. She acts from her heart, not from her instincts like Lillith. Haven't you noticed, Emily, that Lillith has no heart? She comes in darkness and is cold. She wants power over you. Let me free you from her." Will's eyes shone.

As the image of the woman began to slowly fade, Emily was amazed at the depth of the yearning and sorrow she felt in her heart. She cried out to Will, "Why is she leaving? Why doesn't she talk to me?"

"If you choose my way, I will help you bring Sophia closer to you, but you must make a choice. Sophia is the power of the heart. Lillith is the power of the ego."

Turning into her wolfish form once again, Lillith whispered, "Don't listen to him. The feminine he is talking about is weak. Look how she disappeared. I am always with you." She rubbed up against Emily. "Forget him. I belong to you."

Repelled by Lillith in that moment, Emily moved closer to Will. She looked at him. "I'm so afraid my life will go back to what it was. How do I know Sophia even exists? What if she's an illusion? Who can I trust?"

"That's for you to decide. Only your heart knows the truth. Explore your heart, and then all you need to do is call on me. I'll be there to help you bring out your positive qualities so you can live a strong, good life."

He started to back away from her, saying, "I'll keep this creature out of the way for now so you can be with yourself, and I'll leave you alone, too." He then created a circle of light around her, and both he and Lillith disappeared into the darkness.

Emily thought back over the past few days. What do I want? What do I really want? Will is wonderful, but it feels too hard, too painful. I don't want to feel all that pain. And that woman, that wonderful, beautiful woman! Could I be like her? Could I ever? Never! She's seems so far away. I'd have to work so hard. My life is already hard enough.

Maybe I can decide later. Maybe I can do what Lillith says, go with her just long enough to get myself out of this hole and into a better life. Then I'll ask Will to help me. That's it! I can do both. I know I can!

At that moment, Lillith, in her true nature as the crone, appeared next to her. Gripping Emily's arm in her hard fingers, she croaked, "Let's go, my dear. I heard your thoughts. Yes, you made the right choice. There's always later."

My heart! Emily thought, wildly. He said listen to my heart. I forgot to do that! She then felt the wind rushing and heard Will gallop off into the night.

Commentary

In early mythology, gods and goddesses were all powerful and humans were their playthings. Humanity has evolved to the level of consciousness where, endowed with the gift of free will and psychological understanding, we are in a position to make choices, for good or evil. This is not only Emily's story; it is all of ours. It is the choice that faces us as the human race.

Ruel and Lillith represent the rulers of our so-called "lower nature." Split off from love and mired in materialism, they would send Emily whirling through a life steeped in selfishness and narcissism. Lillith plays on Emily's anger and frustration and amps them up to rage. Through Ruel, she offers Emily a sexuality separated from love and connections. The rage and the disconnected sexuality give Emily a rush of power. However, separated from the heart as it is, this power is limited and could well become destructive to Emily and others.

Ruel's masculine counterpart, Will, who was aligned with Sophia, represents the nobility of the soul-infused individual, who uses power to help others and to bring beauty and goodness into the world. If Emily so wishes, he can protect her from Lillith's self-serving ambition. He is the bridge between Emily and Sophia.

Psychologically, Will represents the positive masculine's focus and will to make things happen. If Emily were to go with him, she could make her own way in the world and become the best that she could be in whatever area she wanted to apply herself.

Emily wondered why Sophia was so distant. The archetype that Sophia represents is available to all of us, but we must discover her in our hearts, through her qualities of inspiration, intuition, love and compassion. Perhaps when Emily is a little older and wiser she will reach out to Will and Sophia and join them on their quest to spread the power gained in balancing the positive feminine and masculine energies.

Exercise:

Ask yourself the following questions:

1. Looking back on Emily's story, are there any feelings that she went through that you relate to?
   If the answer is yes, ask: What are they? If no, ask: Why not?

2. What would be your response if the events in the story happened to you?
   If your response would be the same as Emily's, ask: Why?

3. Would you have followed Will more than Emily did?
   If the answer is yes, ask: Why?

4. Did you respond positively to Sophia, the positive feminine?
   If the answer is yes, try to visualize an image of her and place that image in your heart. Really take your time to experience how that feels.

Judith Bach, Ph.D. & Nanette Hucknall

3
The Lost Child

Sloughed by an inattentive mother, Laurie, the young heroine of this tale, discovers the healing power of nature. She learns that nature is the feminine aspect of our planet. Nature gives birth to natural beauty, without which we would be living in a very barren place. Laurie represents the inner child that we each, whether man and woman, have within us and need to embrace.

The following is her story:

She sat alone on a park bench. Her name was Laurie, and she was five-and-a-half years old. Her sandy-colored hair was cut short and tousled, framing her delicate features. Her large hazel eyes stared straight ahead, oblivious to passersby. Now and then someone would pause and look at her. Even though she was small for her age, she had a very mature look on her face, a look that said, 'Leave me alone, I'm okay.' Therefore, no one stopped to inquire where her mother was. There were two women talking on the bench next to hers, so most thought she was with them, but in reality, she was very much alone.

Laurie was wearing a flowered dress, and she tightly held a small red purse. Her straw hat lay next to her on the bench, and once in a while she would pick it up, put it on, then take it off again. This was the only sign of her nervousness. After all, she was alone, but she knew she would be okay because she had done this once before. A month ago, she had left her backyard to come to the park all by herself. She wasn't missed then, so she expected she wouldn't be missed this time either.

The first time she ventured out to the park was scary, but Laurie had wanted to see the ducks and swans in the pond. Her mother never had time to take her, so she came on her own, and no one bothered her. This time, her intent was to go to the zoo, which was ten blocks east of the park. Right now, she was resting after her long walk.

Laurie thought about her home and how hard it was being there. Her parents were always busy, and now that she had a new brother, she felt even more alone. He got all the attention from both her mother and father.

She didn't mind being alone because she could do things that her parents might not approve of, like coming to the park, or digging up her neighbor's flowers and hiding them in the secret garden she'd made for herself. When she got dressed in the morning she wore whatever she wanted to wear, and her mother never said anything, even when she wore her best dress, the one she was wearing now. So, there were advantages to being left alone. Sometimes, though, she got scared, especially when there were people around who tried to talk to her. This happened frequently when she was just walking down neighborhood streets. She usually ran fast to get away.

Today, she had been very careful to walk next to an adult who was preoccupied with another person. This was why she had chosen the bench next to the women.

As she thought about this, the women got up and started walking away. Laurie jumped up and walked behind them after first making certain they were going in the direction of the zoo. She'd been there once before and remembered the general direction.

She followed the women for a long time, until they turned to leave the park. Laurie then stopped to look around, but still couldn't see the zoo. In fact, she was in a place in the park she didn't recognize at all. There were wide walks branching in different directions and very few people around. She suddenly felt a little scared when she realized there was no one on her path, just a small figure way in the distance. She kept on walking. A boy rode past on a bicycle, and she shouted at him, hoping to ask directions. He just waved and kept bicycling.

Laurie was feeling very tired again, but instead of sitting on a bench, she went and sat against a tree out of sight of the path. A sudden breeze arose and whipped around her, blowing her hair and dress in all directions. The wind kept getting stronger and stronger, becoming so intense that Laurie had to hold onto the tree to keep from blowing away.

Maybe it's a tornado, like in the Wizard of Oz, she thought, and I'm going to meet the beautiful witch of the North. For a moment the thought delighted her, as the story was a favorite of hers. Then, she became frightened as a new gust of wind hit her, causing her to squat down closer to the tree.

As the wind blew stronger, the sun hid behind some clouds and didn't come out again; the park grew dim with shadows. Laurie became very anxious. She couldn't get up and walk back because the wind was still blowing, and now rain began to fall like bullets, striking her with increasing vigor. She tried getting up on her feet, but the rain beat her back down again. Huddled there in total despair, she cried out, in a rare moment, for her mother.

A voice said to her, "You'll be all right. Just stay calm. I'm protecting you." She felt a warm blanket cover her from head to toe, but when she looked up, nobody was there. The rain was still pelting her, but now she felt only the warmth of the blanket. She sank down into it, not caring if it was real or not. She felt warm and comforted.

She must have fallen asleep, because when she opened her eyes again the rain and wind had stopped, and she was sitting on the grass in the sun. Looking around, she didn't see the tree any more, just grass everywhere, thick green grass extending down a hill, down and down into a green lake that looked like a pool of spilled green ink. She stood up in wonder and saw that she was standing on top of a green mountain surrounded by more green mountains that were so richly green that even the sky appeared green.

As she looked around, a figure appeared in front of her of a tall man dressed completely in green. The strangest thing of all was that his face, hands, hair, everything about him was green!

"Who are you? Where am I? Why is everything green?" she blurted out.

The man laughed, "You are where you should be, in a safe place, and you will stay here until it's time to go back. Everything is green to reflect growth. Look, even your clothes are green." Laurie looked down at her dress and saw he was right; her dress was now a bright green and even her purse, which she still clutched, had turned green.

"I am your host," continued the green man. "You may call me William." Then he gently took Laurie by the hand, and they started walking down the hill toward the lake.

"Where are we going?" Laurie stopped to ask.

"We are going to swim in the lake so you may experience what it is like to swim in green." They continued to walk down the hill until they arrived at the beach.

"Oh my! I can't believe it. Even the sand is green!" exclaimed Laurie.

William picked Laurie up, walked with her into the lake and gently put her down into the water.

"How strange. I don't feel wet, yet I'm standing in water up to my waist. How can that be?" Laurie asked.

"The green has taken the wetness out of the water. Try to swim in it and feel the greenness."

Laurie put her arms out and floated while moving her arms and trying to swim. As she did this, she saw that the skin on her arms and legs was turning green. The water was even covering her freckles and turning them into green spots.

"It feels wonderful on my skin," she said, giggling. "Like a bubble bath. No, much better, more like what it's like to take a bath in cream. Can I drink it?"

"No, it would make you sick. Try not to swallow any of it. Now you are one of us." William lifted her out of the water and placed her back on the beach.

She picked up the little purse that she had left on the beach, opened it and pulled out a tiny mirror so she could look at herself. "Look, everything but my hair is green. Why didn't my hair get green?"

"You must do more than bathe in the water to make your hair green. When you get older we will talk about how to do that. Now you must go back. It is getting late."

She pleaded, "Please let me stay. It's so wonderful to be with you. I like being with you. Please can't I stay here forever? I don't want to go home!" Laurie's eyes filled with tears.

William picked her up and held her close. "I will be with you forever. When you sleep at night, I will take you here to play with me in the water. When you daydream, you will see and feel me holding you. You will no longer be alone. I will guide you home."

William set Laurie back down, and she realized she was now walking in the park alone, but not really alone, as she still felt William's hand in hers, taking her down a path that led out to the street that connected to her home.

The next day it was raining outside, so Laurie went into the sunroom and pretended to look at a picture book, but instead, she closed her eyes and called for William to come be with her.

He appeared immediately, then smiled and hugged her. "See how easy it is for you to find me again?"

"I'm so happy that you are still here."

"Let's have an adventure. I want to take you to a small town where you can meet people and even make friends with some of the children."

"That's wonderful. I don't have any friends. I used to in the park's playground, but my mother is too busy to take me there, and I haven't gone on my own 'cause some of the mothers would recognize me and ask where my mother is."

Again, everything was green. They walked through a meadow with green flowers and trees whose bark was highlighted in a lemon green. Today, she saw that the green varied. There were dark green plants and trees and also light green ones. The sky was less green, more like a turquoise color.

"Why is some of the green different today?" she asked William.

"Every color has lots of shades, and because we only have one color here, green, our green has even more shades than most colors."

Laurie saw that this was true, not only were there dark greens and light greens, but there were also yellow greens and blue greens. One of the plants she saw had lavender glowing through the green, creating a halo effect around the edge. Looking down at herself, she realized that her dress had turned dark green but her arms were still the clear green color of the lake.

When she entered the small town called Greensville, Laurie cried out in delight. "What beautiful houses. They look like green gingerbread houses!"

Indeed they did. They were town houses that were attached to one another. They had various shades of green on the outside, all with the same dark green tile roofs. The windows had different decorations that resembled swirled icing. Swirls of creamy green and dots of turquoise and teal green continued the pattern, linking the windows to one another.

"What fun!" Laurie reached up to the side of the decorated door and discovered the design was made with paint, not cream.

"Here, you can have this instead." William reached into his pocket, withdrew a huge decorated lollipop and gave it to Laurie.

"Thank you," she said. Contentedly, she continued to walk down the road with him until they came to a large playground full of laughing children.

William introduced her to some of the mothers there, and they brought her over to a group of children and introduced her. The children were very polite and invited Laurie to join them in a tag game. All were wearing jeans and T-shirts with designs on them that were very similar to the clothes that kids normally wore except that they were in tones of green.

"Do you ever get sick of just wearing green colors?" Laurie asked Carol, one of her new friends.

"Oh, no, this is the only color we have ever seen, and it has so many different shades. We all love it; don't you?"

"I don't know. It's weird to have green skin. My skin is very different where I live. It's a whole different color."

"I can't imagine that. This is all we know."

They kept on playing all afternoon until William came over and told Laurie it was time to go home.

On the way back, she asked him, "How come most of the children had white hair, with no color in it?"

"Did you notice that your hair is also white when you are here?"

"No," said Laurie as she grabbed her pigtail and saw that, indeed, it was white. "How did that happen?"

"I took your normal color out as we were leaving so you would fit in more when you met the children."

"You said before that my hair will turn green when I get older. Why is that?"

"I can't tell you now, but when it happens I will tell you the reason for the delay."

When Laurie opened her eyes, she was still sitting in the sunroom and it was dark outside.

Her mother came in with her baby brother, Ruel. "What are you doing sitting here in the dark?"

"Reading."

"You will ruin your eyes. Turn the light on." She then left as suddenly as she'd come. Laurie felt a wave of sadness. She turned the light on and started to read.

Several years later, when Laurie was ten, she asked William if she could bring Ruel to the green land. Her mother had been after her to take care of Ruel and pay more attention to him, so she thought it might be nice for him to meet her friends there. William reluctantly agreed but said he didn't know if Ruel would like the place. He didn't.

"Where are you taking me? This is ugly. What ugly people!" he pouted. When William tried to take him for a swim in the green lake, he refused. Looking at Laurie's green skin, he thought she looked ugly too, and he certainly didn't want to look like her.

"But you'll love it, I promise." Laurie said.

"No I won't. I'm going to tell mother where you've taken me."

"But you promised you wouldn't tell her."

"So what? You're hurting me, that's what you're doing, so I'm going to tell her."

"Please don't. I'm not hurting you. That's a lie."

"Yes, you are," he started to cry. "Take me home."

On the way back, Laurie whispered to William, asking what she should do. "He'll tell my mother, and she won't let me come anymore."

"Don't worry. I'll make it so he forgets the whole experience," William whispered back.

After that, Laurie was very careful with Ruel. She didn't like him at all, but he still was Mom's favorite. Fortunately, as she grew older, she became much closer to her father, and he to her. Her relationship with William helped her; she and her father started to do things together, just the two of them. He took her on outings in the countryside. He loved nature as much as she did, whereas her mother preferred shopping and the city life. Her mother wanted Ruel to join them, but her father said no, he was too young and once, when they had taken him on a hike with them, he had complained the whole time.

Laurie was very popular in school. Her friendships in Greenville, and the love and happiness she felt there, radiated in her personality and gave her confidence to reach out to her peers.

When she was sixteen, she noticed that the hair of some of her friends in Greenville was beginning to turn green. She asked William if it was now time for hers to turn also.

He smiled, "Yes, sixteen is the right age. It's time to meet the Mother."

"Whose mother?"

"The Mother of us all. She is the one in charge of growth and the one that has made us all green. She is not green, though. She is blue."

"Why is she blue?"

"She comes from the heavens, which are blue."

"But why, then, are we and all of nature green?"

"When the sunlight passes through her, everything turns green. The combination of the yellow sunlight and the blue of her being makes green, and it is through her that we all grow."

"Oh, how wonderful!"

He took Laurie by the hand, and they entered a new part of the forest, one she had never seen before. There, in a clearing, sat a woman dressed in a luminous blue gown. As they approached her, Laurie saw her beautiful, transparent blue face and eyes of love. She felt a strong energy enter her being as she came closer. Laurie knew she needed to kneel down in front of her.

The Mother said, "My child, you are entering womanhood and can now absorb my energy," and she reached over and put her hands on top of Laurie's head. As Laurie felt the Mother's incredible energy, she saw the sunlight surround them and felt the light penetrate her being too.

The ceremony took only a short time, but it was a time of innate understanding; when Laurie finally stood up, she felt changed. She was no longer a girl, but was now a woman, and her hair fell over her shoulders, a luminous green.

Commentary

Laurie represents the inner child who lives within many women and men. The park, where we first find her, represents her inner world, where she can escape from her difficult home life. She has learned to create her own world. Making the best of a bad situation, she turns parental indifference into her own declaration of independence.

Her little brother, Ruel, is different. Everyone dotes on him. He is special because he is brand new and he is a boy. Her father always wanted a boy, and her mother is happy because she has given him what he wanted. Ruel is, unfortunately, destined to grow into a negative masculine narcissist.

Sadly, there are vestiges remaining of the patriarchal attitude where boy children are welcomed and where little girls are devalued. This attitude, in a heart-breaking manner, was demonstrated in China, where little girl babies were left to die in state-ordered one-child families. In Western culture, this preference is more subtly embedded in the unconscious attitudes of even so-called enlightened parents.

Laurie's experience of the "green world" represents those special times, in the midst of terror and despair, when the invisible world and the physical world merge in one's consciousness as if to tell us we are not alone. A blanket of comfort comes from her own Higher Self (the wise being within each of us), who, while she sleeps, draws her into a subtle, more spiritual level of consciousness.

Her guide, William, explains that green represents growth. His message is that to become one with the feminine, one must commit to conscious growth. We know that all plant life and trees are, essentially, green, even when adorned by other colors. The fact that everything in Laurie's world, even the mountains and the lake, are green, symbolizes the fact that the planet Earth itself is a growing, transforming being, and the feminine energy is stimulating this process. The ecological concept of "greening the planet" is about transforming the human consciousness so it understands planetary needs.

William's caution to Laurie that she must not drink the substance in the lake or she will become ill carries another message. He is telling her, yes, she must accept, honor and love her feminine nature, but it is not all she is. If she were to fully immerse herself in the lake, inside and out, she would become unbalanced and lose her equilibrium. She would be bingeing on feminine energy, leaving no room inside to grow into her positive masculine qualities. This message is further illustrated by the fact that her head does not turn green. William is telling her that, although she is too young to understand the mind, a positive masculine quality, she will develop it as she grows older.

When a woman or a man heals and embraces her/his inner child, a greater wholeness is experienced; a person's heart opens and is able to then reach out to others. Psychological approaches or good, in depth therapy can help guide people through inner child work.

Finally, at the end of the tale, we meet the one who symbolizes the divine feminine aspect of nature, the nurturing Mother of us all.

Exercise:

Close or lower your eyes, relax your body and take some deep breaths. When you feel you are in a calm place, try to picture yourself as a child about the same age as Laurie, five or six years old. Once you have the image, just be with it for a while. Notice your own feelings about and toward the child you once were, and try to sense your inner child's mood and feelings. She may be playful, or other feelings may be more prominent.

When you are ready, ask your inner child how she feels. Be aware that she may not have names for many feelings, so you may need to trust your own sense of what they are. If it seems okay to do so, name a feeling you sense; for example, if you sense sadness, you might ask, "Are you feeling sad?" Be sensitive as you continue to try to get to know her better.

You may wish to go for a walk with her, or sit on a park bench with an arm gently around her. If so, ask first if she'd like that, and if her response is affirmative, imagine that a gentle sun is shining on the two of you as you walk or sit. Also, ask her if there's anything she wants, and then, what she needs. Sense her responses if she does not have many words.

It's best not to promise what she wants and needs if you feel you can't follow through, but perhaps you can let her know that you do want to get to know her better and will do your best to visit her again.

This is a beginning step for working with your inner child.

Judith Bach, Ph.D. & Nanette Hucknall

4
The Magic Spectacles

Steven, an egocentric bachelor, lives on the surface of life. He has no under-standing of love and relationships. For him, women are mainly sex objects that he can use and discard. He lives in the negative masculine and sees none of the beauty that life and the positive feminine can offer—until he puts on a pair of mysterious spectacles, and, with Sophia's help, his life takes a dramatic turn.

Here is Steven's tale:

Nothing like coffee after a late night with Lillith. God, she's a great lay. Just wish she had a little more upstairs; downstairs is so good. He leisurely went over the de-tails of her beautiful body as he reclined in bed. The coffee tasted great! He always set the timer on the coffee pot he'd installed by his bed so that he could reach over and pour a cup before his legs came to a vertical position.

It was Saturday morning. Steven rose and walked around his apartment, cup in hand. Susie, the cat, followed him closely, patiently waiting for him to wake up enough to feed her.

Picking up the phone on the kitchen table, he listened to his messages as he fed Susie her tuna out of a can.

"Darling, it's been too long, but I'm back in town now for a week. Are you free tonight?" It was Cindy.

Steven smiled. Good, Cindy will be a refreshing change, and she'll stay the night. No 'hurry ups' to be out before Lillith's husband comes home from the night shift.

One of these days he might get caught, and he didn't need that at this stage in his life. He looked at himself in the mirror. In his twenties he'd been a match for any irate lover, but now all the booze and rich foods were making him soft around the middle.

He tried sucking in his belly while pushing out the muscles in his chest. Not bad, he said to himself. He inspected his eyes for any crow's feet, a routine he did every morning before shaving. All in all, I still have a few more years left.

Steven was a very handsome man. Women couldn't resist his blue eyes, deep in color and full of devilish laughter. He had a broad, masculine face with a square jaw and sharp nose. His curly, sandy-colored hair flopped charmingly in short ringlets around his face, adding to his mischievous quality. At thirty-eight, he still could pass for his mid-twenties, and he enjoyed dating both ends of the spectrum, ladies in their twenties and forties.

He was financially sound, having inherited a pile from his grandfather. Since he was a stockbroker, he knew how to make the money work for him.

Steven's freedom was the envy of most of his male acquaintances. The perfect bachelor playboy; it was clear he would never take on the responsibilities of a wife and family. He was much too selfish. Yet, his friends knew that if some day Steven ended up old and alone, he still would feel secure and happy.

Susie brushed against Steven's legs, and he languidly reached down to pat her glossy black coat. "Patience, sweetie. Let me get dressed, then I'll give you a thorough massage." This was a ritual he performed every morning, and even more so on Saturdays when there was extra time.

He dressed carefully, as he had a date with a new woman he'd casually met a few nights ago in a restaurant. She'd been eating alone next to his table while he was having a drink. They'd started talking, and he asked her out. It was her suggestion that they meet in the park today and have lunch together.

Steven thought about how beautiful she was. Sophia was her name: tall, slender, dark-haired, and dramatic in looks, almost sultry. And her legs! He could still see them as she rose to leave and walked toward the door, shapely and graceful. They were long legs; she was almost as tall as he was, around six feet. Legs could make or break a woman, and she knew how to show them off, with a flowing skirt that caressed them like leaves blowing gently in the wind.

His black jeans fit snugly on his narrow hips and matched his tweed black and gray shirt, which was a favorite of the ladies. What to wear for a jacket? Steven rummaged through his closet, then remembered the new black leather jacket he had bought last month but hadn't worn yet.

He found it hanging in the back and put it on. Very good, very, very good, he thought, as he turned to look in the mirror, admiring his image. Sticking his hands in the slanted pockets to get another effect, he felt something hard under his right hand. It was a pair of black sunglasses. What were they doing there? Maybe another shopper had put them in the pocket when trying on the jacket.

Steven examined them closely and liked what he saw. He put them on to see how they looked. Checking himself out in the mirror, he decided they were too big for his face, but when he tried to take them off, he couldn't. For a moment Steven thought maybe they were caught in his hair, so he carefully felt around the ends, behind his ears, and realized there was nothing there. Again, he pulled hard on them, this time trying to lift the ends up from behind. They wouldn't budge. He looked into the mirror again, pushing and pulling at them in vain. Frightened, as if seeking help, he looked around the room.

At that moment, his cat ran toward him. Panicked, he let out a quiet scream, for he could see the insides of her body. Her outer skin covered bones and muscles, and her stomach was full of the food she had just eaten. He could see all of it in perfect detail.

He sat down on the bed in astonishment, and she jumped up into his lap, very much alive and well. Steven automatically patted this strange aberration, and she settled down for a massage, totally unaware of how she was affecting her owner.

Shaken, he wondered, am I dreaming? If so, it was a very vivid dream. He could still smell the strong aroma of coffee and the perfume of his after-shave lotion.

Then he realized that what was happening had to be caused by the glasses. He went into the bathroom. Pouring soap and water into the basin, he ducked his head into the hot suds and, once more, tried to remove the glasses. He pulled at them and lathered around his ears, but nothing worked. Trying to dry off the glasses and his face was a formidable task.

Maybe I can cut them off! He found his scissors and tried to cut the stems, but they were like solid steel. Feeling desperate, he grabbed his keys and left the apartment.

Once outside, Steven walked through the condo gardens toward the parking lot. Again, he felt shocked; the plants looked like they were in another dimension. Flickering lights and luminous colors floated around the flowers. He could even see miniature odd-looking creatures flying in and out of the leaves and branches of the nearby trees. Some looked like fairies from his childhood books and others had gnarled features that resembled the elves of Irish mythology. They waved at him when he walked by, which frightened him even more, and he ran as fast as he could toward the parking lot.

When Steven reached his car he almost did a double take. The car was moving, or so it seemed at first, then he realized there were elf- and fairy-like creatures here too, floating around, going in and out through the glass of the car's windows. He tried to ignore them as he jumped in and began driving. He knew of an eyeglass store near the park where he was headed for his date. Removing these glasses was of prime importance.

At the store, he explained to the clerk that he needed a doctor to remove the glasses. She stared at him incredulously when he showed her that he couldn't budge them. The doctor also was taken aback and pulled as hard as he could. Finally, he took a small screwdriver and tried to undo the small screws on the stems, but they wouldn't move. The doctor gave up and told Steven his best bet was to go to a mechanic. They had heavy wrenches and sharp pliers that might break them off.

Disappointed, Steven looked at his watch and realized he had to go or he would be late for his date. What a disaster that he had to wear these glasses! They were so dark that it was impossible to see his beautiful eyes. It was too late to call Sophia and change the meeting, so he drove off to the park.

Sophia was seated on a bench, basking in the sun. When he first saw her, she looked normal, but, as he drew closer, the creatures were there, flying all around her body. They varied in size and shape but, in general, they were very beautiful, more beautiful than the car fairies, but equal to the blooming flower ones. She smiled at him and three flew out of her mouth. They giggled at him and flew away. He was relieved that, other than the fairies, she looked solid, with no bones showing.

"What are you looking at?" Sophia asked as he sat down next to her.

"Oh, I thought I saw someone I knew." He realized he had been watching the fairies fly off and disappear into a tree branch.

"Those are nice glasses. Where did you get them? Can I try them on?" She smiled again at him.

"No, uh, sorry, um, maybe some other time," he stammered.

She looked at him strangely, and he almost thought she was laughing at him. "Oh, come on. I won't hurt them, I promise."

"No!" Steven's voice had an edge to it. "Let's find a place for lunch," he said, trying to change the subject.

He started to stand, but, when he was halfway up, Sophia grabbed the glasses and pulled them off. "I really wanted to see your eyes," she said, holding them in her hand.

Steven was stunned. "How did you do that?"

"What do you mean?" Sophia put the glasses on.

"Oh no, no, you shouldn't have done that! Oh, no!" He grabbed her hands, but it was too late, the glasses were neatly framing her eyes.

"You really are attached to these, aren't you?" When she smiled, the three fairies flew back into her mouth.

He let out a small moan. I'm still seeing them, even without the glasses. What am I going to do?

"There's nothing to do but enjoy them." Sophia replied to his thoughts.

She suddenly looked larger, even somewhat overwhelming.

"What are you seeing with those glasses?" he asked.

"I'm seeing your thoughts, but I don't need these to see them." She took off the glasses and handed them back to Steven.

"No, you keep them. Don't give them to me."

"But they belong to you."

"No, I told you they don't belong to me. I don't want them!" He was almost yelling at her as she tried to give them back.

Sophia winked at him with her hazel eyes. "They do belong to you."

"You don't understand! They are magic, terrible magic!"

"But I do understand. They belong to you."

"No, stop it!" His hands were folded tightly against his chest when she touched them with the glasses. Immediately, his hands opened and automatically took the glasses and put them back on.

"No, what are you doing to me?" he cried as the glasses again became glued to his nose. "Who are you?"

"I'm a friend. You treat women as playthings because you are afraid to see who they really are. The glasses help you to see what is hidden. That is why you are seeing all the nature spirits, which are hidden from human eyes. More importantly, these glasses will help you develop your intuition and really feel what is happening with the women you are dating."

"Intuition? That's a woman's thing!"

"If it would make you more comfortable, we can call it a 'gut feeling.' That's what a lot of men call it, but it really is the intuition. Now I think it's time for you to see these women differently." She took his hand and started to lead him out of the park.

"Where are we going?" Steven was very frightened. He could not resist anything she did, and he followed after her like a little boy.

In just a short time, he found they were standing in front of Lillith's house. Why were they here? It was Saturday, and her husband would be home.

Sophia led him to the door and rang the bell.

Lillith answered it, and made a small noise when she saw him.

"Why are you here?" She whispered.

"Who's there?" A man's voice called from the living room.

"No one, just a salesman," she replied.

"That's not true," Sophia said, and pushed her way past Lillith, dragging Steven into the living room.

A large, burly man, dressed in jeans and a sweatshirt, was sprawled out on the couch reading the paper.

"What do you want?" When the man stood up he was far bigger and bulkier than Steven. Flying around him were very large dark fairies.

"I want you to look at this man," Sophia said to him. "He knows your wife intimately."

"What?" He looked at Lillith, who was now backed against the wall. "Is this true? Are you sleeping with him?" His face became gray.

"No, it's not true," Steven protested. "I don't even know your wife." But as he spoke the words, they changed in mid-air to "Yes, it's true. I'm here to apologize to you. I will never see her again."

Before the husband could respond, Sophia pulled Steven out of the house and so far down the street it was as if a speeding car had picked them up and deposited them a mile away.

"Why did you do that? He'll kill her. How can you be so cruel? How dare you interfere with my life," Steven protested in a whiny voice.

"No, he won't. What does your intuition say about it?"

He was silent for a minute. Hesitantly, he said, "I felt her power for the first time just now when he confronted her. I might be wrong, but I think she'll cajole him into forgiving her."

"Why do you think he would do that?"

"I saw the way he looked when I told him the truth. His face turned into a tear drop, and he was like a small boy sobbing, all alone," he answered quietly.

"You saw the hurt he's been feeling. He suspected her all along. It's not the first time she's cheated on him. It's a shame. He's a nice man, and he loves her for who she is, not just her body. Someday, he will leave her, and only then will she appreciate him for who he is."

"I never thought about hurting the husband. I figured that's the wife's problem, not mine."

"Well, now you know you're wrong. Come." She again took his hand and pulled him, reluctantly, down the street. This time they arrived at Cindy's apartment.

"Why here? She doesn't have a husband. Nothing's wrong with our relationship."

"How long have you been seeing her?"

He thought for a minute. "Maybe about three years. She travels a lot, so it's on and off. It's been a nice thing; you know, casual."

"Yes, you mean casual sex, right?"

Now he was getting mad, "What's wrong with that? She wants that, too!"

"Maybe, maybe not." Suddenly, they both were standing in Cindy's living room. She was talking to a friend of hers, Anna. Steven realized that neither one could see them.

"Stop doing this to yourself. He's not worth it, and it's too hurtful," Anna said.

"I know, but I can't help loving him. It's crazy, but I do protect myself by pretending I'm away on business trips."

"But why? You know he doesn't love anyone but himself. All he wants is a good lay. How can you degrade yourself? That's not love; that's being a victim."

"I'm not a victim. I'm doing this willingly. I've tried not to see him, to end it, but I miss being with him, even if it's only a week here and there. You know I've dated other guys, but so far I haven't met anyone I care about."

"But this could go on for years. You'll end up old, he'll dump you and then you'll lose your chance to marry and have a family. You've said how much you want that."

"I know, you're right, and I keep telling myself this will be the last time I see him, but then it's such magic for me! I just love him, and I can't help it."

Steven could see tears in her eyes, and he felt suddenly sick to his stomach. Cindy was wonderful to be with, fun, charming, sexy, and intelligent. I never dreamt that she loved me like this, he thought.

Suddenly, he was back in the park, sitting on the bench with Sophia.

"Why didn't she tell me?"

"She knew if she did, you would end it."

He thought about how he always ran from close involvements. "Yes, I guess I would have."

"What does your intuition say about this scene?"

"I don't know." He paused. "I guess I'm feeling her pain."

"Stay with that feeling, and tell me what she is going to do."

"I think she's going to try to end it. Anna was sounding very convincing."

"Yes, that's true. In fact, tonight she's coming over to tell you she's met someone else and it's over with you."

"But why would she do that? That's a lie. Why not just end it?"

"She feels you will talk her out of it. This way you can't do that."

"Oh, yes, I would talk her out of it. It's been a great relationship: casual, no demands, fun, and no responsibility."

"Well, it's over."

Sophia took the glasses off his face. "I think it's time for you to use your intuition more. You're doing well at it, so you won't need these anymore." She stood up, looked at him, her hazel eyes sparkling with amusement, and said, "Goodbye, and have a happy life."

Steven watched her long, beautiful legs carry her away.

He sat there for a long time, thinking about all the women he'd been with, all the casual relationships he'd prided himself on. Suddenly, they all felt shallow. He had never allowed himself to love any of the women. He was the permanent bachelor who never loved. It all felt very sad to him.

He wanted to hold his Susie cat. He could love her, and she never made any demands on him. He suddenly realized that's what he feared the most: demands! His father died when he was twelve, and his mother had made him into the man of the household. He'd had to do everything, taking on all the responsibility until he left for college. Even now, she still called him to do things for her. Oh God, what a mess his life was. He sat on the bench and cried for the first time since he was a child.

That evening, he waited for Cindy to come, dreading it. When she walked through the door, bright and cheery, he wanted to cry again. He held her in his arms for a long time, feeling her warmth and, for the first time, her love.

She finally pulled away from him. "Darling, I can't stay long. I've come to just tell you some exciting news."

"What news?" He asked, looking her in the eyes.

"On this last trip, I met a wonderful man, and we are engaged." She looked down, avoiding his gaze. "So, naturally, I can't see you anymore, but it's been fun and maybe-"

"No." Steven grabbed her as she turned away. "No, that's not true. I won't let you ever leave me. I care about you too much. In fact, I love you." As these words flew out of him spontaneously, he felt love overflowing his heart.

He allowed the tears to return as he drew her back into his arms.

Commentary

This is a story about a man who lives in fear. He is afraid of everything: love, the fullness of relationships, even the unexpectedness and novelty of life. He is like a musician who has learned to play only one note. Because of his fear of commitment, he walks on the sands of life and leaves no footprints. His heart is cold, constricted into a defensive 'self-love.' Lillith becomes his companion, and great sex his measure of happiness. He is not a bad man, only a fear-based and selfish one. He lies when it's convenient, but so does everyone else; he might tell himself if he thought about it at all.

With the arrival of Sophia and the magic spectacles, he is forced to look through the superficialities of his life and into its essence. Though scared nearly witless, his magic glasses make his eyes fly open and see not only the fairy-like creatures that surround everything and everyone, but the impact of his narcissism on Lillith's husband and on the woman he discovers he really loves. Steven's so-called freedom, which had become his prison, vanishes as Sophia opens the doors to his heart.

Exercise:

This exercise can help you determine your way of accessing the intuition and clarify how you can use it.

Try to recall a time in your life when your intuition was trying to tell you something, when it was prompting you in some way. It might have been expressed as a dream, a "voice," a thought, a feeling, a sensation, or a hunch. Or, you may have experienced it as a subtle inner sense of knowing.

When you remember something, ask yourself:

What was the message?

Did I act on it or ignore it?

What were the consequences in either case?

Did it affect my life in any way?

You may wish to keep track of how your intuition comes through for you and of the messages it brings you in an intuition notebook for a time.

Judith Bach, Ph.D. & Nanette Hucknall

5
The Many-Faceted Feminine

Women are so conditioned from childhood to meet their needs through manipulation that this behavior becomes second nature. Unfortunately, not only do most mothers model such behavior, it is also a common theme in our popular culture, like in movies and television. Men too can use this negative feminine characteristic and be manipulative. To change this trait to a positive one, it is necessary for men and women to connect to their inner masculine and to use the positive masculine characteristic of being direct.

The following story illustrates manipulative behavior:

The restaurant was crowded when the four women wove through the tables to an outdoor terrace and sat together at their usual table. Set apart from the others, this table was reserved for them throughout the summer months. In cold or wet weather they met inside before a gas fire; as Lillith once commented in her snappy fashion, "Better phony warmth than nothing at all!" She was tall and dark-haired, with a handsome face, bordering on exotic. Generally, she looked and acted sophisticated, with a somewhat 'holier than thou manner.' Today, she was wearing a tailored brown pantsuit that flattered her slim figure.

In contrast, Edith was fair in coloring, short and slightly plump, with a round, girly baby face. Her redeeming features were her well-shaped legs and full breasts. She always wore flowered skirts, as she felt they were more feminine and sexy, and, for the same reason, she wore high-heeled sandals even when she walked over rough terrain.

Betty was as tall and thin as Lillith, but with a longer torso and none of the stylish flair of Edith. She was wearing her usual jeans and a good quality T-shirt. She walked with a slight limp as a result of childhood polio. Betty used very little makeup. Her most arresting feature was her azure-blue eyes. When she remembered to enhance them with eye shadow, her face changed from plain to striking.

Joyce, like Edith, preferred skirts, though not because she felt they made her look sexy, but because they were cooler in hot weather. During the winter months she preferred pants and jeans. Recently divorced, she was going through the emotional challenge of facing the world as a single woman. Of the four, she was the prettiest, with long blond hair, gray-green eyes and a wide, full mouth that readily curved into a smile, though recently less so.

The others were married, and all were well into their forties, with children ranging in age from 13 to 18.

After ordering, they relaxed and began generally catching up as they enjoyed their pre-lunch drinks. A cool breeze wafted across the terrace, rustling the leaves of an ancient oak that shielded them from the midday sun.

"Mmm, does that feel good!" said Edith. She opened her purse, fetched a mirror and quickly applied some lipstick. After blotting it with a tissue, she looked around at the others. "What's our subject today? Anybody got an idea?"

Lillith said, "I'd like to talk about how we use our feminine wiles in relationships. Ruel is starting to drive me crazy with his demands, and I need to hone in on my skills in order to take charge."

"Why do you need to take charge?" Edith asked.

Lillith looked at her with intense eyes. "Come on! I've seen you control Thom far better than anyone I know."

"Well, I don't call it control, but …" she paused and, with a dimpled smile, said airily, "I do manage to get my way most of the time."

"Just a minute," Joyce piped up, "if he does everything you want, that sounds like control to me."

"And to me too," agreed Betty. "Come on, admit it!"

"Well maybe that's true, but I use my femininity in a way that I don't feel looks controlling." She thought for a moment, her hand raised to keep them from interrupting. "Okay," she continued, "here's an example. If he happens to be in a stubborn mood, I come up and hug him from behind. Most of the time he caves in. Sometimes I do it deliberately in order to get him to let go of a rigid point of view, but mostly I do it because I just want to."

"How does he respond?" Joyce asked.

"Generally, if he's in a negative mood, he'll relax and be more positive, or if he's feeling good, he'll grab me and kiss me. Once in a while he'll push me away because he's feeling too irritated."

"Okay," said Joyce, "you've got him out of his mood. How do you get him to come around to your point of view?"

"If he responds positively, then I make suggestions about the topic in question in a lighthearted manner; or, if I want him to do something, I will kiss him and gently ask him to help me. It all depends on how direct I have to be. If I'm too direct and just ask him, he generally resists, but if I act sexy and coy, he definitely responds better."

"But isn't that a lot of work?" Betty asked.

"Yes, but it's worth it in the long run. Believe me, the only way to get a man to do anything for you is to strategize."

"I agree, but your husband's a pussycat," Lillith replied. "My Ruel is a control freak. Even though I hide a lot from him, he's too smart not to notice."

Betty frowned. "I would hate being married to someone like that. It's bad enough to have a husband who's lazy. John never does any work around the house unless I threaten him with no more sex. Early on I discovered that he responds to that fast enough."

"You actually tell him no more sex?" Lillith was surprised. "If I tried that, Ruel would probably have an affair."

"John wouldn't dare do that. I've already threatened telling his born-again Christian mother, who would disown him big time."

"I would think he'd be happy about being disowned," Joyce observed.

"No way. A part of him would believe her if she said he would fry in hell. I would love to have the power she has over him. When he acts like her, it's really unnerving. He goes into a rage, and sometimes I'm afraid he might hit me."

"Has he ever done that?" Joyce asked.

"No, because he knows I would leave him if he did. My way of handling him is to laugh at him. The more I laugh, the crazier he gets, and then he stops."

"That's an interesting tactic. Where did you learn that?" Lillith asked, looking at Betty with sharpened interest.

"When I was younger I told my uncle about a friend, Jerry, who always yelled at me when he got angry. He advised me to simply laugh at him when he did that, and it really worked. My laughing made Jerry so upset that he finally stopped yelling, which was great, as otherwise I was ready to break our friendship. I've used it with John a lot."

"Hmm, seems like you're attracted to volatile men," Edith observed.

"Lets get back to how to manipulate our husbands," Lillith interrupted, "because that's what it's about, ladies. How to keep our husbands in line by manipulating them."

"I hate that word! I never manipulated Steven," Joyce added.

Lillith responded with a slight smirk, "Maybe that's why you're divorced. I, for one, think it's one of the best attributes women have. How else can you deal with demanding men?"

Joyce, obviously upset, retorted, "Steven was never demanding! That wasn't the problem. You know it, and I would appreciate you not suggesting the divorce was my fault. It was mutually decided."

"Mutually decided by him and his girlfriend," Lillith muttered under her breath. Then she said, "Come on, ladies, let's not lie to each other. We all manipulate, otherwise we couldn't survive in a man's world. We do it every which way."

She looked at Betty. "You do it by refusing to have sex."

Betty frowned, then murmured, "I guess that's true."

Then, turning to Joyce, Lillith spat out, "Joyce, you did it by planting bits of knowledge to make Steven a little insecure. I remember you once told me how you put a woman's handkerchief in his coat pocket, pretended to find it and then asked him whose it was. He swore, rightfully, that he didn't know, and you acted as if you didn't believe him. A week later, when you wanted to go on vacation to Europe, he readily agreed, when before he had been reluctant. That was a grand manipulation— and you just claimed you never manipulated Steven!" Lillith laughed.

Joyce, her face flushed, admitted, "Well, that's true." With a defensive edge, she retorted, "But then he did end up meeting someone else." She then sighed and said, "You know, my cousin would call it 'karma' because of what I did."

Ignoring her, Lillith turned to Edith. "And guess what? You very carefully groomed your pussycat husband to be the way he is by using your charms to persuade him to do things that he really didn't want to do. The charming bit is really very effective. I remember when you wanted him to buy you a new car. Thom never would have given in to that one if you hadn't talked him into buying a new set of golf clubs. You kept saying how much he deserved them, that he needed to have the right equipment, and so on and so on. Then, a month later, your car supposedly broke down, and you said that maybe you deserved a better one because you're always shopping for the family. You kept at it every day until he gave in. Over the years, Thom has become so accustomed to your charms that he now automatically gives in." She threw out her arms and proclaimed, "Ladies, that's real control."

They all laughed.

"I have to admit you're right, Lillith," said Edith. "I remember my mother saying when I was a teenager, 'Edith, you'll never be a beauty, so you need to develop other ways to catch a man.' Charm was the main one that I learned, and as you know, I landed him; he was the top of the class and the smartest and wealthiest man at the university, and I've kept him." She glanced at Joyce when she said that.

Lillith turned to Betty. "You've been awfully quiet. Don't you have anything to add?"

"Yes. I've been thinking, it would be so much easier to just be direct with men. Why do we always have to play games and be conniving when we want something?"

"Ah," said Lillith. "That's what makes us women. We've always had the advantage because we really are smarter than men. Our problem is we sometimes let ourselves be subjugated by our partners, instead of owning our power. We have the ability to take charge and survive male dominance by using our feminine wiles."

Betty said, "I guess you have a point. Survival, that's what it's really about, isn't it? We've always been weaker than men, a weaker species, so, in order to compensate, we've had to develop these methods."

"But that's changing," commented Edith. "Younger women who work don't have to use those kinds of tactics. They are much more direct and much more powerful."

"I don't agree," Lillith replied. "I work with these women. They'll be assertive and perform the same way as their male counterparts, yet when they talk to their lovers they act differently. They switch from being strong and direct to being cooing and attentive. I hear them talking on the phone to their partners, and they use the same old tactics that we do."

"I know," Joyce said. "Hopefully, now that I'm alone, I can just try to be myself. I never told you this—I guess I was ashamed—but last year Steven came home one evening and I knew he'd been drinking a lot. He reeked of alcohol. He claimed to be out with his friends from the office. Of course, it was a lie, which I intuitively felt. While he was taking a shower I grabbed his wallet, found a restaurant receipt and copied the number. Later, after he went to bed, I called the restaurant and described him. Fortunately it was a small restaurant and one of the waiters knew who he was. It turns out he was quite a regular there.

"The waiter described the woman he was with. I wrote it all down, and the next day I hired a detective to follow him and get some evidence. That was the best thing I could have done. It gave me great grounds for divorce and much more money in the end. It was much better than letting myself be victimized, but what really hurt me the most was all the lies that he tried to lay on me; he knows I have a very strong intuition and pick up on everything."

"Men aren't all that way," Edith said. "Thom would never do that to me. It's unfortunate, Joyce, that Steven was so deceitful."

Lillith snapped, "Why do you think Thom is so different? When it comes to a piece of ass—that's Ruel's expression—all men are susceptible. I'm sure Ruel has had some flings, but I haven't caught him yet. He's very good at covering up, but even if I do find out about something going on, I'm not certain I would leave him. I would just use the information for added fuel for my wish list. Besides, ladies, how many of you have had some outside activities?" Lillian looked at each woman in anticipation.

There was silence as they looked at each other.

"You mean you've all been faithful babes?" Lillith laughed, and said to Joyce, "I can remember early in your marriage you met a man on a business trip and had a little extra curricular activity."

Joyce blushed, "Well, only once. I never had an affair that lasted a year like Steven's did. That was different." Then she countered, "How about you, Lillith? I do remember something about an Edward."

"Oh, Edward! Yes, he was fabulous in bed. Ruel nearly discovered us one afternoon when he came home early. It was the old window routine, with me tossing out his clothes and shoes and Edward running for cover before the neighbors or Ruel spotted his naked butt. I barely had time to throw on a robe. It was the last time I ever brought a man home. It's stupid to do. From then on it was motels."

"But how could you do that? I could never be unfaithful to Thom," Edith said, and Betty agreed.

Lillith replied, "How do you keep the sex interesting without some diversion on the side? It's just as much a part of our nature as it is a man's."

"I don't think that's true," said Betty. "A woman is naturally faithful, whereas a man just isn't. It's bred in their genes."

"Bullshit!" Lillith grimaced and shook her head. "How do you think the genes produce the sex drive? That comes from the head and the eyes: looking at women and thinking about them. It happens in both sexes, take it from me. Tell me none of you noticed that hunk of a guy over there?" Lillith glanced at a table in the corner where a good-looking man was eating alone.

"Can we change the subject?" Edith was frowning.

All three looked at her. "Maybe there's something you're not telling us?" Betty asked.

"Well, I've always been faithful, that's true! I've never actually had sex with someone else, but ..."

"But what?" prodded Betty.

"About ten years ago, when I was thinner, Thom was away on business and I went to a bar to have a drink, just in the spur of the moment. You know, I was lonely, and just wanted to be around people."

"Yeah, yeah," grinned Lillith. "Go on!"

"There was a great looking man there. His name was Ben, and we talked and drank and even danced. He was traveling on business and was staying in a hotel nearby, and I, foolishly, went to his room with him. We played around. I refused to have intercourse with him, but we did everything else. End of story."

"End of story? How did you get out of the final act?" Joyce questioned.

"I lied and said I had caught an infection from my husband and I was being treated at the time. The doctor said no intercourse until it was cleared up."

"I'm surprised he fell for that one. But you did everything else?" Lillith asked.

"Yes, and it was nice, I must admit."

"Did you see him again?"

"Heavens no, but he did call me when he came back to town, and I was tempted for a repeat, but Thom was home, and I really don't believe in doing those things." She looked at the others. "Now can we change the subject?"

Betty said, "You know, I'm tired of men trying to grab me or seduce me. One of the reasons I got married was to leave all that behind, but it still goes on." She shook her head in disgust.

"I should be so lucky," Lillith said. "Is that why you never wear makeup anymore?"

"Yep! I try to play down my looks and body for that reason."

Edith said, "But that's crazy. You're so beautiful. It's crazy not to want to have people stare at you. Look at you. You're in your forties, and you look late twenties. I would give anything for that."

"Not if you're constantly pestered."

"So, have you been faithful to John?" Lillith enquired.

"Yes, and that's never been a problem for me. Remember, I got married only seven years ago, and I had many love affairs before that, so I certainly don't need any now."

"Well, there's still the seven-year itch factor." Lillith stopped talking while the waiter served their lunch, then she resumed. "About the seven-year itch, you never know when that's going to happen."

"I thought that only happened to men," Edith said.

"That's what men want you to think."

They all thought about that for a minute.

Then Lillith smiled, a wily look on her face. "I've got an idea! Let's play a trick on our husbands."

"What kind of trick?" Betty asked.

"I don't know. Let's brainstorm it."

After a few minutes of back and forth talking, Betty suggested, "How about having a party and each of us will make a pass at someone else's husband to test if any of them pick up on it?"

"That would be too much, but we can pick one husband to do it to," Lillith said, and looked at Edith. "You claim Thom would never be unfaithful, but I bet you he will succumb."

"I don't want to do that to him."

"Are you afraid?" Lillith asked, an edge of challenge in her voice.

"No, of course not, but who will be the one to try?"

"Joyce, it has to be you. You're single now, and the one most likely to try something. Besides, I think you may like Thom a lot." This sly remark went over Edith's head.

"Alright, but you all need to help in some way," Joyce responded enthusiastically.

"We'll find a way to keep Edith out of the way."

When the waitress appeared with the desert menu, they took a break from their conversation to look it over.

They had been so involved in their discussion that they hadn't noticed the woman that had sat down at the next table in earshot of the conversation. She was very lovely, dressed in a blue silk dress and sandals. Her hair was brown and coiled in a French roll that enhanced her oval face. Her deep blue eyes had been watching the group with interest.

She got up, and pulling her chair behind her, approached their table. She surprised them when she said, "May I join you? I've been overhearing your conversation and think I can add something to it that might be of interest to you all."

Her voice was high and sweet, and her face lit up when she talked. Not waiting for them to answer, she edged her chair into an open space and took over. How she did it was amazing. First, she asked their names in such a way that they immediately responded, then, she explained that she was alone because her date couldn't make it at the last minute. She smiled sweetly, with incredible charm, as she told them she not only agreed with all they were saying, but felt they might also need a new perspective.

"Men aren't very complicated, the way we women are. That's why we can really control them if we want to. The problem is, most women don't realize this. It certainly sounds like you all are very bright women and do understand though, especially you, Lillith. You are extremely clever and can teach your friends a lot. You sound like an expert in handling men."

Lillith, flattered, asked, "What did you say your name was?"

"I didn't," she replied. "But you can call me Janet." She quickly turned to Betty.

"Betty, my suggestion is to do what your friends are saying. Play up your looks, and you can do anything. Certainly your husband wants to see you beautiful, and I assure you he also loves to see other men stare at you and know you are his. Beauty is a wonderful attribute to have.

"And you, Edith, obviously have done very well with a delightful personality. What a wonderful mother you have, to give you that advice when you were young. You listened and accomplished everything you wanted by developing your charm."

"Joyce, be happy you aren't with that ex of yours. You deserve more. You are still adorable and can capture many a man's heart. Keep smiling, that's your best quality."

Stunned by the compliments, the women were totally captivated by Janet. Even Lillith was without words.

"Now, about your plan to seduce Thom. It's the right man, but the wrong woman. Just imagine it. Thom has been faithful all these years. He's a good businessman with a good mind. If he were going to have an affair, it wouldn't be with anyone who knows his wife. That would be stupid and unnecessary. There are a lot of women in the world who would go after him. He's good-looking and wealthy, what more would they want. I'm sure he has already been approached."

Janet paused and looked at Edith.

"So instead, my suggestion is that I be the one to seduce him. He doesn't know that I know any of you, and I'm beautiful enough that he's going to notice me. I'm the perfect woman to play out your plan."

They were nodding their heads when Lillith came out of her stupor. "Wait a minute. We don't even know you. How do we know you won't go through with the seduction? Thom is a good catch."

"Oh, I assure you, my husband is all that Thom is and more. You can trust me. My only intention is to play the game with you. I really am enjoying the idea of duping Thom."

"It's okay," Betty said. "I feel she's sincere."

Lillith started to protest, and Edith interrupted, "But Thom may go for you and that would be terrible."

Like Lillith, Janet said, "Are you afraid? You should know that the bond you and Thom have together is stronger than any pretty woman. You need to keep that trust. You said he would never be unfaithful."

"I know, but you're so beautiful."

"I promise you, I'm only going to flirt with him."

"That's all I was going to do with Ben, but it ended up a lot more."

"Your friends will be there and not allow more to happen."

"What do you mean we will be there? What's the plan?" Joyce asked.

Janet turned to Edith. "Is there a favorite bar that the two of you go to?"

"Yes, it's also a restaurant, and we do both."

"Good, you will tell Thom you will meet him in the bar at a certain time. Then, at that time, call him on your cell phone and make an excuse that you can't come. I'll be there and engage him in conversation. If he buys me some drinks and dinner, that will be a good indicator that he's interested, and if he gives me his card, that also means he wants to see me. If he does all of that, he needs to be caught. The three of you will come into the bar and restaurant an hour later. He and I will either be gone because we didn't connect, or having dinner. If Thom is there, he'll see the three of you and, obviously, be upset."

"How will we know you didn't go off together to another place?"

"You will know because Thom will be home, and you, Edith, will be home earlier than you thought you would be."

"Sounds like a good plan to me," Joyce acknowledged, and the others agreed.

"Let's shake hands on it." Janet held out her hand, and when they shook hands with her a shot of energy went up their arms.

"What was that?" Edith jumped back in her seat. They looked at Janet and, spellbound, watched her brown hair change into a glowing blond; her features became even more beautiful, radiating light.

"My real name is Sophia, and I am the positive feminine that is part of all of you."

Lillith snarled, "I should have known. Damn you!"

The three looked at Lillith, shocked to see her grow almost ugly, her face suddenly shadowed as if a cloud had passed overhead.

"What's happening?" Edith cried.

Sophia looked at the three of them. "You have been sitting here, entirely immersed in the negative aspects of the feminine, because of the influence of your so-called friend, Lillith. You have been manipulative and underhanded, used your husbands for your own purposes, lied, cheated, and even planned to hurt a friend by proving her husband won't be faithful. The only positive quality of the feminine that you used was, momentarily, intuition and a little affection. Love, kindness, consideration, compassion—none of my positive qualities were part of this conversation.

"You were so beguiled by my flattery that you never questioned a stranger joining your table and never questioned that I had so easily dropped in on your conversation. You even listened to my plan and accepted it without much questioning because I was so convincing with my charm. What I did was take everything you have been doing to your husbands and did the same to you. I seduced all of you. Even you, Lillith, were fooled into believing me."

"I know," she said bitterly, and gave Sophia a nasty look.

Sophia ignored her and said, "Ladies, look at yourselves. You are all a lot more than these negative qualities. I assure you, men do like directness and will respond to it if it is done with a loving heart rather than a manipulating mind.

"Stop listening to Lillith. She's not your friend. She wants you to lose your husbands. Edith, she was already calculating to tell Thom that you planned this trick on him."

"But I thought you were a friend," accused Edith, and she looked at Lillith angrily. Lillith's face was twisted with rage. Muttering, she stood up, glared at Sophia and Edith and stalked off the terrace and out of the restaurant.

The others sat stunned.

"Let her go," said Sophia gently. "She's not your friend. She's destructive and extremely negative."

"But who are you?" asked Betty.

"Let's just say that I have a very different approach to the feminine than Lillith. You can be strong, caring and inwardly beautiful at the same time. You don't have to resort to the tricks that she was goading you to do. You have extraordinary qualities within you that you need to discover and nurture. The world needs these qualities. You need these qualities, and you can become compassionate and strong leaders in whatever direction your lives take you."

The three women, moved by Sophia's words, stared at her.

"But how...?" Edith began.

Sophia's smile seemed to light up the terrace. "All you need is to find me in your hearts and work with my inner beauty. Realize that my positive aspects will help you in any relationship, and a loving heart will never fail you. Develop my aspects, and let go of hers."

With these words, Sophia disappeared.

Commentary

Manipulation is the opposite of directness, a positive masculine trait. Learning to be direct is not about being masculine. As we have pointed out, the ideal for all of us is to become balanced in relation to masculine and feminine energies, which has nothing to do with being male or female. It is possible to be direct without being harsh. It is possible to be direct without hurting another person. When directness comes from a loving heart, the other person can "hear" us better and is more likely to respond in the same heartfelt way.

It is not easy to change our style of communication. It takes time and conscious effort. First, we must become aware of our tendency to be manipulative. The following is an excellent exercise for learning how to recognize any manipulative behaviors and change them into more direct and honest ones:

Exercise: The Nightly Review

At the end of the day, while you are still feeling alert, look back on the day's events in 2-hour time blocks. You may start from when you first got up in the morning and move forward to the present time, or, start with the present time, moving back. For example, remember what happened in the last 2 hours—were you with someone, or alone? What were your behaviors, your thoughts, and your feelings? Without any self-judgment, simply notice whether or not you were manipulative in any way. Make a note when you discover a manipulative tendency. Then move on to observe the next 2-hour block of time, and so on. If you feel you're not manipulative, then don't continue with this exercise.

Once you finish reviewing your day, choose an incident where you recognized that you were manipulative. Take time to imagine how you could have acted more directly; play that out in your mind, noticing your energy, feelings and thoughts.

If you do this several times a week, or every day, you will begin to get a handle on your manipulative behaviors and gradually become more direct, honest and caring;

those around you—friends, family, and co-workers—will benefit from your positive feminine characteristics.

6
Sophia Unveiled

The positive feminine believes in working with others to find the most creative solutions; it is open to change. The negative feminine uses power to generate separateness and fear, inciting people to hold on to what is familiar; change of any kind is too frightening. The negative and positive aspects of the feminine are within all of us. It is up to us to choose which positive one we want to nurture and bring into our consciousness.

The following story shows the dual sides that we can fall into. We can be Sophia or Lillith: it is up to us:

The lowering sun cast its departing shafts of light over the small town as the taxi moved slowly along Meg Richard's street. The taxi stopped at the small house next to hers and a woman stepped out. Meg, who was sitting on her porch, was transfixed, utterly spellbound, by the beauty of her new neighbor. She had never seen anyone like her. The woman radiated both the setting sun and the rising moon. Her hair was an ashen blond that glistened in waves down to her shoulders, and, even though dusk was turning into dark, her face and body seemed silhouetted with a golden glow.

The taxi driver pulled out two suitcases and set them on the ground. "Where do you want these?" he asked, looking toward the house.

"This is fine. I can carry them." She smiled at him as she paid him.

Meg kept staring at her as she walked up the stairs to the porch, unlocked the door and went in. As soon as the door closed, Meg was on the phone.

"Francis, she's here! The new owner is here!"

"Already? What's she like?"

"All I can say is, in all my 62 years, I have never seen anyone like her. Wait till the men here see her. What a looker! Tom Dailey will surely go nuts."

"Yes, probably, but he is engaged."

"Oh, c'mon. You know that won't stop him." Meg settled deeper into her armchair.

"You're probably right."

"Tell you what! Come over in the morning, and we'll be neighborly and introduce ourselves."

"Good idea," said Francis. "I'll be there at nine."

"Great, see you then!" Meg hung up and closed the blinds against the impending darkness.

The next day was chilly and cloudy, without a hint of sunlight. Meg, with Francis right behind her, rang the new neighbor's bell. After a moment the door opened, and a small thin woman with sharp features stood there. Meg, startled, asked, "Is your mistress at home?"

The woman frowned. Her lips telegraphed a smile that failed to reach her eyes. "I am the mistress of this house. Can I help you?"

"I'm Meg Richards, your next door neighbor, and this is my friend, Francis Libby. We just wanted to welcome you to the neighborhood, but I saw someone else arrive last night, a tall blond woman, and I thought she was the new owner."

"You must have been mistaken. I'm the only one here, but it's very nice to meet you. My name is Lillith. Would you like to come in for a cup of coffee or tea?"

"Yes, we'd love to," said Meg, after looking at Francis, who nodded and cast a puzzled look at her as Lillith led them through a parlor and into the kitchen. Lillith prepared a fresh pot of coffee as Meg and Francis settled themselves at the kitchen table.

As they sipped their coffee, Lillith dominated the conversation with stories about herself and her life. After what seemed like hours, Meg and Francis, feeling drained and exhausted, almost stumbled down the front steps. It seemed that they had talked about everything and nothing. They went next door to Meg's house and sank into the deep, flowered cushions on her couch.

"Whew, she seems nice enough, but I feel like I've been through the ringer," said Meg.

"Me, too," agreed Francis. "And can she talk! It was all about her! I couldn't get a word in," she complained. "Now tell me, Meg, where is the tall, outrageously beautiful woman you talked about? Lillith is small and not even very pretty, nothing like you described."

"I really don't know," Meg said, shaking her head. "But I do know what I saw, unless I'm really losing it."

During the following weeks, the puzzling situation continued. Some people saw Lillith and others saw a young, attractive woman with blond hair who seemed kind-hearted and warm. Her name was Sophia, and the people who conversed with her raved about how wonderful she was, whereas the people who talked to Lillith described her differently. They said she was friendly at times, but often cold in manner and even a bit sarcastic. Both women lived in the same house and said they owned it, but, when asked, they appeared not to know each other. A woman inquired at the Department of Records in the town hall and was told that the ownership of the house was under the name of Sophia Lillith Morris.

The Lillith/Sophia phenomenon soon became the talk of the town. The people who had met Sophia wanted to meet Lillith and vice versa, but that never happened. When one or the other went out for any reason, they encountered only the people who they had met previously.

Meg was becoming more and more frustrated. After all, this was her neighbor, and she wanted to meet the pretty, nice one, not the cold, distant one. She tried everything, even resorting to looking through a window with binoculars, but she only saw Lillith.

One morning, as she was watering her plants in the living room, she heard the sound of her mailbox lid outside her front door. The mailman! Of course! She rushed to the door just in time to catch him as he was starting down her porch steps.

"Greg! Please, could I speak to you for a moment?"

The elderly, cheerful-looking man turned around and gave her a big smile.

"Yes, of course. What can I do for you?"

"Come in for a moment, please. I have something to ask you."

"How are you, Mrs. Richards?"

"I'm just fine, Greg," she said as she closed the door quietly. "I just want to ask you about my new neighbor. This might sound strange, but I'm really puzzled."

"What about?" he asked.

"Well…when I first laid eyes on her it was when she arrived. She was Sophia. No doubt about it! That's who she was."

Puzzled, the postman replied, "But I don't understand. That's who she is!"

"But no," replied Meg, quickly. "There's someone else living there, also. Did you know that?"

"No, Mrs. Richards. Who could that be? I really don't think so." He frowned thoughtfully. "Perhaps she has a friend staying with her?"

"But I've met this friend, who's there all the time, and I never saw Sophia again! What do you make of that?"

"What are you suggesting…" stammered the postman, looking positively alarmed as he regressed into one of the mystery and fantasy novels that he was addicted to reading.

"I don't know what I'm suggesting. Only that it's really strange that I haven't seen Sophia going in or out of that house again."

"But," protested the postman, "I see her often when I deliver her mail. I don't understand..."

"Please, indulge me," Meg interrupted. "What does she look like?"

"She's quite beautiful—tall, slim, blond, and very pleasant."

Meg frowned and shook her head. "I just don't get it! I can't figure out that other woman. She said she owns the house, and she didn't seem to know anything about Sophia! She doesn't even resemble her!"

"I'm sorry, Mrs. Richards, but I can't help you," the postman mumbled as he moved toward the door. "I must get on with my mail deliveries."

After the door closed behind him, Meg stood and shook her head. Determined to get to the bottom of the mystery, she decided to sit in her car the next day, wait for the postman and follow him up to her neighbor's door. She could bake some cookies and pretend that she was just being a good neighbor.

The following morning she put her plan into action. She waited in her car for the postman, who was very prompt, and as he approached Lillith's door, she left her car and walked swiftly behind him with her plate of cookies. The startled postman turned around to see who was behind him.

"Oh, hello again. Would you like a cookie?" Meg asked, feeling awkward as a flush moved up her neck to her face. At that moment, Lillith opened the door, gave Meg a sarcastic look, took the mail and closed the door. Meg was left standing there with her plate of cookies, her cheeks hot with embarrassment. At the same time, she realized this was a perfect moment to get to the truth. She whispered to the mailman, following him closely as he was turning away and walking down the path. "All right, Greg, now tell me who you saw just now."

He waited until he reached the sidewalk, handed her some mail, and, frowning, replied, "Sophia, of course. Isn't she lovely? She is such a nice person. Oh, thanks for the cookie."

Meg watched him walk away, shaking his head.

Exasperated, Meg was even more determined to uncover the mystery. She arranged a meeting with people who had met Lillith. Many of them were friends she had known for years. Generally when they met, much of the talk was gossip, so they immediately started in on Ray Bagley, who had just lost his wife and was already dating, but Meg interrupted, "We need to decide what to do about this Lillith woman. Ray can wait for another day."

"We wish he would," someone replied, and they all laughed.

"Do you think maybe it's a wig?"

"And she's playing a joke on us?"

"No, it can't be a wig. Everyone talks about Sophia's blue eyes, and Lillith's are black," Meg insisted. "Besides, the Sophia I saw getting out of the taxi was much taller than Lillith."

"Why not ask her outright about her and Sophia?"

"I did, the first time Francis and I met her. She just laughed and said she didn't know what I was talking about."

"What gets to me is how she knows everything about us. Who's been talking to her? She knows our whole history and makes digs at us all."

"Yes, that's true. She asked me how my brother Tommy was and how much longer he had to be in prison. Only a few people know about him, and I've asked that it be kept private." Frowning, she looked at each of the people in the room.

"Well?"

"I haven't said a word to her about any of us," protested one woman. "Who has?" Everyone denied the accusation.

"Well, if no one here has been talking to her, who can it be?"

"It could be anyone in Sophia's group."

"It's probably Rebecca. She's a talker."

"Yes, but I've never heard her say anything about anyone that was unkind."

"True, but you never know what happens inside someone's home. Her husband is quiet, but it's the quiet ones you have to watch out for."

The meeting went on for some time as they speculated about who the informer could be. Finally, they all agreed to try to find out and meet again in a week.

At the same time, the Sophia people were curious about what this Lillith woman looked like and why they only saw Sophia. When they asked her, Sophia said that maybe someone was impersonating her and that she would look into it.

In the meantime, Sophia was spending a lot of time at the town hall talking to Mayor Hankins. The town was faced with an economic crisis because the state budget had been cut. Some jobs were being eliminated, and the work was being allocated to other staff members, which soon became a burden on them. Sophia asked to be of assistance, explaining to the Mayor that she had a background in team building and corporate training. She suggested bringing the remaining employees together to do some creative brainstorming for ways to eliminate the extra work. She also felt more money could be raised from the townspeople and gave him some fund-raising ideas.

Mayor Hankins was very impressed by all of Sophia's suggestions and asked her to be in charge of both projects, which she happily agreed to. Again, some of the workers there saw her as Lillith, while others, at the same time, saw her as Sophia.

After discussing it, the Sophia clan decided that they should let go of their need to meet Lillith. The impression from those who dealt with her was always negative, and they all agreed it was best to just appreciate Sophia and be glad they saw her instead of Lillith.

One late afternoon, Meg was sitting dreamily on her porch. Suddenly, she spotted Sophia walking down the block away from her. Excitement coursed through her body. Finally, at last!

She stood up and followed her, walking quickly. As she came close, she realized that Sophia had changed back to Lillith. It happened in a flash, and Meg was so frustrated that she screamed Sophia's name. There was another flash, and Sophia was back, standing in front of her.

Meg, trembling, demanded, "Please don't do that again. That's very scary."

After gazing at her for a long moment, Sophia said softly, her voice lyrical, "Well, I wouldn't have to change for you if you would remember who you really are."

"What do you mean? I'm Meg Richards. I know who I am."

"The real you used to be a warmhearted woman, but that was before you turned into a lonely, gossipy old lady. Your beauty was in your heart, but you've let bitterness and loss cover it up."

A wave of defensive anger exploded from Meg. "How do you know about my losses? Who told you?"

Unperturbed by Meg's emotion, Sophia replied calmly, her gaze direct, and her words piercing Meg's defenses. "No one told me, but I know about your husband. You told people he died, but he ran off with another woman and left you with two small children to raise. When he came back a couple of years later and wanted to see the children, you wouldn't let him. They still think he's dead. Don't you think it would be nice to let them see him? He is still alive and lives alone in the next town."

Sophia turned and walked away, leaving Meg standing in the middle of the street in shock. Sophia's clarity and directness had hit their mark.

When she returned home, she sat on the porch in the darkness of the descending night and thought about Dave for the first time in many years. Her children were married with families, and living in different parts of the country. She only saw them on holidays, and even then it was a strain for her. Her bitterness had made them dislike her, and she always felt unwelcome in their homes. But, Dave was in the next town? How could that be? He would be 62 by now, as they were the same age. They'd married at 22, much too young, she thought. It was true that he'd returned and wanted to see the children. He'd even apologized and asked to come back, but she couldn't forgive him. Throughout the years, money would be deposited in her bank account, enough to support her and the kids, and she never told them about any of it.

How did Sophia know all of this? How was it possible? Somehow it didn't really surprise her, nor did it bother her. She'd felt Sophia's energy when she stood next to her. It was such a loving energy, something she hadn't felt for a long time. She had only experienced that with Dave.

Suddenly, she heard someone walking up the steps to her porch. In the darkness, she didn't recognize her at first. Only when she came close did she see it was Lillith.

"Good evening, Meg. I hope I'm not disturbing you." Without asking, she sat down in the rocking chair next to her. "It's such a nice night, I thought you would be sitting out here. I wanted to talk to you."

Meg felt all the warmth she had been feeling leave her. "I'm really tired. Maybe we could make it another time."

"Oh, it will only take a minute. I saw you talking to Sophia, and I thought it important to warn you about her. She is very deceitful and can cause a lot of trouble."

"What do you mean? I found her warm and charming. She hasn't a deceitful bone in her body."

"Oh, but that's how she does it. She flatters people and makes them feel like they have an inner depth they haven't explored. Then, she slowly worms her way into their affections, and before they know what is happening, they are supporting her financially. Really Meg, I own the house, and she wants people to think it's her home and she has money. She's running a fund-raising campaign for the town, and when the money comes in, she'll run off with it all. Quite a con artist! I'm sorry to have to tell you this, but my advice is to stay as far away from her as you can." Lillith got up and left as quickly as she'd come.

"Wait, wait," said Meg. "I thought you didn't know her. You said you didn't know her. What's going on?" she called to Lillith's retreating back.

Lillith ignored her as she swiftly mounted her steps and slammed her door behind her.

Meg's stomach was roiling. Too much, too much! Was Lillith telling the truth? Was Sophia? She felt a whirl of confusion. Was Sophia really a con artist? If she was, maybe she'd found out about Dave that way. In fact, she could have met him and been told all about what happened. Doubts flooded her. She felt terrible. Loneliness descended over her, and feelings of wanting to die penetrated her being like cold ocean waves. She still missed him, her Dave. Why hadn't she forgiven him and let him back into her life?

Suddenly, Meg felt a warmth come over her, as if someone was hugging her and whispering, "It's not too late. Call him." Then, fearful thoughts invaded her mind—thoughts that said, "It's too late. You'll be hurt again. It's too late." She shook her head, wearily stood up and entered the house.

Meanwhile, next door, Sophia was sitting on the porch opposite Lillith. "You won't win this one, Lillith," she said.

Lillith smirked, "I wouldn't be so sure about that. She has a lot of negativity in her, and you know how good I am at drawing it out."

"Yes, but at bottom she has a good heart, and that's where the battle is always won."

"We'll see. Our agreement is only for a couple more months, and right now we are pretty even. The real battle is just beginning. Tonight, I have the house." Lillith got up and walked inside, leaving Sophia sitting in the tranquil light of her own reflections.

Days later, the fundraising campaign commenced with a community supper and auction. Individuals and businesses donated goods for the auction mainly because of Sophia's efforts. She had personally gone to each of the businesses asking for donations, and very few could refuse her. The evening was very successful. Not only were thousands of dollars raised, but also, for the first time in years, there was a genuine feeling of community building. People who seldom left their homes became involved, and many volunteered to be part of the fundraising committee to continue the effort to help the town out of its financial crisis.

Lillith was there of course. Many saw her, and some of those that did left early, feeling that most of the evening was nonsense and a waste of time. The others stayed and enjoyed themselves. Meg didn't come, and Lillith glowed about that. Winning Meg to her side was somehow symbolic that she would surpass Sophia's influence in the community.

The team building work went well from the outset. Some people had skills that the others were not aware of, leading to a shift of some of the workload. Others, strongly influenced by Lillith, felt that the changes were wrong and began a campaign against Sophia.

The team process inspired the Sophia group, whereas the Lillith group felt it took up too much of their time and lacked direction. The mayor, bombarded from both sides, was perplexed and frustrated. Sophia suggested that he send complaints to her, and she would give him a weekly report on how the work was progressing. He was ambivalent about the fairness of such an arrangement, but she convinced him that it was her job to make the new system work. It was a difficult challenge. Those who were against the process often browbeat others to join them, which intensified the angry resistance. Finally, Sophia brought the two groups together in a meeting that she mediated.

The meeting was held in the Town Hall on a cold December evening. Darkness had enshrouded the town, and streetlights and holiday decorations blinked on to compensate for daylight's early retreat. The room was large and warmly lit. Photographs of early days in the community shared wall space with oil paintings of the town made by local artists. Sophia had arranged the chairs in a large circle to indicate that the two groups should, at least, start off by blending together.

The meeting was scheduled to begin at 7 p.m. As the time approached, people began to pour into the room and take their seats.

Sophia, dressed in a soft green pantsuit, began with an exercise that helped relax everyone and ease the tension. The participants were asked to tell a story from their childhood that impacted them the most. It could be a story that they heard or something that actually happened to them. Most of the stories were positive ones, but several people talked about an illness or a loss. Some of the positive stories stimulated laughter from the group, and the sad ones evoked feelings of sympathy and even compassion. In general, the experience allowed for greater intimacy, so that people felt emboldened to speak from their true feelings.

Then Sophia brought up the real issues of what was happening in the town. Those who objected to change were able to express why they felt that way and were listened to. Both sides compromised, and after three hours of deep discussion, they decided to meet again to continue the process. After several meetings, some new procedures were tried out, and finally, after several experiments and more mediation, most people were working well together. The mediation process itself helped people to learn about each other in a new way, destroying many of the barriers that had existed before.

Throughout the mediations, Lillith was constantly sabotaging the process by supporting resistance to Sophia's efforts, making her work more difficult. The unseen battle was at its height when something happened to help Sophia. The two main opponents were William, head of the Ecology and Conservation Commission, and Ruel, head of the Planning Board. William was advocating for change and Ruel wanted things to remain the same. They were locked head to head, and neither one would compromise.

Sophia arranged a meeting with the two of them. When she attempted to mediate with them, they sat and said nothing at first. William finally was forthcoming in his beliefs, but Ruel wouldn't even respond. While he sat in stubborn silence, Sophia stood up and pulled her chair in front of the door. She said, "The two of you need to talk. I don't care how long it takes, but you are not leaving here until you have come to a working agreement." She then sat down and waited.

"You can't make me do this!" protested Ruel like a stubborn little boy. William was shaking his head, frowning. "Why are you so against making changes?" he finally asked Ruel.

"Just because you want to make changes in your department, it doesn't mean I have to do the same. Things are fine with my people, and we get the work done."

"Yes, that's true, but it's not fine with your people. They work ten-hour days, and that isn't fair to them."

"Then it's up to the Mayor to give us more money to hire people instead of downsizing."

"You know the town hasn't the funds."

"Instead of wasting time in team building, we can do some fundraising." Ruel mumbled.

"Why are you afraid of the new structure?" William asked.

"I'm not afraid of anything. I just think it's stupid and a waste of time."

Finally Sophia interrupted them. "I'm authorized by the Mayor to let people go if they don't try to comply with the new structure. I don't want to do that, but, Ruel, I will be forced to fire you if you won't work with William and come to an agreement."

Ruel glared at her with such hatred that Sophia felt as if a sword was running through her heart. She immediately armed herself against him by imagining metal armor covering her whole body.

Ruel turned to William. "I can't afford to lose my job over this. I will work with you on this, but I refuse to have her in the room."

William looked at Sophia. "I thought you liked Lillith."

Ruel replied. "That's not Lillith. That's Sophia. She's responsible for all of this mess."

"So you can see them both?"

"I've only seen Lillith up to now. Now, for the first time, I see Sophia, and I don't like her."

Sophia smiled and winked at William. "I'll leave you two alone." As she left the office and walked down the corridor, those who had never seen her before gasped at her beauty.

She arrived home at the same time as her next-door neighbor Meg. They stood together on the sidewalk, admiring the clouds racing across the moonlit sky. Sophia spoke first.

"I heard you were vacationing. Did you have a good time?"

"Oh yes, yes. Thank you for telling me about Dave. I've been with him, and we plan to remarry. I've told the children, and they're coming up for the wedding. They haven't forgiven me. I guess it will take awhile. The main thing is, Dave has, and he still loves me. Thank you so much."

"You're welcome. I'm so happy for you. By the way, my work is done here, so I'll be selling the house."

"I'm selling mine, too. Dave's place is much bigger, and quite frankly, this place reminds me of long years of loneliness. Where are you going?"

"I don't know yet. I'll go where I'm needed. Goodbye, and be happy." She gave Meg a big hug and disappeared into her house.

Commentary

This story is about the Law of Attraction as it relates to the feminine. Simply put, the Law of Attraction is that we are responsible for creating our own destiny through our beliefs and the choices we make. In this story, those with goodness in their hearts are privileged to see Sophia; those with anger and resentment can only see Lillith.

Sophia, represents the positive feminine. She is a force for change and transformation. Lillith is self-involved, fomenting gossip and divisiveness.

The positive feminine supports collaboration and creative change. The negative feminine plays on self-centeredness and fear of change. We, men and women alike, each have a preponderance of Sophia or Lillith within us. Sometimes both, at different times, affect us. It is up to each of us to recognize when we have fallen under the influence of the Lillith archetype and to take responsibility for our ensuing actions, which can be destructive not only to ourselves but to those around us. When we recognize the influence of the negative feminine, we must call on our knight, the positive masculine. It is this archetype that, for all of us, men and women alike, that helps us find the "I"; a centered space beyond our personalities from which we can make clear choices.

The following is a very effective process for beginning to get to know your inner knight:

Exercise:

Sit quietly and imagine that you are in a large meadow on a beautiful, sunny day. Take time to feel the sun on you, and enjoy the beauty of the meadow.

Notice a forest at the far end of the meadow. As you look, a knight in shining armor appears. He is on a stunning white horse, and is riding toward you. Even while he is at a distance, you can sense his positive energy. Soon he is near. If he is wearing a helmet, he removes it and smiles at you. Take time to connect with him and experience his energy: strength, uprightness, directness, and clarity.

He dismounts and hands you his sword. You hold it up in front of you and feel the power of the positive masculine within you.

You ask him if you can ride around the meadow with him. He tells you "yes," helps you onto the horse, and then gets on in front of you. You can feel his energy more distinctly now: it is strong and clear. Let yourself absorb some of it.

As you ride slowly around the meadow with him, you might want to imagine the negative Lillith in the scene. You are completely protected by the knight, and can simply observe her. She may shrivel up and disappear, or run away, but that doesn't mean she won't try to come back. It is up to you to recognize when she tries to influence your thoughts and interactions with others. Know that whenever you recognize that she is influencing you or is about to influence you, you can call on your inner masculine – your knight.

Imagine that your ride with the knight comes to an end. You both dismount and simply stand together for a few moments. As you stand with your knight, let yourself realize that the more aware you become of any attempts of the negative feminine to take you over, and the more clearly you can say 'No,' the more you can open up to your inner Sophia, the positive feminine, and the more your inner Sophia can flower and eventually become part of you.

The inner marriage occurs when your two inner energies, your positive masculine and feminine, are in tune with each other and are of equal strength.

Part Two: The Inner Masculine

7
The Pedestal Seat

Perfectionism is a negative masculine characteristic that blocks creativity and the joy of accomplishment. It makes a person feel like they are never satisfied with any completed task. Dissatisfaction with one's work also causes a person to do a task over and over again to try to improve it to 'perfection.'

People with a prominent perfectionist aspect usually developed it in childhood because they were never praised for accomplishing anything; instead, they were always expected to do everything better. A perfectionist parent makes a child feel inferior.

The following tale describes perfectionism:

The evening began with low clouds that hovered over the countryside and veiled most of the fields and houses in a dewy gray mist. The sun had just set, but the darkening sky still gave off enough light for easy driving. The two vehicles were moving slowly on a dirt road, a short-cut that William, the lead driver, had suggested. As they bumped over ruts and ridges, Lillith, sitting next to William in the front seat, said in a surly voice, "This is impossible! It's going to take us forever to get to the main road now. It's already getting dark."

"The last time I drove here, the roads were in good condition," William said, defending his decision. "I don't think it's too much further. Unless, of course, we get lost," he added with a little laugh.

"Lost, you're lost?" In the back seat, Erick suddenly woke up, and Rosalind, who'd been dozing with her head on his shoulder, sat up, hyper alert.

"What's happening? Where are we?"

"No, no, only a joke. We're fine. Go back to sleep."

The occupants retreated into silent boredom.

In the meantime, those in the second car also began to wonder if they were lost. "I think William made a mistake." Ruel's voice was tinged with anger.

"No, he never makes mistakes about directions," Sophia calmly observed. "Besides, I'm riding with you instead of Will because I also know the way, remember?"

The low hanging clouds began to take on an ominous look, forming larger clouds that were turning black. The atmosphere thickened with humidity. Back in the first car, Rosalind said what everyone was thinking, "There has to be a storm ahead. Look at those clouds. I hope it's not a big one."

"Surely not," William said, beginning to feel tired of driving.

At that moment, rain began to pelt the windshield in a fury of drops, making it difficult for him to see. Both cars slowed to a crawl.

"We need to stop and wait until this is over." William's voice was full of concern.

As they drove around a bend, a house appeared through the fog and rain. William honked his horn and swung into the drive, stopping a short way up to be certain Ruel had seen him. Then he continued to drive to the building.

The storm was now casting bolts of lightning into the sky with rolling thunder. The cars pulled up as close to the house as possible. Fortunately, there was a long covered porch. William jumped out of the car and ran toward it. Behind him, Ruel left his car and followed. Huddled together and dripping wet, they rang the doorbell and could hear it resounding throughout the house. No answer. They walked along the porch, peering into windows, but could only make out dim shapes, which they realized were pieces of furniture covered with sheets. The house was deserted, obviously closed down for the season.

"Now what do we do?" William wondered.

"Well, let's see if anything is open," said Ruel. "The storm doesn't look like it's going to let up for a while. It'll be better to wait it out inside than in our cars."

They tried all the windows and finally found one at the end of the porch with a lock that appeared to be broken. It didn't take much to release it, open the window and crawl in. Once inside, they unlocked the front door and called to the others.

Elise, Harry and Sophia grabbed their bags and jumped out of Ruel's car, followed by Lillith, Rosalind and Erick from William's car, and all ran into the house.

Flipping a switch, William was surprised that the lights came on. "They must be planning to return soon. Why else would the electricity be on?"

"Just thank God," Elise said with relief. "I could use a john," she said and wandered off to find one.

"We shouldn't be here. It's not only illegal, it's not right!" Sophia said emphatically.

"Look, if the people were here I'm certain they would invite us in out of the storm," Lillith rationalized. "Look how bad it's become." Indeed, the thunder and lightning had escalated.

"I'm surprised they're not here. It's the beginning of summer and this place can't be too far from the coast," Rosalind said.

"Who knows, maybe they're taking a trip abroad. In any case, we lucked out. Let's take some of these sheets off and get comfortable." Harry grabbed a sheet and yanked it off an old, but lovely, leather couch. "Not bad." He continued removing sheets as he went around the room.

"Don't do that," Lillith protested. "You're making a mess. Don't dump them on the floor!" She picked up a sheet and began to carefully fold it.

"Let me help you," said Rosalind, who began to fold another one, placing it carefully on top of Lillith's.

"I personally don't like objects with sheets on them. It gives me the creeps." Harry kept pulling off sheets, and Rosalind and Lillith followed him around, folding them and putting them in neat piles.

Soon the room was fully back to a normal sitting room. Ruel and William fell onto the couch, tired from the long drive. Sitting together, they provided a direct contrast in appearance, both were tall and thin, but William was by far more muscular and filled out, while Ruel looked like he had never picked up a bar weight or tossed a football. When compared to William's warm smile and soft face, Ruel's sharp features made him look more masculine.

Elise returned and asked, "Where is the radio? It should give us the forecast for this area." She disappeared into the hall and came back with the radio. She found the station, and they listened with growing dismay: "Severe storm warning over the area. Expecting two to four inches of heavy rainfall and very low visibility. There is a flood watch for low-lying areas. The storm will continue throughout the night and possibly clear late in the morning."

"Well, I guess we were lucky to find this place," William said wearily.

"Come on, Elise, why don't we see what we have here in the way of bedding?" suggested Sophia. The two women went off to investigate the upstairs of the house.

"I can sleep here." Ruel yawned and lay down on the couch, forcing William to move to a chair.

"Just like him," William whispered to Erick, who, seated next to him, nodded slightly.

The women had discovered four bedrooms upstairs, and even though there were no sheets on the beds, they found some in a cupboard. "Let's just sleep on top of the beds," Sophia suggested when Elise starting pulling out the sheets.

"That would mess up the bedspreads. No, it's much better to make the beds, and first thing in the morning we can wash the sheets."

"But we need to clear out of here fast. Who knows if the people are on their way here now and also got stuck?"

"Don't be silly. The chances of that happening are slim."

Elise carefully laid two sheets on each bed as the two women moved from room to room. Then they proceeded to make up the first bed. With pursed lips and deep concentration, Elise smoothed out each wrinkle and lined up each top sheet perfectly, folding it over under each pillow. She fluffed up the pillows, flicking off specks of dust that Sophia, watching her in fascination, couldn't even see. They had started working together, but soon it became clear that Sophia's side of the bed was falling short of Elise's expectations. She walked around to check Sophia's work, straightening and fussing as she examined the corner at the foot of the bed to make sure Sophia had tucked it in properly. This routine continued until all four beds were made. After the task was completed, Sophia, half annoyed and half amused, commented, "Are you sure you never owned a Bed and Breakfast?"

Elise responded seriously, "Why do you say that?"

Sophia shook her head slightly. "Never mind. Let's go back downstairs."

They entered the kitchen to find Lillith and Rosalind rummaging through the pantry. Lillith, who was married to Ruel, looked very much like him. They might have been brother and sister. She had dark hair and eyes, was tall, and wore a black shirt over dark green pants. She had a strange face that at first appeared very attractive, but when she smiled, became almost ugly. Rosalind was black and very exotic looking, with a sensuous mouth and ebony eyes. Both she and Lillith were thin, appearing almost emaciated. They were both very conscious of their weight.

Opening some cupboards, Lillith said, "There's not much here, but we can open a few cans and packages of pasta. All in all, it's not bad, and I even found a couple of bottles of wine that smell okay."

"You opened them?" Sophia was taken aback. "You can't do that. It's bad enough that we're even here!"

"So what? As long as we don't get caught." Lillith drank some of the wine she had already poured for herself.

When the meal preparations were completed, they called the men in and sat down at the round table. Sophia sat next to William and gave him a little hug. She could see how tired he was. Her long, light brown hair fell against his shoulder. She was attractive and radiated a quiet charm and femininity that made most men stop and stare.

Erick and Rosalind were the only unmarried couple. Somewhat hefty, Erick dwarfed tiny Rosalind, who was curled up next to him.

The last couple was Elise and Harry. They were good friends of Lillith and Ruel, but didn't know the others well. Harry was neatly dressed in a buttoned-down shirt and slacks rather than jeans like the others were wearing. Elise was very quiet and somewhat mousy. Her features lacked distinction, and she was the kind of person who, after meeting her, you forget about meeting her if introduced a second time. In contrast, Harry was very talkative and filled her silences.

All the married couples and Rosalind were in their late twenties. Erick was a little older at thirty-five.

The food was a mixed bag. Even though it wasn't great, it at least filled them up. The wine seemed to make everything taste better.

"I know this wine. It's very expensive," William said.

"Good, let's see if we can find more." Harry was already getting a bit tipsy.

Lillith pushed her chair back and, as she stood up, looked at the floor. "You know, these floors are dirty, and everything is dusty. I hate to sleep in these conditions. Anyone want to help me clean?"

"I agree. I'll join you," and Elise also got up.

"Well, as long as you two are doing it, I'll help." Rosalind offered her services.

Frowning, Sophia started to clean up the kitchen.

Ruel observed, "You know, I like this kitchen, but the paintings are wrong here. I think the one in the hall would look better than that one." He pointed to a scene of an apple orchard hanging on the nearby wall.

He stood up and fetched the painting from the hall. He then switched them, stood back admiringly, and said, "Yes, I'm right. Look how perfect that is."

"Are you nuts? Put it back! Remember, we broke into this place," exclaimed William.

"It doesn't hurt to help them out," Ruel retorted sharply, adjusting the painting on the wall. He sat back down at the table and glared at William.

"What're you talking about? You don't even know them," said William.

"I don't need to know them to help them out!"

"Oh, come on. That's ridiculous. You're intruding on their space!"

"What's wrong with you? Clearly they have no aesthetic sense. This really improves the look of the place. Anyway, I'll bet they won't even notice."

"That's not the point. This whole business is wrong. Here we are, taking over the place. Okay, we needed shelter, but let's not be dishonest about it and pretend what we're doing is good for them." William was staring fiercely at Ruel.

Annoyed, Ruel stood up abruptly and said, "C'mon, Harry. Help me help our hosts out. I've seen a few other things that would look better in other places." He walked out of the kitchen with Harry in tow.

Looking after them, William said, "I can't believe those guys! The storm must have affected their senses."

He then moved over to the window to see what was happening. The thunder was louder, and the lightning was clearly striking closer to the house. As Sophia joined him, they gave each other a look that spoke volumes.

"Maybe we should go to bed before they invade our room," she said in disgust.

"I don't like what's happening here. I think we need to be more vigilant and keep them from going too far."

"It's gone too far already," she replied loudly over the noise coming from another room.

"Let's see what Ruel and Harry are doing," he said. "By the way, where's Erick?"

"Don't know. He left right after dinner."

When they entered the living room, they were shocked to see that all the furniture and paintings had been rearranged, and the two guys were busy deciding what to do with a large mirror they had taken down from over the fireplace.

"Stop it!" Sophia cried. "Will is absolutely right. We're intruders here, and you're rearranging these people's house. What in the world do you think they'll say when they see it?"

"I would hope they'd be delighted." Harry protested.

"Right!" said Ruel. "Don't you see? We're helping them out with all our work." To her astonishment, Ruel seemed to really believe it.

At that moment, Erick walked into the room.

"Where have you been?" William asked.

"I thought I would surprise everyone," he replied, placing four bottles of wine on the table. "I brought these for the weekend. Now we can have a real party." He removed his dripping wet coat. "Wow, it's really a mess out there!"

"I think we've had plenty of wine, but it would be nice to leave these for our unseen hosts," Sophia suggested.

Just then the door opened, and Lillith and Elise came in with all their cleaning gear.

"We're going to have a party. You can clean later." Erick pointed to the wine.

"No, we'll clean first so the room will be more comfortable."

Lillith then added, "And of course, we'll give it a last run-through after the party."

"C'mon, Erick, give us a hand!" Ruel and Harry left, with Erick following, leaving the women to start cleaning. Lillith assembled all the cleaning material that she had found under the sink, and the vacuum cleaner that she had also discovered. She began to delegate tasks to the women.

"Rosalind, you dust, then you can polish the furniture with this," she said, handing her a bottle of liquid and a rag.

Before Lillith could say more, Elise volunteered to vacuum.

"That's good. Then I'll mop the floor. I couldn't find any floor polish, so we'll have to stop there. It's a shame. These floors could be so nice." She wheeled around and said, almost accusingly, "Look, there's a scratch, and another one over there!"

William grabbed Sophia's hand and pulled her into a small sitting room that was off the living room. "First they take the sheets off the furniture, then they take over the place. This is nuts!" His voice was strained.

If we don't watch out, they'll have us polishing the silver—if they have silver," she said lightly. Then, in a more serious tone, she added, "Did you notice how Ruel and Lillith instigated the others to follow suit?"

"Yes," he replied. "I've always thought they were too extreme. You know, obsessed in a way. Everything has to be just perfect. Their house is overly neat. If you put anything on a tabletop, one of them is always moving it."

They looked at each other worriedly. He continued, "What's happening here is wrong, but we're overruled. No one seems to see what's going on."

"Will, I know the storm is bad, really bad, but I'd feel better if we slept in the car. Then we can take off as soon as the rain stops. It might seem crazy, but I don't want to be part of this. In fact, I don't want to spend the weekend with any of them."

"Okay, I agree, but what about my passengers?"

"Well, Lillith will replace me, and their SUV has a third back seat. There's plenty of room for Rosalind and Erick. I'm sure they can find their way in the morning since we're almost there."

"Let's write them a note, though, and tell them we're going home," he said.

"I think we should also tell them how we feel about what they did."

"I agree."

They found some paper and a pen and wrote a long note stating how they felt, adding that it was important to put everything back the way it originally was. By now, they could hear the party starting and loud music playing. They found their bags in one of the bedrooms, but stopped to take off the sheets and put them back in the linen closet.

No one heard them leave, as the music was deafening. Only when the party was over and they were cleaning up did the others discover the note.

Concerned, Rosalind said, "I thought they went to bed. Didn't you?" she asked Erick.

Before he could respond, Lillith, looking disgusted, said, "They're deadheads; I'm glad they left."

"Me too. We'll have a much better time without them," agreed Ruel.

The others mumbled their assent, except for Rosalind and Erick who looked very upset. They were closest to William and Sophia, and the note had sobered them up.

"I think we should do what they said about putting everything back," Rosalind finally spoke out.

"Never! It would take all morning, and we'll lose more time from our weekend." Ruel gave her a dirty look.

"If you want to stay and do that, go ahead, but I think you're going to have to ride with us now. Some friends!" Lillith's voice was nasty.

Ruel grabbed Harry's arm, "We still need to hang that mirror. Come help me."

Harry protested. "No way, I'm going to bed. Coming, Elise?"

He grabbed her around the waist and they left, as did Ruel and Lillith, leaving Erick and Rosalind sitting alone in the clean, neat living room.

"Oh, lord, what have we done?" whispered Rosalind. "I feel terrible. How did we just go along with all this?"

"We finked out, that's what! Will and Sophia are right. Maybe we can at least put some of the stuff back where it belongs."

In tears, Rosalind said, "I feel so bad, and I refuse to go home with any of them! What'll we do?"

"Look, it's still storming. Will and Sophia can't drive in this. They must be planning to sleep in the car. I'm going outside to check."

"Okay, but be careful. I'd rather stay up all night than stay here. I'll get our stuff together. Boy, do we owe them an apology!"

"Right." And, throwing his still damp coat on, Erick plunged into the storm.

Commentary

In our society, perfectionism is considered a virtue. In fact, this trait has nothing to do with virtue, but rather is often an obsessive and destructive aspect of the personality. This story dramatically exaggerates this fact by unfolding the ethical dilemmas represented by the six characters: The morally defunct Ruel and Lillith play out a pattern of super cleanliness, whereas Will and Sophia are completely unfazed by the dusty household. Their concern is for the larger issue of invading someone else's house and rearranging their possessions. When Ruel starts moving the furniture, he is exhibiting his need for control, a negative masculine trait that deludes him into thinking he is helping people who have not asked for help. His and the others' perfectionism has absolutely nothing to do with concern for others.

An extreme perfectionist can only see what is wrong. The mind closes down into a negative thinking pattern. If you are an extreme perfectionist sitting by a beautiful lake, you will only see the weeds or the dead fish floating by. In our story, the callous behavior of Ruel and Lillith, as well as of Harry and Elise, illustrates that there is nothing positive or helpful in their perfectionism. On the contrary, their only concern is for the objects around them, not for people.

When it takes over, perfectionism deadens creativity. Nothing is good enough. If you are writing a story, painting a picture, or planning a meal, this trait can creep in and demolish your self-esteem, and thus your ability to perform. How does this happen? Underneath a perfectionist mindset there is often the belief that one is not good enough. If I have this belief, then I will compensate for it by being "perfect" in everything I do. I will most likely also have an inner critic, working in tandem with the perfectionist, who is constantly yammering at me. If I look at my lawn and see a weed, the critic points it out and the perfectionist takes over. I go to the garden shop, buy some weed killer, and go on and on into a depressing scenario.

Years ago, a relative was visiting Judith Bach in the deep woods where she lived. The relative looked around and announced, "You really should clean out these woods, then it would be very nice." Astonished, Judith looked at the acres of beautiful trees around them. The relative could only see the underbrush and failed to take in the beauty of the trees.

This is the point. To be a perfectionist is to miss the beauty of the positive feminine and to fall into negative masculine action that is destructive and uncaring. In the story, Ruel and Lillith collude, through perfectionism, to create a negative situation that illustrates their lack of moral principles.

Exercise:

Think back to your childhood and teenage years. When you were a child, did you feel that you should always do better? If the answer is yes, reflect on your parents' responses to the things you did. Did they believe you were doing very well, or did they always want you to do better?

If you feel that being a perfectionist is part of your personality, then do the following:

Link with your heart, and ask: How can I begin to change this perfectionist characteristic?

What is the first step to helping me accept who I am and not be driven by a need to be better?

8

Lost in Inspiration

Many people have great ideas and beautiful visions that have never been manifested. This is because, although such individuals are in touch with the creativity and inspiration of the positive feminine, they have very little of the positive masculine needed to manifest those ideas into reality. It is disappointing to see great ideas never take form, because they are lost and may never appear again.

The following tale illustrates this situation and indicates what is needed in order to change it:

Startled into wakefulness by a sound in the room, Sara held her breath, blinking and staring into the darkness. Was someone there? No, she realized as her eyes accommodated to the dark and her chairs and dresser took shape in comforting familiarity. She turned on the light and realized she must have been dreaming. She struggled to remember her dream, then turned off the light and let herself fall back into a doze. There had been something beautiful. Ah, yes, she'd been walking down a long path lined with rose bushes of every color of the rainbow in full bloom. What was so extraordinary was that the flowers were twice their normal size, and the fragrance was luscious. Never had she experienced such beauty.

Before she reached the end of the path, the bushes became tall and formed an arch over her head. Inside the arch were chairs made of wicker, with deep flowered cushions that invited her to rest. When she sat down, the scene suddenly changed to a very different place. She was now seated on a bench on a small village street, and the people who walked by her resembled characters out of a nineteenth-century play. The women were dressed in long skirts, and the men were in knickers and flowing, blouse-like shirts. When she looked down at herself, she was wearing a long skirt made of blue striped cotton with a white apron tied over it, and buttoned, brown shoes.

I must be seeing a past life, she thought. Opening a cloth bag she was carrying, she found a small antique mirror and looked into it. Her features were almost the same, but her brown hair was lighter, almost sandy colored, and her eyes were a blue green instead of a dark blue. It was almost the same nose, though, small and delicate looking, and it was the same full mouth, just uncolored with the deep red lipstick she normally wore. It was a pretty face, but her eyes looked sad and distant, with none of the sparkle and life Sara had now.

Suddenly, a tall, good-looking man came over to her, greeting her by the name of Jennifer. "Why are you sitting here, Jennifer? Everyone is waiting for you at home."

He took her hand and led her along several streets until they came to a tall white townhouse with green-shuttered windows. They hurried up the walk and entered a long hallway.

She heard someone call to them. "Did you find her?"

He answered, "Yes, we're here."

The scene that followed was hazy in Sara's memory. The man was her husband, that much she knew. When she walked into a living room with Victorian furniture, she was aware of several people gathered there. Some were old, and others were more her age, in their late twenties. It seemed to be a family meeting, but why they were meeting wasn't clear. All she knew was it was a very serious occasion, and the outcome would be one that she wouldn't like. She also knew it concerned her.

Something jarred Sara awake again, and this time she felt someone standing next to her bed. Her body was paralyzed and numb, as it hadn't completely awakened yet. She struggled to regain consciousness and open her eyes. It took her what seemed like an eternity to finally do so, and when she did, the figure she saw was the man in the dream.

"Who are you?"

He smiled at her and disappeared.

The next moment, she closed her eyes again and found herself flying through clouds, with the wind blowing hard against her body. Oh, what a wonderful feeling, she thought. I want to fly back to that rose garden to smell the roses again. Immediately, she was back, seated in the wicker chair under the arbor of roses. Her thought was to stay there and not go forward to the other scene, but somehow she had no choice, and she found herself back in the living room with the same people. The man who was her husband was still holding her hand. He was much taller than her, around six feet; he was taller than most of the people there. His grey hair was curly and long, and she could now see he was much older than her. Someone spoke his name, Ruel. Again, she went in and out of the scene, not knowing what was happening, except that it concerned her.

When she returned again, the others had decided to send her to some kind of institution.

They think I am insane, she thought. He has convinced them that I am crazy, and that's not true. He just wants to get rid of me.

In the scene, she started to cry. "Please don't let him do this to me. He's the one who's insane. He beats me if I talk to people, which is why I'm so quiet. Please believe me." She ran to the woman who she knew was her sister.

Her sister hugged her and quietly said, "I know, I know. It will be alright. This is for the best."

She screamed, "You don't believe me! Doesn't anyone here believe me?" When she looked around the room at their vacant faces, she knew they didn't. Ruel took her by the arm and led her out of the room.

Then Sara was back in the rose arbor again, but this time she left quickly and found herself flying over an ocean, with waves pounding a sandy beach. After she landed on the sand and sat down, she woke up again. This time she could see the sun rising over the trees in her yard, and her dog, Ginger, jumped on the bed for his early morning belly rub.

Later that morning, Sara thought about the lovely visions she had seen in her dream: the glorious roses, the clouds floating in a turquoise sky, and the rolling sea with sparkling sand. She took out a sketchbook and tried to draw some of the images, but soon gave up. Sara had always wanted to draw and paint, which is why she had some art supplies, but somehow, even when she felt inspired, she didn't really know how to do it. Once, she'd signed up for an art class, but she only went to one session. The class was half an hour away, and when it was cold out she didn't like to bundle up and wait for the car to warm up.

Then she thought she should write about her dream experience. It would make an interesting short story, and she'd always liked the idea of being a writer. In college, her English teacher had encouraged her to pursue that career, but it seemed like a lot of work. Writing a novel would take forever, and then she'd have to try to sell it, or even self-publish, and that too was a no-win effort, as then it would have to be marketed. She did take a course in creative writing and really enjoyed it. She was, once again, encouraged by the teacher to continue, but other things came up, so she dropped the creative writing venture.

Fortunately, she had enough money from an inheritance to not have to work full time. She mainly did some volunteer work at the hospital, and, once in a while, she would help a friend who had a cottage industry in pottery.

Sara had lots of friends, so she was never lonely, and her dog was her constant companion. He was a lot easier to take care of than a man.

When she was alone in her house she often made up fantasies. It kept her mind busy, and it was fun to imagine scenes. Her friends always told her she had a vivid imagination. Maybe it was because her favorite books were science fiction. She loved the Harry Potter series and even thought about writing her own series, which would also be about magic and a teenager.

After a long walk with her dog, Sara went to town to shop. Her one love was buying clothes, and she had to admit, she was a good-looking woman with a nice body, due to her daily visits to the gym. She had been married in her early twenties, but that only lasted a couple of years, and since then she had no desire to remarry. Dating was fun, and now that she was in her early forties, the urge to have children had left her. Back in her thirties she'd contemplated having a child or adopting one, but when she really got serious about it, the thought of changing diapers and being a single mom made her drop the idea.

After buying a couple of skirts—she preferred skirts to pants when it wasn't cold out—Sara went to her favorite deli for a cup of coffee. Seated at a table, she was reading the local paper when a voice said, "Do you mind if I sit here?"

She looked up to see a tall, thin man with gray hair looking down at her.

She almost jumped out of her skin. It was the man in her dream!

"I'm sorry. I must have startled you."

"No, uh, yes, I guess you did. Please sit down."

He put coffee and a sandwich down on the table and pulled up a chair. "Please don't notice me. Go back to your reading."

"Thanks, it's okay. There's nothing important in this paper. Are you from around here?"

"Yes and no. I live in the city, but just bought a second home here. May I introduce myself? My name is Rudy Green."

"My name is Sara Evans. I've been living here most of my life. I'm sure you'll love the area."

Soon they were deep in conversation. It turned out that Rudy was in his late 50's and was hoping to retire soon in the house he'd just bought. He was divorced, with grown children. It was amazing how much he resembled Ruel. The features were almost the same, except Ruel's nose had been longer and more pointed. Sara had to keep from staring at his face, and somewhere inside she felt a twinge of fear, yet also a lot of attraction. When it was time to leave, he took her phone number, and they made a date to have dinner the next evening.

Sara went home and collapsed in her favorite chair.

What to do? This guy must be a reincarnation of Ruel, and he was terrible to me. I can't see him again. It would be awful, yet maybe he's changed. It was a couple of centuries ago. Maybe it would be different now. He's so attractive and available. How can it hurt to go out with him?

That night Sara had another flying dream. This time she flew to Paris just as dawn was breaking over the city. It was lovely to see Notre Dame with the sun rising beyond its tower. Then, suddenly, she was in another rose garden. It was different from the one the night before. There were long-stem single roses instead of bushes, and the roses were glowing in their luminosity, waiting to be cut. She imagined cutting one and holding it in her hand as she walked down path after path of red roses, then pink, then yellow. Sara cut one rose of each color and ended up with a small bouquet of four roses in her hand. The last path had a mixed rose that went from yellow in the center to white and sometimes a hint of pink at the tips of the petals. It was her favorite; it was called the Patience Rose. At the end of one of the paths, she sat on a stone wall and closed her eyes. Suddenly, she was in another scene.

This scene was dark and dreary. She was sitting in a bare room with only a bed, a table and a light high up on the wall. There was one window with bars on it and a heavy door that she knew was locked from the outside. The rocking chair she was sitting in was hard, with no cushion. The horrible part was that there was nothing to do, no books to read, no knitting; there was nothing to do but rock. She began to cry, but then stopped, knowing that crying never helped at all. Her only hope was to stay very calm and convince the doctors that she was sane enough to leave.

The door opened and a nurse came in with a tray of food, which she put on the table. She didn't look at her or even say good evening. Jennifer called to her, "Lillith, is it possible to have a book to read? I love reading!"

Lillith turned to look at her. She was thin as a rail, with an ugly mouth that turned down at the corners. "Books, books in this place? Even the doctors are too stupid to read books." She laughed as she left the room.

Jennifer ate her meal slowly to make it last. It was time to sit and make up stories to keep her mind busy and to keep from going mad.

Sara woke up with a start. Ginger was barking at something outside. She got up to look but saw nothing when she put her floodlights on. Probably a raccoon trying to get in the garbage can. She didn't feel like going to sleep again, so she picked up a book she'd been reading and sat back on her bed. A wave of depression came over her when she opened the book. Making up stories in her mind had kept her sane in the life she was dreaming about, and in this one, it was her form of creativity. But did she ever get to write her stories down in that life? Would they have given her a pen and paper? Probably not! How long was I in that awful place?

Her eyes closed, her book fell on the floor, and she found herself in yet another rose garden. This one seemed barer and less beautiful. The roses were a normal size and needed a lot of pruning. In fact, that was what she was doing. She was pruning the roses and clearing up the weeds around them. The only tool she had was a spoon, but that didn't stop her. As she was working, she heard someone approach her. Looking up, she saw a young man with brown hair, gentle brown eyes and a smile that lit up his handsome face.

"Jennifer, you are doing fine work with this garden. We wondered who was working here. I should have known it would be you."

"I'm sorry if I'm not supposed to do this. I thought if I told anyone they would stop me. I'm just so bored. I have to do something! So when I'm allowed to walk in the grounds, I come here to help the roses. I used to have a lovely rose garden in my home, and even though we had a gardener, I always attended to the roses myself."

"What are you using to weed?"

"Please don't tell on me, but Lillith dropped a spoon from my tray and didn't notice it was gone." She held up her spoon for him to see.

"Come, let's talk about this some more." He took her hand, helped her up and went to sit on a bench near by.

"Please, Dr. William, don't tell my doctor, or he may take my spoon away."

"I promise, I won't. What else can you do?"

"I love to read, and I used to write when I lived at home. My husband hated my stories and forbade me to continue writing. I think he was afraid that I would write about how mean he was and someone might read it. I don't know what is worse, having him abuse me or being a prisoner here. At least at home I could write and hide my writing, and I had a huge library of books. He never stopped me from reading, thank God, but here, I have nothing but this sick little garden."

"I think I will talk to your doctor, Jennifer. I don't understand why you can't have books to read or paper for writing your stories."

"Thank you, thank you, that would be wonderful."

"And I will give you a better tool to garden with. Just hide it from the others, as some of them are violent. I know you wouldn't harm anyone or yourself."

"No, I wouldn't. Thank you."

Sara watched as Jennifer returned to her work, and then she found herself flying to a scene in the mountains. It looked like Switzerland, with snow on the peaks and small villages nestled in the hills. She flew slowly, taking in the scene, and trying to let go of the feeling of isolation that she had felt in Jennifer. What a terrible life. What a horrible man her husband had been.

She awoke with a headache and remembered she was having dinner with Rudy that evening. His card was in her purse. She found it and called the number on the bottom.

"Hello, good morning."

"Hello, Rudy, this is Sara. I've been thinking about our date tonight. I'm going to have to break it. There's somebody else in my life who I also just met recently, and I'd like to see just him for now, but thank you for the invitation."

When she hung up, she felt a wave of relief throughout her whole body. Even the headache left her as quickly as it had come. She found herself going to her computer. Feeling an edge of excitement, she sat down, opened to a blank page and started typing Jennifer's story: a story about an abused woman who wrote fantasies. If Jennifer never sold a book, she will now! Sara thought.

A year later, Sara finished the book. She made an appointment with an agent recommended by a friend. It was fortuitous that, when she talked to him on the phone and told him the story, he was really interested, and instead of telling her to send it to him, he wanted her to bring it in person.

When she walked into his office, a lovely young woman was sitting at a desk.

"I'm Sophia, Walter's secretary," she said. "You must be Sara. Please just go in. He's waiting for you."

Sara knocked and opened the door to his office, and there was the William of her dream, sitting at the desk with a huge grin on his face.

Commentary

When we first meet Sara, she is living in a dream world. She's like a balloon that is blown here and there by the wind, completely ungrounded. Rich in inspiration, she is incapable of expressing herself in the world. This is what happens when an individual is overbalanced on the feminine side. Without the masculine, dreams evaporate into the ether, inspiration is short-circuited, and nothing is manifested in the world. Not only does the individual suffer from the frustration of an inability to follow through, but those who could be helped by a "grounded" expression of inspiration—be it a painting, a musical composition, a scientific inspiration, or an invention—also miss out! We once knew a man who had wonderful ideas for business ventures, but they never saw the light of day. Such opportunities could affect not only the individual who has the ideas, but also those who could benefit from them.

After going through many years where her dreams vanished into thin air, our heroine discovers the source of her inability to write—the very activity that would "ground" her inspirations. The source was the horrendous experience of being a victim to her husband's dark intention to hospitalize her in a mental institution in a past life. From a reincarnation perspective, such a traumatic experience would leave its mark on the next life, in the same way that a childhood trauma leaves its mark on the current life.

You may wonder, then, why Ruel's reappearance as Rudy in her current life was initially an interesting and seemingly positive occurrence for our heroine. The fact is, we tend to repeat our previous experiences, feeling the power of an old connection in the same way we did in the past. Had Sara stayed with Rudy, she would likely have repeated the old interaction in a new way, feeling, after a time, even more unable to act out and manifest her dreams. Fortunately, she saved herself from repeating the pattern by saying no to a date with Rudy. Taking this action immediately freed her to write, thus opening her up to a new relationship with William, who represents the positive masculine. Everyone needs the masculine to manifest the inspiration of the feminine. Action, the masculine, grounds the feminine, and achievement is the outcome.

Exercise:

Most people have been inspired and have let that inspiration fade without following through. Think about inspirational ideas you may have had but never followed through on. An inspirational idea may be anything, from wanting to create something to experimenting with a project. If you have several, choose one that particularly excited you.

Link with your heart, put the inspirational idea in your heart and ask yourself the following questions:

What caused me not to follow through?

Is not following through a pattern of mine?

If the answer is yes, ask: What caused this pattern?

Is it too late for me to take this inspirational idea and follow through with it now?

If the answer is no, ask: What would be the best way to do this?

If the answer is yes, it is too late, ask: Is there another inspirational idea that I could follow through with?

9
Overtly Masculine

An imbalance between the masculine and feminine has limiting consequences for leadership. In the past, the masculine leadership style prevailed, and even the women who were managers used primarily masculine energy. Team building, an aspect of the positive feminine, was not known or considered. Today corporations realize the importance of developing the type of cooperation where every member of the group can participate fully. This change in leadership style, which has moved towards a balance of the masculine and feminine, has led to more integrative solutions, and more harmonious work environments.

The following story is about how this change affected an overtly masculine man:

Managing a large department of employees and doing well in his career, Nathan was unexpectedly laid off. His company, Jenson's Department Store, was bought by a competing company that wanted to keep its own top executives and had fired him and most of his colleagues.

Nathan was given a week's notice to pack up his office and leave. It was a fierce blow to his ego. He had worked very hard to achieve his high position, and even though he had a healthy severance package, being laid off caused him a lot of pain, as he had been with his company twenty-five years.

Looking back at his rise through the ranks, one would say it was spectacular. He had started working in the mailroom when he was just out of high school. Without any further education, he'd managed to work his way up. Part of Nathan's success was due to his strong, aggressive personality. He also was good at analyzing people. With great care, he'd chosen the right people to develop a friendship with, avoiding those that he felt were politically incorrect. Nathan displayed an ability to do the work, but he also had the commanding personality that it took to be a manager. He'd accomplished many tasks by being authoritarian, telling his staff what to do and how to do it.

Some people admired his leadership skills, whereas others really disliked him. Obviously the ones that admired him were the top executives, which is why he'd been promoted into a high position.

Now that Nathan was no longer working, he found looking for a job difficult. The executive search companies told him that he might have to take a lesser position since his lack of education did not look good on his resume in today's market. Also, he was in his forties, and most places liked to hire younger men. Fortunately, he looked younger than his years. He was a nice-looking man—medium height, blond hair and blue eyes. Playing golf and working out regularly in a gym helped him keep his athletic build.

One headhunter suggested that he consider a job in a small company where he could fit in, but Nathan didn't want that kind of job. He wanted to be back in a large corporation where he could again climb the ladder and earn a salary that was at least equal to that of his last position. Three of his four children were in college, and his wife, Mary, had never worked, so he needed to earn a good livelihood.

Being unemployed not only bored him, but it also made it difficult for Mary, who found his commanding manner much too overwhelming on a daily basis. In his last job, Nathan always worked long hours and expected his staff to do the same. Mary saw very little of him during the week, and on weekends, he played golf with the company executives and went to functions that clients also attended. His life was his work, so now that he was home with nothing to do, all the negative traits of his personality became energized.

After looking for a few months, Nathan finally had to let the executive search teams send him to companies that weren't to his liking but were now his last resort. One of the first places he went was a newly formed company that was developing computer software and other accessories. It had grown quickly because of a new technology that they had developed, a piece of software that was outstanding for its database. The position was for a Sales Manager. Nathan's specialty was in the computer field, and his background was in sales, so it was a perfect fit for him. When the president, William Fields, interviewed him, Nathan did his best to make a good impression, talking at length about his management skills.

William was younger than Nathan, in his mid-thirties. His warm brown eyes and relaxed demeanor were a welcome contrast to other interviewers Nathan had met.

"The people in the sales department have just been hired," he informed Nathan. "The original manager took another position closer to his home. The department consists of ten people, some who are experienced salesmen and saleswomen and a few that are right out of college and will need training."

"I've always been very good at training staff. That should be no trouble, and if you check my references, they will tell you how I topped the sales record."

William thought for a moment, and then said slowly, "I'm certain that's true, but my main concern is your management style. I can tell from what you've told me so far that you belong to the old managerial school, where the manager is the authority and makes all the decisions."

"But that's what I'm good at! I would think you would want someone who is knowledgeable!"

"Knowledgeable, yes, but making all the decisions, no. I believe in teamwork, where an employee's skills are utilized by letting him or her be part of the decision-making process. Instead of talking down to the staff, it's about bringing out their creativity."

"My previous employer, Jensen, talked about doing that and even brought in a facilitator to do team building in one of the departments. It just didn't go well, so they didn't continue it in the other departments."

"Well, it will work fine here if we do it right. Since this is a new company, unlike Jenson's, we are interested in creating a corporate culture that's very different from the ground up. I would guess that, in your situation, it was like trying to screw a golden arm onto a clay statue."

He then grinned, his face lighting up, and said, "I do think you have potential. I feel it could be a good fit if you're willing to learn how to develop your department into a team that not only cooperates, but also develops creative ideas for how to sell our products. Are you willing to try? Don't forget, most of the members of your team are also new to this kind of thinking, so it will be a challenge for all of you. If you agree to take this on, I'm willing to have you be coached by a trainer, and I'm also going to ask you to take some courses to familiarize yourself with this process."

"Of course, I'm always willing to learn. Acquiring the right skills in my last job is what brought me to a top position there."

"Good, let's give it a six-month trial. I'll have a contract drawn up right away."

The tension that had been building up in Nathan's body drained in a flood of relief. "Thank you. I look forward to working for you and this company."

That evening, when Nathan told Mary about the job and the team-building requirements, she laughed. "You'd better keep looking for a job. You're so bossy, there's no way you can let your staff have a say in making decisions!"

His dark eyes flashed as he answered stiffly. "That's not true. I can learn anything."

"Not that, dear. It would drive you crazy if someone comes up with a better idea than you."

"Well, I just won't let that happen. My ideas will always surpass anyone else's. You'll see. I'll keep this job. Besides, the pay is better than I thought, and you know how much we need the money."

"Good luck, but try not to be so controlling; otherwise we'll be dipping into our retirement savings."

In the first few weeks, Nathan took her advice and proceeded cautiously, taking time to learn about each person on his staff: six men and four women. In the beginning, he was disturbed by the women. He'd deliberately hired men for his sales teams in the past because they were more aggressive, and he preferred working with that salesmanship style.

He was pleased that three of the women on his team turned out to be very masculine in their approach to work, but one woman, Sophia, was very feminine. Initially, Nathan was convinced that she would be a weak link. He watched her carefully so he could have a reason to fire her in the near future. Strangely enough, her sales record was extraordinary! He concluded that the reason for this was her looks. She had an interesting face, with strong features, a dark complexion and arresting hazel eyes. Obviously her looks must be getting her the sales. One other woman also rang up the sales. Her name was Lillith. The opposite of Sophia, she was tall and heavy-set, with sharp angular features, blond wavy hair and blue eyes. He realized that she handled men very shrewdly by manipulating them. These two women were the top performers in the group. The others were all good, but not really up to their caliber.

Nathan took the team building courses and the coaching, but he found all of it tough to follow. His habit of taking charge had become automatic. Ruel Jones, an outside consultant, handled the first team building meeting. He was a handsome man with long, thick blond hair that he tossed whenever he spoke. Ruel explained to Nathan that this process would help him determine who should be on the team and who should be let go.

"How will that work?" Nathan queried.

"I'll ask some personal questions so you can have more insight into their personalities."

"But do I have to take part in that? I mean, will you be asking me the same questions?"

"Of course, but I'll make it easy for you and give you the questions ahead of time so you can prepare or even make up an answer."

"Great, I appreciate that."

"Well, you are the boss. In the long run, that's what counts."

"I thought everyone had to be equal in these meetings. Glad to hear that's not true."

When Nathan arrived home after his meeting with Ruel, he was feeling queasy about the whole process. Mary studied him for a moment as he greeted her and asked, "What's wrong, honey? You look awful!"

He slumped into his easy chair, looked out the window into the tree-shaded yard and told her what was going on at work. "I'm not sure this is going to work out, but it has to! I'll never find this kind of a deal again, and I have to prove myself tomorrow."

"So, tell me what's going on. Maybe I can help," she said, perching on the edge of the couch. She was a small woman with short, ash-brown hair, warm, dark eyes and a direct manner.

After he explained the meeting he was to go to in the morning, he showed her the list of questions that Ruel had given him.

"You mean you have to answer these, too? But you're in charge!"

"That's the problem. I haven't a clue how to answer these, and besides this idiot, Ruel, the boss is going to be there, too! I mean, I could handle Ruel, but I really have to look good for the boss or I'm out of a job again."

"I'll tell you what," said Mary. "Let's do this together. Why don't I ask you the questions and you answer them?"

"Good idea. When? Is Mildred home?"

"She's staying over at Joanie's house tonight. Let's eat now, and do this after dinner."

"Great! I'll wash up, we'll eat, and then we can look at this stuff."

The following morning the sales group settled into the conference room. Sure enough, William sat in on the first meeting, which made Nathan very nervous. He had the list of questions Ruel had given him tucked away, out of sight, in his notebook, and he thanked his lucky stars for Mary's help, because he himself hadn't a clue about what to say.

The first question required each person to talk about why he or she decided on a sales career. To Mary, the night before, he'd responded, "Because it pays a lot." She'd changed that to, "I believe in the products and want others to benefit from them."

When the question was posed to the group, a couple of the men stated they liked the salary that came with sales. Sophia said she enjoyed meeting new people and the versatility of the job. Lillith said it was a challenge that she liked to take on. One other man claimed that he started out selling lemonade as a boy, and ever since then he had wanted to sell to the public.

The questioning continued with, "What was the most important thing you did as a child?"

Nathan's answer to Mary had been, "I beat my older brother in a roller-skating contest."

Mary advised him to change it to, "I won a rolling-skating contest and got a trophy and $50, which I shared with my siblings. We all ordered double ice cream sodas." Of course, that wasn't true. He had kept the $50 for himself.

He was looking good so far. All the others had stories of winning something or making A's on their report cards.

Sophia's answer was different. She said, "When I was a child, my parents sent me to an exclusive private school that was mainly white. I was eight years old and a new girl came into our classroom. She was black, and some of the girls started to make fun of her. Every time they called her names, she cried. So one day, when that happened, I put my arms around her and told my friends to stop it. I told the girls if they continued to be nasty to my friend, I would no longer talk to them. I guess I was pretty popular, so it stopped them. Jeannie, my black friend, is still a good friend of mine today. It made me realize for the first time how hurtful prejudice can be."

Lillith laughed at Sophie's story and muttered under her breath, "I think that was stupid. She could have lost all her friends and been called names herself." Ruel heard the remark as well, but chose not to comment on it. When Nathan saw William give her a hard look, he realized he'd better not praise Lillith to him anymore.

The session was mainly about sharing such stories, which was difficult for Nathan to do. A couple of times, William stepped in and asked Nathan an additional question, which really threw him off track. One of the questions was, "If you could do your life over, what would be the one thing you would change?"

Nathan answered, "There's nothing I would change. I'm happy with my life so far."

Of course, that wasn't true. He'd always regretted not going to college, and could he truly do his life over, he would definitely change his very abusive father.

In response to Nathan's answer, Ruel said, "That's good," and quickly went on to the next person, but William interrupted: "I can't believe there's nothing you would want to change!"

Nathan thought for a minute and finally said, "Even though it's never bothered me, I guess if I had to do it over again, I would go to college."

Lillith, her eyes slits and her voice sharp, exclaimed, "You mean you don't have a college degree?"

Nathan, feeling shame for the first time, admitted, "No, my family didn't have the money to send me, and I had to support myself at a young age."

Sophia broke in, "I think it's wonderful that you've achieved so much. I know you were a VP in your last job."

Everyone agreed except for Lillith, who was scowling and shaking her head.

After this first team-building session, Nathan grew very worried. When he trained two of the new salesmen, it was difficult to refrain from telling them what to do. Increasingly, he asked his wife for help. Somehow, she seemed to know a better way of teaching people. She suggested that he was too aggressive; he needed to develop his feminine aspects more. It was good to be direct, but just be softer. He found that almost impossible.

"If I'm softer, I won't make sales."

"I suggest you go out with Sophia on her rounds and listen to how she does it."

"But she's doing well! I only go out with the new guys to help them. If I did that with her, she might think that I'm checking up on her!"

"Tell her the truth, that your way of working is overtly masculine, and you would like to understand how she does so well, as you observe she is very feminine."

"I don't know…but I certainly do know if I don't change my sales style, I'll be fired when my contract is up, and if William ever finds out that Ruel gave me the questions before the meeting, that would be the end, too."

"Don't you think you're ready to share without knowing the questions before-hand? You've made some wonderful changes. Even the children have commented on it. Sharing isn't difficult if it comes from the heart."

Nathan felt like he was hearing her for the first time, and was amazed at her wisdom. He suddenly felt his appreciation of her wrap around him like a warm blanket. Before, she was just the mother of his children, and a good one, but there was little time for any deep conversations. Now he was home early and had a lot more freedom because William didn't believe in overworking his employees. It was a 9-to-5 job with no weekends.

The next week, Nathan got up the courage to ask Sophia's permission to go with her on her rounds. She readily agreed.

It was a very strange experience for him. First, after a handshake, she talked to the buyer about his or her family. She knew all their children's names and asked what was happening with them. If there was an illness in the family, she asked for details and compassionately put her hand on the person's arm, especially if it was a woman she was talking to. Only toward the end of her allotted time would she smile, talk about the products and emphasize a new one that the customer hadn't ordered yet. Her knowledge of each product was excellent, and she was able to translate the technical language in a way that illuminated the product's function and desirability. He could fully appreciate why nearly everyone gave her an order.

It was nothing like the men he had worked with. Usually, salesmen had a whole list of jokes they started with, and then they would talk sports if they were talking to sports fans. A woman would be given compliments. He noticed Sophia never complimented anyone. Sometimes men would ask about families, but just briefly, not with the depth of Sophia's inquiries. Also, after each meeting she would take out a notebook with a section under each name and write any new personal material in it. Then, if she had already met the individual, she would read what she had written earlier before a subsequent meeting. Great planning, he thought. Nathan asked her if it would be okay to use some of her techniques when he trained the new people, and she immediately agreed, "Of course!"

Mary was thrilled when Nathan recounted the story, mainly because he'd followed her suggestion and went out with Sophia on her rounds. "Maybe it would be good for you to go out with each of your people. At the next group meeting, why not ask them how they would feel if you did that?"

"But I don't need to ask them if I can come. I'm the boss."

"Yes, I know, but asking is a nicer way to do it, and when you ask, say you are interested in their style of selling."

"What if they say no?"

"Then ask them why!"

At the next meeting, he asked the question. The only person who said no was Lillith.

When he asked why, Ruel, who was there to see how Nathan was progressing, interrupted and said, "Lillith, you don't have to answer that. He's putting you on the spot."

"That's not true. Lillith can say no, but I would like to know why."

She replied, "Mainly because I have to focus on each client, and your presence there would interfere with my doing that. I'm one of your top salespeople. If I wasn't doing well, I could understand you wanting to watch me, but I am doing well. So no, I don't want that."

"Okay. Thank you for answering me."

Nathan's suspicion was that she was responsible for some underhanded practices. He'd noticed her studying catalogs from other companies longer than most salespeople did. It's good to know the competition if a customer is comparing products, but she was writing down a lot about any product that had similar functions to one of theirs.

One day he asked, "Why are you doing that, Lillith? I'm curious."

"Well, it's good to know the competition," she stated breezily. "That way, I can emphasize how much better our products are than theirs. And, in case that's not true, it helps me to find something to say, even if it's only a detail, that makes ours look better."

Many salespeople practiced this, but Nathan then thought about Sophia and remembered that when a customer had asked her about a competitor's product, she answered truthfully: that the product was a good one, but ours was just as good and had similar features. Even when the other product was a couple of dollars cheaper, she got the order.

Ruel continued to come in to lead the team building process. Nathan took him aside one day and said, "Ruel, I appreciate what you're doing, but I think it's time that I take over the facilitator's role. I'd be fine if you observed me and gave me feedback."

Ruel looked at him steadily for a moment and, with a slightly supercilious grin, commented, "You know, I really don't think you're ready. I'll let you know when you can try leading the group."

"But," Nathan protested, "I've been taking courses in team building. I think I have the idea. I really need to practice it."

His dislike for Ruel was becoming a problem, so he finally went to William and told him how he felt. He even told William the truth about Ruel initially giving him the questions he was going to ask.

"You know, I wondered about that. Your answers were almost too perfect. That's why I asked you some more questions." He paused and looked squarely at Nathan, "I want you to know I appreciate your honesty in telling me about this. I'm going to hire another consultant to coach you."

Ruel was furious when he was let go, and he told William that Nathan had asked him for the questions beforehand. Fortunately, being truthful was the best thing Nathan could have done.

The new man, Ralph, was excellent. He immediately had Nathan lead the team "conversations," as he called them. When Nathan asked him why he used that term, instead of "discussions," Ralph explained that a "conversation," or even a "dialogue," allows the team members to participate more genuinely. "It strengthens the emotional force of the group, so there's a greater balance between the head and the heart within the team."

He went on to say that the word "discussion" implies that there's a right and a wrong, whereas "conversation" or "dialogue" allows more richness and complexity to emerge in the group.

After each meeting, Ralph would go over what happened and make suggestions to Nathan in terms of his style, which still could come off as authoritarian. Ralph asked Nathan about his parents, in particular his father, and Nathan finally told him how controlling his father had been and that he had gotten some of that from him as a defense mechanism.

With great gentleness, Ralph commented, "You know, something like that... like having a parent like that... can be really hard to change. You have a lot of talent, that's clear, but maybe you should go into therapy. It could be a great help for finding your own style of leadership, instead of automatically following your father's path. Believe me, I know! I've been there. What do you say?"

Ralph was looking straight at Nathan, his eyes riveted on him. Yet, there was a kindness accompanying his words that warmed Nathan somehow, even though his first instinct was to object. He suddenly flashed onto his relationship with the kids. Dismayed, he realized that he was treating them the same way he'd been treated. He was authoritative in the same way that his father had been. In fact, to his shame, he realized that he treated them in the same way he had treated the workers at his last job, like he was God!

With this realization, he reluctantly agreed to try therapy. Over time, his therapist encouraged him to enroll in an online college program. Mary was proud that he was doing this, and his kids, who were in higher grades, were delighted, and even gave him some good advice.

During this time, the team had become very productive and sales were at a high. Much of it was due to Nathan's leadership. He understood the products very well, and if he saw something that he believed could be improved, he would go directly to the designer and work it out with him or her. Even though that wasn't his job, he felt that if his people were selling a product, the product should be the best one on the market.

His staff came to admire his ability and was very happy to have him as their boss. When the six-months trial period was up, William called Nathan into his office.

"Nathan, I know this has been a big challenge for you, a challenge that I've seen you tackle with the kind of energy that I know helped you achieve the position you had in your previous job."

His body flooded with relief. Nathan agreed, "Yes, I must admit this has been the hardest challenge I've ever faced. I didn't think the team building would work, but it really has, and, fortunately, I have a great working staff."

"Well, your staff thinks the same of you. I gave them questionnaires about you. After all, part of the team-building process is having the right leadership heading it."

"Thank you."

"But, unfortunately, they're going to lose you."

Nathan felt shocked. I can't believe this. I've worked so hard. I can't believe I'm being let go after all!

"Don't be upset. I'm promoting you out of that job." William smiled warmly. "I'd like to make you a Vice-President of this company. I also know about your work with the designers. They really like working with you, so part of your new job will be directing new product development. The sales department will be directed by Sophia, and she will report to you."

Nathan struggled to keep from crying as the thought that only women cry flashed in his mind, but a tear or two managed to escape as William embraced him in congratulations.

Commentary

Nathan represents the unadulterated masculine. He is a good, fair man, but he is very limited because his inner feminine is frozen within him. As happens so often with couples, Nathan and his wife cleave together like two magnets. They are polarized, playing out the inherent need for balance between the two primal energies.

Look around you, and perhaps at yourself, and you will see that most couples exhibit this phenomenon. Such a union can be very comfortable, until a crisis arises, such as separation through divorce or the death of one of the partners. When such an event occurs, as is inevitable, the surviving partner often flails around and even goes into crisis mode; this can happen with older women who lose "overtly masculine" husbands who had handled finances, were handymen and who took out the garbage, an amusingly symbolic representation of the male role.

Widowed men often rush into marriage as soon as possible if their feminine side is undeveloped, like Nathan's was. It often takes a crisis for men and women to develop their "other half," and if they are conscious of the need for internal balance, life can offer up some surprising and challenging adventures.

Nathan was fortunate that, during his many crises at work, the job loss, job search, and then the challenge of adapting to a radically different management style, Mary, his wife, actively supported him with wise suggestions and more companionship than they had previously enjoyed. In the process, as Nathan gradually integrated qualities of the positive feminine, his creativity blossomed, he was able to relax and enjoy life more, and, of course, his relationship with his wife blossomed, as did his relationships with his kids.

There are two major styles of leadership: One, the style demonstrated by Nathan in his first organization, is primarily masculine. Sophia and William, who are well balanced in their expression of masculine and feminine characteristics, exemplify the other.

Fortunately for humanity, leadership styles are beginning to change, but it is happening so gradually that it takes special notice to discern this fact. In the past, the model for leadership was "overtly" masculine for both men and women. Julius Caesar, Napoleon, Joan of Arc, and Catherine the Great are examples. Along with the founding of democracy, foundations were laid for a softening, feminization of governance that is now gradually permeating the world. Certainly, the French and Russian revolutions, in addition to the American Revolution, were dynamic markers for the advent of democratization.

There are a fair number of women Prime Ministers and Presidents around the world, but just because they are women, it does not follow that they are well balanced in relation to masculine and feminine energies. However, the fact that women are moving into national leadership positions more often is a powerful indication that a balanced type of leadership is beginning to emerge.

Finally, it might be useful for you, the reader, to examine your own leadership style in your organizational and parental relationships.

Exercise:

Think about your personal leadership style. If you are working, how is it displayed in your job? Are you overtly masculine, or do you also use the feminine?

If you have children or are married, think about the leadership style you use at home. Is it balanced, or are you more masculine, or even more feminine, in the relationships?

You can also consider your style in other relationships in your life.

If you feel you lean more to one side, link with your heart and ask yourself the following questions:

Did I learn this style from my parents?

If the answer is yes, ask: How did it play out? What was the relationship between my mother and father?

Then ask: Do I, in any way, emulate one of them?

If you find that you do emulate a parent, ask: What do I need to do to change this?

If you didn't learn your leadership style from a parent, ask: Is there anyone else in my life that I emulated and followed, or was there a situation in my life that made me develop my leadership style?

After you have determined where you may have learned your leadership style, link with your heart and ask yourself the following question:

Do I like my style of leadership, or do I need to bring more balance into it?

If the answer is that you need to bring more balance into it, ask: How can I begin to do this?

Also ask: Do I know anyone who is an example for me to follow and from whom I can learn?

10
Stranded in Time

Being afflicted with a dominance of negative masculine energy has absolutely nothing to do with whether you are a man or a woman, although it is likely to be an issue more often with men than with women. We know many women who, like our heroine in this tale, have had various partners who were more balanced in feminine and masculine energies than they were.

People with a major predominance of negative masculine energy need to understand their imbalance before they can change and move on to a healthy relationship.

The following is Marian's journey with this issue:

It was a gloomy day, with the beginning of winter casting cold weather upon the countryside. Marian walked quickly, as she wanted to get home before nightfall. Her walk became a run, then a walk, and then a run again, her lean body swaying precariously. She wore long, baggy pants with a loose, raggedy T-shirt. A torn sweater around her shoulders flew like misshapen wings behind her as she moved. When she came to the turn in the path that she should have taken, she missed it, only realizing this when the path ended in a large meadow.

Startled by the abrupt ending of the path, she froze at what she saw. It was a large round object, about the size of a space capsule. In fact, that's what it was, an astronaut's space capsule.

She walked slowly over to it. The cone-like shape was pointed upwards, as if ready for a launch, but there was no launching pad.

"I wonder where it came from?" Just as she voiced her thought, the door of the vessel opened and a good-looking man walked out. As he stepped onto the ground, he saw her and greeted her with a warm, captivating smile. He was dark, quite tall and looked East-Indian. His dark brown gaze was steady and penetrating. She felt seen somehow, seen from the inside out.

"Oh, I'm sorry to disturb you. Uh, isn't that a space capsule?" she asked, flustered by the man's appearance and his powerful charisma. "Do you live here?" she added lamely.

"Sometimes." He put out his hand. "My name is Viraj, but you may call me William. Who may you be?" he asked, his voice exuding warmth and a smile lighting up his refined, almost delicate features.

"I'm Marian Lambert. It's nice meeting you."

She suddenly felt awkward about her appearance, wishing she had changed her clothes before her walk. She'd been working in her painting studio and always wore old clothes rather than a smock. Her brown hair was normally tied back, and when she wore makeup, she looked much younger than her forty years. Her most striking features were her dark eyes, black eyebrows, and full mouth, which could be very provocative when painted a deep red. Her ancestry was Greek, and it showed in her exotic looks. Some men thought her beautiful, others only okay, but she wasn't interested in the latter anyway. Now, when she looked at this stranger, she felt a tinge of attraction and regretted that she didn't look her best.

Viraj was not only good-looking; he had an air of strong manliness that she liked. He also was taller than her, a rarity as she was almost six feet and usually towered over the men she dated. Sneaking a look at his hands, she saw no ring. "What is this thing? It looks like a space ship, and what's it doing here in this remote area?"

"Well, it is a kind of space ship, even though it doesn't fly through space."

"What do you mean?"

"Come inside and experience it for yourself." He opened the door for her.

"Oh, thanks, but I don't think so. I have to get home." This guy could be a whacko for all she knew.

"Look," he grinned. "I was just on my way out. You would have looked inside if I hadn't been here, so do the same. When you leave, just close the door behind you. It has an automatic lock on it." Before she could protest, he was walking down the path from which she'd just come. Marian watched him disappear around a bend.

She stood there for several minutes to make certain he wasn't coming back. Then, curious, she opened the door and climbed in. What she saw was extraordinary. It did look like a space vehicle, with two seats behind a control panel, but around it were windows that looked out on a wide, sandy, desert-like plain instead of the New England meadow. The sky was a cloudless expanse of azure blue, rather than the dark cloudy one she had just left. Marian quickly turned back to the door and opened it. There was the meadow again!

Turning back to the cockpit, she sat down in one of the chairs and sank into a deep, down cushion that seemed to enfold her. She was astonished to see that her name was written above one of the controls. How did my name get there? This is weird! At that moment, a great lassitude overcame her. Her eyes closed as vivid flashes of light opened her inner vision to statue-like figures that were standing, motionless on the sandy landscape looking at her. Startled, she opened her eyes. They were still there.

When she tried to stand up, she found she couldn't. The seat had folded over the lower part of her body, and she couldn't get out.

What to do? As she started to cry out, panic gripped her throat. Then she saw the screen on the panel light up, and words appeared: "It will be alright. Yours is only a temporary stay. When you finish the program, you will be free to leave. Just press the switch under your name."

She suddenly realized the people looked familiar. She knew them. They were all from her past. She saw her mother and father standing in the far distance.

Slowly, her childhood friends moved forward, and, one at a time, greeted her with a quick gesture. There were Sally and Andrew, her next-door neighbors. She liked Andrew best. Sally played with dolls, and Marian hated dolls, no matter how cute they looked. She would much rather climb trees with Andrew and play baseball and tackle football. It made her mad that boys had all the fun. They got to go on camping trips with their dads and played all the best sports. Her mother had wanted her to stay in the kitchen with her and learn to cook. Ugh, she still hated cooking!

Ann was her best girlfriend. She was standing there too, looking as cute as ever wearing one of her many frilly dresses. How they fought over clothes! Marian cringed at putting on a fancy dress, whereas Ann just loved to dress up. Really, they had little in common, but Marian liked her as a friend, because secretly, she knew she could boss Ann around. She would go along with anything Marian wanted to do.

The colored lights flashed, and Ann was the only one standing on the sand. She was a teenager now, wearing designer jeans that fit her small body like glue. Her blond hair was curled and long, almost to her waist. Marian saw herself at that age standing next to her. She looked as unkempt as ever. Her jeans were baggy and loose, and she wore a boy's T-shirt that hid her maturing breasts as much as possible. This was in contrast to Ann, who wore a tight, embroidered blouse that conformed to her budding bosom. They'd been so different. Why had they been such good friends? Marian even made fun of her flirting with the boys. She herself didn't know boys existed until much later.

There was another flash, and she was in a scene with Ann, who was sobbing. Oh no, I don't want to see this, Marian thought as the entire scene unfolded before her eyes.

"Stop crying! It's stupid to cry over a boy. Dick's a jerk. If you want, I'll punch him out for you."

"No, no, I don't want you to hurt him. He just likes Elaine more than me. If anything, it's my fault. I should have been nicer to him."

"What, let him touch you? Are you crazy? Ann, you need to understand boys. All they want is sex. That's why he's trying things out with Elaine, and she'll probably be stupid enough to do it with him. Dick never cared about you. Don't you know that?"

"But he said he did." Ann cried even harder.

"They all say that. Boys are different from us. You can't believe anything they say."

Marian went on and on until Ann was in hysterics, "Stop it, stop it! I did it. I did have sex, and I'm stupid, just like you say, stupid!" She ran off before Marian could say anything.

The next day, Ann's mother called her. "Marian, I know you'll want to know. Last night Ann tried to commit suicide. She slashed her wrists, but, thank God, we found her in time. She's in the hospital. Can you tell me anything about why this happened? I know she tells you everything."

She stammered, "Uh, no, I can't. Can I see her?"

"Not now. She has to be under treatment and supervision so she won't try it again."

When Ann returned to school, she ignored Marian. When Marian tried to talk to her, she said, "You know Marian, I've been thinking about our friendship. You didn't help me when I needed help. In fact, you made it worse with your attitude toward boys. You don't know the first thing about being a girl, so I don't want to be your friend anymore."

Marian's eyes watered as she watched this scene play out. "Damn, why am I seeing this?"

The answer came on the screen. "See yourself."

"Bull!" Her guts clenched in anger.

The flashes happened again, and a group of young men stood in front of her on the screen. To her astonishment, they were all ex-lovers, guys she had dated in her early twenties. Laughing out loud, she thought, maybe this will be better, but it turned out to be worse.

One at a time, they came into view. Larry was her first lover. Nice guy, but a pushover. She'd grown bored with him, mainly because he'd followed her every wish. He was heart-broken when she left him. Not only was he in love with her, but he also had plans for them to be married. She'd been very sarcastic toward him, and even a bit mean when he proposed to her. She didn't exactly laugh in his face, but nearly. Again, she saw the look on his face when she turned him down and said goodbye. As he stared at her from the screen, the look turned into disgust and loathing, and she felt a stab in her heart.

The next man was Alan—a sweet man with a loving heart. Marian felt his affectionate nature for a moment. It had been nice to be hugged and held a lot. She had even become more romantic with him, but again, her cold nature kicked in, and she grew tired of the affection. When she told him so, he was genuinely surprised and said, "I thought you liked being affectionate."

"No," she'd said, "I just went along with it, but now it's enough. It makes me feel sick to be tugged at all the time."

He'd replied, "Okay. If you don't want my affection, I guess I need to find someone who does."

Marian was a little upset that he would break up with her because of this. But really, how juvenile, she had thought, and she happily let him go. Now, though, seeing him on the screen looking at her, she felt a pang in her heart. The affection wasn't so bad. Maybe she would have learned to like it. She heard her voice when she told him off, and it had been extremely cutting and cold. *Maybe I would have ended up with him instead of Arthur. That would really have been a hell of a lot better.*

When Alan left the screen, Walter replaced him. Marian felt some regret when she saw his face. He was very handsome and tall, with a Brad Pitt type of looks. His blond hair was long and shone in the sun, and those fabulous blue eyes! But again, she hadn't handled the relationship very well. It came down to her wanting what she wanted. With Walter, she was never satisfied. He raised her libido a lot, and she only wanted sex, sex, and sex with him. He was very accommodating, but, eventually, he felt used and said so.

Marian now saw the scene when she had responded angrily. "How dare you say it's just me that wants to screw all the time? I don't hear you saying no. You're a liar. You know damn well you want it as much as I do. Every time you look at me you have a hard-on."

"I can't help it when you start to maul me," he protested. "Of course I like sex, but not every day, and besides, we haven't even gone out for dinner or a movie in a couple of weeks."

They'd ended up yelling at each other, and that was the end of that relationship. Seeing him now, standing in front of her, Marian wondered how she could have handled it better. She realized that, if a man had ever treated her the way she'd treated him, she would have been really pissed off. She'd made him a sex object. Walter, watching her from the screen, pointed at her and said, "You got it. I was starting to feel that way. It could have been different. I really was falling for you, but you didn't see me." He then turned and walked away.

Following him came Gary, John and even Marvin, all short-term affairs that left very little impression on her; they were mainly sex-driven, with not much heart involved. She wondered how she had gotten so brazen. They weren't important to her at all. In fact, if they hadn't appeared on the screen, she wouldn't have remembered them or their names.

There was another flash and the men were gone, replaced by three others, her two husbands and her present-day lover, James. Marian groaned, "Not you guys. Do I have to see this all over again?"

The screen lit up with the words, "They played an important role in helping you begin to know yourself."

"But why do I have to know myself? I know enough! I'm fine with who I am."

"Were you fine a few hours ago, after your fight with James? Do you want to add him to your list of lost loves? You need to know yourself and change." The screen flashed back to the three men standing in the desert and looking at her sadly.

Arthur, her first husband, stepped forward. "We were good at first, you and I, but then you became demanding and controlling. Why couldn't you see that and understand how I felt?"

"I was controlling? I never knew what you meant by that. It was just the reverse. You were the controlling one!"

He shook his head. "What about when we decided to spend our vacation in France? We were supposed to plan the trip together. Instead, you made all the plans and wouldn't let me share or help in the decision making."

"But that's because I'd been there and knew the best things to do and see."

"You still don't get it, do you? You still don't understand how you made me feel when you took over and didn't let me in. It was always you, you, you, what you wanted, and you always verbalized it as, 'I know what's best for us.'"

His face then hardened: "You tried to wear the pants in the relationship, and that's the true reason I left you."

"That's a lie. It's not about me. You cheated on me with Rachel."

"Yes, I needed a real woman. If you'd been that, I never would have left you. Back then you looked beautiful, feminine, but look at you now. This was always the real you, hidden beneath fancy clothes." As he looked at her sloppy appearance and unkempt hair through the screen, Marian felt undressed and vulnerable. She shuddered and couldn't answer him. Somewhere deep inside, underneath her usual protest of, "but I'm working," arose a sense that he was right.

She finally said, "Would you have preferred me to manipulate you instead of being direct? That's not who I am."

"No, I wouldn't want to be manipulated either, but what you call directness, is more of an assault."

She couldn't answer that. It was true; she'd always had a short fuse and still did. It came from a rebellious nature, the part of her that wanted things to happen a certain way; this much she recognized about herself. Maybe it was time to look and try to understand why she felt this way so often.

Arthur said, "I asked you to do some therapy and even suggested couples counseling, but you refused."

"I know, but later, after we split up, I did do a little therapy. It didn't help much."

"Maybe you didn't have the right therapist."

"Maybe so."

He shook his head and said, "It's time to go. Goodbye. I'm sorry you didn't want to stay friends." He turned away, leaving her feeling regret over the fact that she'd lost his friendship.

Paul then appeared in front of her. She'd met him on the rebound, six months after her first marriage ended. Marian was thirty-two at the time, still very attractive and eager to make this marriage work. She'd even agreed to have children, something she hadn't wanted in her first marriage.

He was a lawyer and well connected. They'd met at an art opening, and it was a whirlwind romance. She'd felt fortunate, as he was considered a good catch. Not only was he wealthy, but he also oozed masculinity. His face was strong and rugged, and he had a great body that seemed like it wanted to burst out of his tailored suits. He was the opposite of Arthur. Arthur had been taller than her and very blond, and he had blue eyes and a fair complexion that kept him out of the sun, whereas Paul was of medium height and was swarthy, with dark brown hair and laughing, fun-filled eyes. His light-hearted personality and quick witticisms kept her constantly laughing.

It was fun all the way to the marriage, but then things changed. When the reality of being married again sank in, Marian became irritated at small things Paul did, like leaving the toilet seat up and tossing his clothes on a chair. She'd known these habits beforehand but never took much notice until she actually had to live with him. His jokes didn't seem as funny anymore, sometimes she felt they were demeaning, and she told him so. He'd responded, "You always laughed at them before. Why not now?"

She'd said, "I felt they were funny before. I loved your sarcastic wit, but now I feel it can be overdone and even a bit nasty."

He'd claimed, "I haven't changed the way I am. I've always talked this way. You're just hearing me differently. Now that we're married you want me to change my personality. Are you nuts?"

That's when the fights really began. She did want him to change; otherwise she couldn't stand to be around him. Having children then became an issue. Again, she remembered their dialogue: "But you agreed to have children before we married. I wouldn't have married you if I'd known you didn't. I want a family."

"I'm not saying otherwise. I just want to wait a few years."

"Why wait? You're already in your thirties, and I'm thirty-seven. I don't want to start a family in my forties."

So there were more fights, and, on this issue, there was no compromise. Since the marriage had started off badly and was continuing to get worse, having a family really wasn't what Marian wanted to do. The marriage lasted a year before the last fight that ended things.

Paul looked at her now and said, "Why did you change so much? I asked you that several times and you never answered. Can you answer me now?"

"No. I just don't know. I wasn't seeing the real you when I dated you. We got married too quickly, and you didn't want to live together first. Living with you made a difference."

"You knew because of my job that appearances were important, but you lost your happy nature and became incredibly domineering. Nothing seemed right to you. You wanted everything I wanted beforehand, but as soon as we were married, that changed. I really loved the you that I dated, and I felt deceived when you changed so much." He looked at her sadly.

For the first time, Marian realized he was right. She had changed as soon as the ring was on her finger. She'd sabotaged her marriage to him from the start. "I don't know why," she said. "Maybe I started reliving my first marriage. I think it was too soon for me to marry again."

"I agree. We should have waited, but I didn't want to wait. I wanted a family, and I have one now. My wife is very different from you. She loves having children as much as I do. You were an adventure, a passion, but it's impossible to be married to someone like you and be happy for long. You had it all, the beauty, the creativity, the energy, but you aren't giving or loving. I feel sorry for you."

He turned and walked away.

Marian was devastated by his words. Was she so heartless? James said as much this morning. He was still standing out there on the sand, at a distance. She looked at him with great longing. Of all the men, he was the one she loved the most. He wasn't even that good looking, not the way the others were. He had a nice, pleasant face and grey eyes that seem to know more than he expressed. He was her height, with a good build. He also had a good mind; she always needed that in a man, but most of all, he was kind and gentle. Just two days ago a friend had called and asked James for his help, and he had dropped everything to go and just talk to him.

James had many friends because of his generosity of spirit. Marian initially thought it was a weakness in him, but now she realized that he simply had a warm, loving heart that even she could feel, and she realized that that was a wonderful way to be. What she'd thought was a weakness was really an inner strength.

He didn't move forward; he just stood there. I must have lost him, she thought. Why doesn't he confront me like the others? How could I not have realized how I acted, how scared I am to be feminine in any way?

Marian had been living with him for a year now, and, again, it looked like it was over. He probably would leave her, and her heart was broken already. There had been too many fights; it was too much to handle. He had two small children who spent the weekends with them. Even though she cared about them, she hated being bothered with them every weekend. She'd told James that every other weekend would be fine, but definitely not the whole two months of the summer time. This didn't sit well with him.

As she watched him standing in the distance, she felt a sensation, as if she was whirling back in time: back, back to her childhood, back to her infancy, and back to before she was born. It was as if she were suspended in endless space. There was no fear; there was nothing to fear. She experienced a state of absolute calm and deep peace. An exquisite rainbow sky, with ever changing brilliant shades of orange, pink and purple, felt like it was penetrating and filling her heart with absolute beauty. Her heart yearned for James and for his goodness.

Then she was back in the cockpit. Oh, how wonderful I feel, such a deep, deep peace. She became aware of the flashing screen and opened her eyes to see, "Do you want to be with James, to maybe marry him?"

Her immediate response was, "Yes, oh yes, I really do love him."

"Then are you willing to change, to really look at your actions?"

Instantly, she felt the hot tar of her rebellious nature rise up in her, and the words, "Why can't he love me for me? Why do I have to change and not him?" tumbled out.

The screen flashed, "Didn't you learn something about yourself today? Can you see your controlling behavior and unyielding attitude? Do you see how you took on all your father's traits, especially the negative ones, and rejected your mother's?"

"I guess I did. I never wanted to be a fragile, sniffling woman like my mother. Ruel, my father, was strong, and so am I!"

"But in that strength there is no heart. Feminine strength is loving. In rejecting your mother, you also rejected the feminine. Look at all the relationships you have seen today. Every one of them failed because you were afraid of the feminine within you. The men you were with had more of the feminine than you did. Even James has more nurturing within him than you do. You haven't even allowed yourself to love his children, and they really want to love you, to become a family."

She started to protest, then stopped herself and forced herself to consider what she was being told. It was true, all of it. That incredible experience with the rainbow—how could she turn her back on that? She'd felt so different…what was it? She had felt like a woman; she had felt the wondrous beauty of being a woman, inside and out. Finally, she understood.

Then she was back in the cockpit again, looking out the window. James was still there, standing quietly in the distance and looking at her. She realized that he was the one for her, and she had a deep sense that something had happened to her that would change her and her relationship with him. It was as if she'd stepped over a barrier that had been keeping her from knowing herself and what she really wanted. For the first time in her life, she felt energy in her heart, as if it had softened, and that softness was spreading throughout her whole being.

Marian looked at James in the distance and felt the depth of her pain. "I know what you say is right, but I've already lost him. I know I have."

"No, you haven't. Not yet." The screen flashed, and James was standing in front of her, looking at her. She reached out to him and touched the screen. When she did so, it went blank.

"Oh no, I want to talk to you! I want to make it work. Please come back." She sat and wept for all her losses, all the people she'd failed to understand. She cried so hard that she wasn't aware that the cockpit windows now reflected the meadow, not the desert. She cried so hard that she wasn't aware of the opening door and of William walking into the cabin.

"Someone is looking for you. I think you need to meet him. He's coming down the path right now."

Marian jumped up and ran to the door. In the distance, she heard James calling her name. "Thank you so much. Thank you, thank you for my trip."

William smiled at her, "You're welcome. Make good use of it."

"I will." She ran down the path and into James' arms.

Holding her close, he said, "You've been gone a long time. I've been so worried about you. It's almost dark; where were you?"

"I was spaced out, thinking about how much I love you." And when she kissed him, her face lit up and her eyes were full of happiness.

"Let's call the kids and have them over this weekend, and every weekend we can!"

Commentary

Afflicted with a preponderance of negative masculine energy, Marian had blotted out any possibility of a healthy relationship. How does this happen? The reasons can range from having an abusive father and/or abusive male siblings (and often along with that, a passive, weak and non-protective mother), to having an offensive, domineering mother, who is possessed by primarily negative masculine energies. If, like Marian, a woman lives primarily out of the negative masculine, she will lack the ability to open her consciousness to the power of love and compassion, the positive feminine.

As Marian is brought face to face with her past and is taken through her list of relationships, the pain of her losses opens her heart, and she experiences the positive for the first time. Now she can begin to enjoy the richness of her life in a more balanced way.

Exercise:

Look back at your life and your important relationships. Have they been good ones, or, as in Marian's case, have they been imbalanced? Also notice if the imbalance was just in your partner, or if there was some imbalance in yourself as well? Then ask yourself:

Is there something I can learn from Marian's story?

Do I lack a quality of the feminine that affects my relationships?

If the answer is yes, link with your heart and ask what that quality is.

Then ask: How can I best develop this quality and use it in my relationships?

11
General Wayne's Dilemma

General Wayne's dilemma is that he has been leading a one-dimensional life, tilted precariously to the masculine side of the spectrum. Without the influence of the feminine, he has not been able to develop his heart qualities, and thus he is blocked from feeling compassion and living a balanced, full life. Without such balance, the richness and depth of life passes one by.

The following is his story:

The house was old and deserted; maybe that was why it stank so badly when he opened the door. The smell at first made him gasp, even cough. Entering the hallway, he turned on the light and saw that the cleaning crew had been there. But why does it still stink? It smells like a dead animal. Had one gotten in and died? Before he investigated, he needed to pour himself a stiff drink and relax from the long journey home.

I guess I should at least check everything out first, he thought. So, in a regimented way, he opened each door in the long hallway, inspecting each room to see that it had been cleaned properly. All was in good order, just the way he liked it, and there were no dead animals. Maybe it's a mouse in the wall.

Upstairs, the smell was faint. Everything was neat, and in the master bedroom the sheets had been turned down for his use. It all seemed too big for him; he probably would close up most of the rooms and live in only a few. It seemed like a long time ago when his huge family occupied all of it. Then, it was full of games and mock battles of the boys against the girls. His father was in the military and taught them all strategies of warfare. His sisters married of course, two of them to soldiers, and his brothers served, but later left the army. He'd remained and became a leading commander of the soldiers in Vietnam. He had made his dad proud of him. Maybe that's why the house was left to him, only him—which caused some resentment in his siblings.

So what? He was a loner anyway. He had never cared for most of the family, and he had broken all relations with them years ago when they disputed the will.

He never did use this house though, except once in a while when he took a vacation here, but now, of course, all that had changed. He'd retired and would now be here permanently. Without a doubt, this was home; it was the only home he'd ever known. Most of his career was spent in various countries, fighting on the frontlines; he was always fighting. The last place he was stationed was Iraq; it was the bloodiest war of them all. So many civilians died there because of the bombings. But that always happened in war. God, Vietnam was brutal. His mind always pictured the children he had seen huddled in a hut after all the men and women had been killed. Authorities took them all to God knows where. Some said the army used them as slaves to clean up barracks and supply sex. Not my troops! I'd never have tolerated that!

Back in the living room, he built a fire and sat down to enjoy his drink. He was tired. The journey home had been a long one. His large body sank back into the chair. Wayne was the big one in the family, six foot four and very muscular from all the training he'd gone through. He still lifted weights to keep in shape. His face was rugged and not very handsome, with cropped, graying hair, a nose too large for his square-shaped face and brown eyes that squinted a lot from his many hours spent in the sun.

The smell, more intense, woke him from a drifting sleep. Looking around the room, he saw something move in the corner. Grabbing his gun, which he'd laid on the table, he walked in that direction, turning on a lamp along the way. What he saw was truly astonishing: A dark shadow in the shape of a man, moving upwards and floating in the air. A ghost, it's a damn ghost!

"What are you doing here?" he asked.

"Look at my face; don't you recognize me?" the ghost replied.

The face illuminated, and he recognized it as the first man he'd killed in Vietnam. He would never forget that face, mainly because the soldier's gun had been pointing straight at him, and he'd ducked the fire and shot the soldier instead.

"What are you doing here?" he asked again.

"We are all here." Suddenly, the room filled with figures of women, children, and men. He knew they were all the people he'd killed in all the wars he'd been in.

"My God, what's happening here?" he demanded, his voice belligerent.

A chorus of voices replied, in unison: "We are here to keep you company in your retirement. We are the corpses of your destruction; you have corpses to keep you company."

The General sat down and laughed. "If you think any of you can scare me, you're wrong. Believe me, after all I've seen, nothing can frighten me. There's a lot of room in this old house. You can wander around as much as you want. It's not going to bother me."

He paused. "Is the stench coming from you guys?"

"Of course. We are decaying corpses."

"The smell I don't like. If you plan to stay to try to haunt me, at least cut the smell out."

"We can't do that," the chorus responded.

"I'm going to have to buy a lot of deodorizing spray then. That should work."

In the next few weeks, the General put deodorizers in every room, and whenever he saw a spectral figure, he would spray it. It helped, but only a little. During this time, any figure he encountered would illuminate its face and rant at him about its death. Even a young soldier from his platoon showed up; he'd mistakenly shot him, thinking he was the enemy. That happened a lot in war. Then there was the young Asian woman who'd come up to him; fortunately he'd noticed a hand grenade that she was trying to hide. He'd shot her through the head, and the hole now glowed with a strange light. There were also the young boys who were used as bomb carriers: no one could chance getting blown up by them.

The General was skilled in detecting deception; it was a skill that kept him alive through many battles, and it was one of the reasons he'd moved quickly up the ladder. He was a no-nonsense guy. He was proud and arrogant, sure of himself and a true commander of men, and the higher-ups saw his talent and kept promoting him. He was only in his forties when he became a General in the first Iraq war. He was one of those who had tried to get Bush to keep moving on to Baghdad. It would have saved a lot of money if they'd been allowed to do the job on Saddam in the first place.

When the stench took a turn for the worse, Wayne decided it was time to eliminate the corpses. Using a list of exterminators from the yellow pages, he made several appointments. The first man who came said there must be dead animals in the walls; when Wayne said no, the smell was from dead people haunting the place, the guy looked frightened and unbelieving. Some of the ghosts appeared with a gush of elevated aroma, and the man fled.

This happened time and time again, so the General offered more and more money, which finally made one company decide to take on the job, but that lasted only a few hours. The crew of workers kept surrounding the corpses, trying to catch them in a net. They would drag the full net outside, but as soon as that happened, the figures would break through the net and fly back into the house. The crew even brought a big-lidded dumpster and tied down the lid with ropes. That was successful for about half an hour. Just as they were planning to pull the dumpster away, the ropes broke and the spirits pushed the lid up. It was impossible, and the exterminators quit. One of the workers gave him the name of a man in the village who he thought could help. "William is known to see and talk to ghosts. That's what you need, a ghost whisperer who can send them away."

"Good idea," the General said, and he immediately called William to set a date.

William arrived early in the morning. He was a tall, middle-aged man. He was nice looking, with silver-gray hair and a face conveying a hidden wisdom that made people want to talk to him and ask him for advice. His blue eyes shone with open frankness. When Wayne told him the problem, he showed no surprise, just curiosity.

"Do you know these ghosts?"

"No, I never knew any of them, but they all died in battles I commanded and fought in, and, for some reason, they all blame their deaths on me."

"Why wouldn't that be correct?"

"What do you mean by that? I was following orders. I'm not a murderer."

"Well, not directly, but you did kill them. Are they all soldiers?"

"Mostly. Some women and children died under artillery. That always happens in war. It doesn't matter; I just want them out of my house. Their decaying bodies stink. Can you help me?"

"Yes, I can smell them. I need to talk to them. Which room do most of them use?"

Wayne led him into the living room and, immediately, a few of them appeared. William addressed them collectively: "I'd like to hear your stories, and I also want to know the reason you don't want to move on, but prefer to be here, haunting this man."

A spectral figure, the first ghost who had confronted Wayne, stepped forward. "I want to know who you are and why we should tell you anything."

"Good point," William replied. "My name is William Hayley, and I'm here to help you."

"Help us! We don't need help. He's the one that needs help: big time help. He has no heart." He pointed to General Wayne.

"What's my heart have to do with this?"

William looked at Wayne. "Maybe they feel you have no regrets about their deaths."

"Of course I don't. If I hadn't killed some of them, I'd be dead instead. It's about self-preservation."

A small Asian woman stepped forward, with some children and other women surrounding her. "What about me? I didn't own a gun, and you and your men slaughtered a whole village of us!"

"We were told you were hiding weapons," said Wayne, his voice hard. "Go haunt some of the other men. I was just following orders."

There was a roar of protest from the group, and the stench increased a level.

William turned to Wayne and said, "Why don't you go outside for a moment? I'd like to talk to them alone."

Wayne, his face a stubborn mask, stared back at William, then turned and stalked out the door.

"I'll be out in a minute," called William before the door slammed.

William then turned to the ghosts, who'd grouped together in a ghostly crowd.

"All right. Now, what do you want from him? Can one of you tell me?"

One of the ghosts said, "All we want is for him to feel some sorrow for his actions. We don't want to stay here in his house with his miserable moods."

"That makes sense," said William, nodding as the other ghosts made sounds of agreement. "Let me talk to him privately," he added, and he left to join Wayne at the edge of the woods that surrounded his yard.

The day was sunny, with a mild breeze moderating the heat of the sun. The two men moved to a path that led into the woods. At first they walked in silence. Then William stopped, turned to Wayne and said, "Your situation is very difficult. It will take some special work."

"I don't care how long it takes or how much it costs."

"It's not about that. It's work that you have to do."

"What do you mean? I don't know how to get rid of ghosts. That's what I'm hiring you for!"

"Let me explain. These ghosts feel that you caused their deaths and that you won't even acknowledge your part in what happened to them. Your work is inner work. It's about you trying to understand who these people were, and, in that understanding, feeling some regret for having killed them. If you can get them to forgive you, then they will be willing to leave."

"Forgive me! That's absurd. I keep explaining to them that I followed orders. None of their deaths are my fault."

"You also gave orders, which I know was your job, but did you ever question the results of those orders, orders that caused many people, including women and children, to die? Surely you could have stopped some of the massacres that took place."

"Well, I agree; I was upset about that village, but I was a Lieutenant then, and I was following orders. When I was in command I never did that."

"Never?"

Wayne looked away, frowned, shrugged, and then turned back to look William straight in the eyes: "Well, there was one incident with some men from another village. When we went in after them, one of the soldiers got gun-happy and shot a couple of women. You know, things like that always happen in war; no one can be blamed."

Looking straight back at him, William replied, "Even if you feel it wasn't your fault, try at least to understand what these ghosts are experiencing and have some compassion for them."

"Compassion? That word is for monks and women, not for military men!"

"But you're out of the army now. That's the past. You're now a civilian. Believe me, with a little compassion, you'll be able to speak to them in a way that will earn their forgiveness."

"You're sure? No other way of getting rid of them?"

"No, they won't leave, no matter who else you hire or what else you try."

"How do you know they'll leave?"

William looked at Wayne for a long moment. "When you went out, I asked what they wanted from you, and one said, 'All we want is for him to feel some sorrow for his actions.'"

"Harrumph!" Wayne grunted.

William then added with a slight grin, "They also said they don't want to stay here because of your miserable moods."

"They said that?" His eyebrows arched in astonishment.

"That's what they said!"

Wayne shoved his hands in his pockets and studied his shoes. "So, how do I learn – uh – compassion?" He screwed up his face like a little boy.

"Look," said William, "I understand this isn't easy for you. War is difficult. It hardens a person."

Wayne looked at him, his lips pressed together. "You been to war?"

"No," said William. "But I know people who have, and they've had to find a way back to being fully human again. Some manage that; some don't."

"So, what do you know about it?"

"You know, Wayne, that's not the point. The fact is, you're in a situation that's forcing you to learn compassion. That is, if you want to live in your house."

"All right," Wayne agreed with a sigh. "What do I need to do?"

"I have a friend named Sophia who has a beautiful, compassionate heart. You can take lessons from her."

"What? Lessons from a woman? I can't do that!"

"Then I can't help you." William turned to walk away.

"Wait! Why can't you teach me? You strike me as being knowledgeable, and the ghosts seemed to like you."

William planted himself in front of Wayne: "Look, trust me. You asked for my help. This is all I can offer. You'll learn what you need to from Sophia just from being around her. Take it or leave it."

"Okay, okay! I give up. Bring her on! It sounds nuts, but I'll try it. I'll try anything at this point."

Later that day, William brought Sophia over to meet Wayne. She was tall and very fair, with a complexion that glistened as if she bathed in morning dew. Wayne's heart pounded when he looked into her blue-green eyes and glanced at her slim but curvaceous body. Well, these lessons might be fun, he thought. I'm an old man, but looking at her makes all my juices come back. After William left, Wayne, embarrassed by the stench in the house, suggested that he and Sophia sit in the gazebo in his backyard.

"Good," she said, as they entered the little gazebo. "It's nice out here. Let's sit opposite each other now," she suggested. "This is about working with your heart, not your mind. It will take a lot of effort on your part."

"What do you mean, working with the heart?"

"Not your physical heart," replied Sophia. "I'm talking about a center of energy in the middle of your chest. Right here," she said, pointing to his chest. "Have you ever felt a kind of emptiness there? Or a pain that's not quite physical, but maybe more emotional?"

"No!" he said abruptly.

Sophia watched him quietly, then asked, "Have you heard the expression 'he or she is a warm-hearted person?'"

"Well, uh, yeah, maybe."

"That's what I'm talking about."

Wayne said, with a slight grin, "You mean like you?"

"Well," she smiled, "You can become that, too."

Wayne frowned, shaking his head slightly. "It's too late for me. I'm a soldier. I've seen too much death."

Sophia put up her hand. "It's never too late. It's just not going to be easy. Tell me something, Wayne; have you ever been married?"

"Nope! I joined the army when I was eighteen, and that was that!"

"How about a relationship?"

"I had a girlfriend once, but because of my schedule, we never spent much time together. She got fed up and married someone else." He looked away.

"That must have been painful," said Sophia.

"I couldn't put any woman through that again. I guess I turned my heart off."

"Well," said Sophia with a smile, "how about turning it back on? We can get rid of the ghosts, and who knows? You might let yourself be a happier person."

"Hmm! Well, what would it entail?"

"I'll show you. Let's try. It's about working with the energy of the heart center. Now, close your eyes, because that will help you concentrate on what's happening. I'm going to link my heart with yours energetically. All you have to do is try to feel the energy in your chest."

They both closed their eyes. Wayne concentrated, and after a few minutes, said, "I feel something! It's like a kind of warmth that's coming into my chest. Is that what you mean?"

"Yes, exactly. Now try to respond to that warmth by sending it back to me with your heart."

They sat silently again. After a moment, his eyes popped open, and he said, "I don't want to let it go."

"It's reciprocal. You will still feel the warmth, and so will I, so try it again."

They worked on this exercise a few times until Wayne really experienced his heart linking with hers.

"Now you need to practice this. Do you have a housekeeper?"

"Well, yes. Why do you ask?"

"Does she see the ghosts?"

"Oh, no. Only I have the good fortune of being able to see them!" he said ruefully. "When she comes around, they stay away. I'm their major attraction."

"I want you to practice this on your housekeeper."

"You mean like we just did? She'll think I'm loony!"

"You don't have to tell her what you're doing. Just put your attention in your heart center, right where you feel the warmth. Do this every time you talk to her. Try to remember. Also, practice when you go out to eat, or to see a friend. Just practice whenever you're with someone. I think you'll be very surprised. If you don't practice it, it will fade away."

Sophia then added, "Let's try something right now. Is your housekeeper here?"

"Yes," he said, looking at his watch. "She probably got in a few minutes ago."

"Good. You need to start practicing this with her. Remember, link your heart to hers in the way I just taught you, and then talk to her. I'll wait here. Come back and tell me how it went."

"Hmm, well, all right. I'll give it a try," he said reluctantly. Leaving the gazebo, he was surprised at how he felt; his heart was alive with warmth and his stomach was twisting in fear. Jeez! He thought. This is worse than going into battle. Weird!

At the back door of the house, he stood in the sunlight, took a deep breath, straightened his shoulders and put his attention on the center of his chest as Sophia had taught him. When he entered the kitchen, Anna, his housekeeper, was at the sink. She looked up, startled, and said, "Oh, hello, General Wayne! I thought you were upstairs."

Wayne stood inside the door, smiled uncertainly, and tried to beam a connection between his heart and hers. "Good morning, Anna. I was out in the gazebo with a friend." Not only Anna but also Wayne himself was surprised at how he sounded: His voice was calm, soft, and even warm. It felt as if another person were inside him. Anna responded with a big smile.

When he rejoined Sophia, she asked how it had gone.

"I could see she wasn't expecting me to talk like that, and I didn't expect it either. It's strange!"

"How is it strange?" asked Sophia.

"I don't know," he said, his voice gruff. "It's not me!"

"Maybe it's you with a heart!" she replied with a little smile.

"Well, I'm not sure about this. I mean, why am I doing this, and how will it help me get rid of the ghosts?"

"The plan is for you to listen to their stories with your heart. When you do that, you will begin to understand how they feel."

"Oh, no," he protested. "So, that's it!" With his jaw set and his eyes hardened, he said, "I don't want to listen to their stories. If I'm doing this for that purpose, forget it. It's not going to work."

He argued back and forth with Sophia until she finally left without making a date to return.

The next morning, an old woman came to the door. She looked in her seventies, with white hair, a very wrinkled face and a jaw set in stubbornness. Her voice was strong. "My name is Lillith, and I've heard you have a ghost problem. I can help you get rid of them."

"Ah, that's good," he said. "I'm getting sick of them. They were so noisy last night I barely slept. Enough is enough! I'm tired of the smell." He then told her about Sophia and her lessons.

"That's nonsense! Using your heart with ghosts will just make them want to stay longer. They love that kind of energy."

She headed for an armchair, sat down, and indicated for Wayne to sit too. "Now, you listen to me! I've been around a long time, and I know how to handle ghosts, believe me!"

"Thank God! Someone with experience!"

"Yes," snapped Lillith. "I have plenty of that! Now, this is what you must do. You must do exactly the opposite of what that woman Sophia told you to do. Listen to their stories, and tell them once and for all how each and every one of them is responsible for what happened. Don't let them blame you. Once they all have a chance to talk it out, they will leave."

Wayne readily agreed. He called in the Asian woman and had her tell him her whole story in detail. It was pretty ghastly how she had to witness her boys being killed one at a time when they refused to show where their ammunition was. She also saw a soldier take her daughter to a corner of the room and rape her, and when she tried to save her, he stabbed her with a bayonet.

As she related her story, Wayne felt a pang in his heart. Realizing this, Lillith glared at him, waggled her finger and shook her head. Wayne steeled himself as if he were going into battle and questioned the woman in a cold voice.

"Don't you think it's foolish to try to fight a soldier? Of course he would kill you! That's his job. What you should have done was hide. You could've helped your daughter later."

"Are you mad? He killed her after raping her. They all did the same: rape and kill. Luckily, I was dead before he could rape me."

"Well, it's the spoils of war."

The woman turned away in disgust.

He talked to three others, including the first man he had seen, the man he had shot in Afghanistan. "I was defending myself," he told him. "Why are you here?"

"You didn't even notice that I dropped my gun and was raising my hands to surrender."

"That's a lie."

"No it's not, but now you will suffer. I did this. I brought them over from the other side to make you suffer."

"What do you want from me in order to leave?"

"You're an old man. We're staying here until you die, and then we'll have great fun fighting your ghost. Believe me, we can wait. We've nothing better to do. In the meantime, we can haunt you."

The prospect of never getting rid of them really bothered Wayne. "Did you hear him? They're not leaving." He turned toward Lillith and caught her gloating, with an evil grin that sent a chill through his body.

"Out! Get out!" he yelled at her. "You're a fake! You just made it worse!"

Lillith stood up, grabbed her bag, muttered, "You're an old fool!" and left, slamming the door behind her.

Shaking with rage and his heart pounding in his chest, Wayne headed out the back door and crossed the lawn to the gazebo. He sat there, trying to calm down. This is impossible, he thought. Maybe I'll have to sell the house. No, he argued with himself, I won't give up. They won't drive me away from my own house. I've never surrendered in my life. I won't let a bunch of ghosts defeat me.

As he breathed deeply, he experienced a flash of Sophia sitting opposite him. Just the thought of her serene beauty began to change his mood.

The next day, he called her. "I need help. I'm willing to try anything you suggest." He told her what had happened with Lillith.

"She's made it worse now, but we can still try our method."

For the next several weeks, Sophia worked with Wayne. She made him go into the village and talk to people using his heart. Soon he had made friends with many of the locals. It was tough at first to listen to their stories without taking over and steering the conversation. After a time, he was able to just listen to what they had to say. They started asking him to their homes to meet their families. Suddenly, he felt how nice it was to socialize, something he had never done in his life. He even met a widow, Julia, who was his age and very attractive. Wayne hadn't dated in years; his life was always his work, but now he found it very pleasant to spend time in the company of a woman.

He wanted to have a party and invite his new friends over, but he couldn't with the ghosts still there. They would haunt the scene, and, in fact, some in the village had already heard his house was haunted. He brushed the idea aside whenever he was asked about it.

He decided to redecorate the house and then have a party. Liking that idea, he hired a decorator and began to brighten up the rooms with new furniture and paint. Life was great, except for the evenings at home when the ghosts came in to surround him.

Finally, Sophia said she felt the time was right to start the real work with the ghosts. Again, the Asian woman who had lost her family appeared. This time he listened with his heart, saying only how awful it must have been for her and apologizing for the soldiers from his platoon who were the perpetrators.

"If I could punish them now, I would, but I don't know which ones did this terrible thing to you. Did any of your family survive?"

"Yes, one son who was in the fields that day."

"Is he still in Vietnam?"

"Yes, I have seen him there."

"If you give me his name, I will write him a letter from you and send it to him."

Astonished, she said how much she would love to do this and immediately dictated a letter to her son, mentioning things that only he knew so that he would realize the letter was from her.

"Thank you, thank you. You are kind."

He could feel love coming from her in his heart.

He continued talking to each ghost in this way, and they all responded to him and felt genuinely heard. In some cases, where they had relatives he could find, he wrote letters; in others, there was no one to write to, but they knew he would do what he could for them.

But they still stayed on, only because they had all agreed to come and leave together. Except now all those he had talked to kept a distance and didn't try to bother him. Sometimes he could hear them protesting to the Afghan soldier, whom they called Ameen, saying that they wanted to go on. They no longer blamed Wayne. When Wayne finally asked their forgiveness, they all gave it, except Ameen. He still wouldn't budge from his position. In fact, when Wayne tried to talk to him, he refused to listen.

"What should I do about him?" Wayne asked Sophia.

"You need to get enough of the others to demand he talk to you. They can pressure him into it."

Finally, after much persuasion, Ameen approached Wayne, looking sulky.

"If you say you were surrendering back then, I believe you, but please believe me when I say I didn't see you do so. If I remember, it was dark, and difficult to see in the moonlight. I really am sorry. Please forgive me."

"I could never forgive you."

"I can understand that, but is there anything I can do for you now? Is there anyone you would like me to write to or help?"

Silent, he waited a long time for an answer, then Ameen looked at him, and a thought penetrated Wayne's heart.

"Ameen, did you have a daughter who died? Would you like to see her again?"

"How did you know?"

"My heart told me about your loss. Did she die before you, so you haven't seen her on the other side?"

"Yes," he replied, with deep sadness. "She was only ten years old. We were very close."

"You know, if you leave and go on, you will see her in the other place."

"What do you mean?"

"People, when they die, follow the light and go to a place where they await rebirth. That's part of your religion, I know. She's there, waiting, and you will see her if you let go of your need for revenge and feel my sorrow for having shot you."

"How do I know what you are saying is true?"

"Ask some of the others. They know. Now they want to go on so they can meet their loved ones."

"I'll think about it."

Ameen left to join the others. For the first time, Wayne felt a deep sorrow for the ghost. Turning to Sophia, he asked, "What made me say all of that, and how did I know about his daughter?"

Her smile was radiant. "When you open your heart, you can bring wisdom into your consciousness from much higher places."

That night, his room was filled with all the ghosts, and one by one, they said goodbye and thanked him for his kindness. Ameen was the last to leave, but he only said, "I hope you're right," as he vanished.

Wayne frowned, and asked Sophia, "If I'm not right, can he come back?"

She laughed, "No, he can't once he's gone on, but you were right. He will see her."

"Thank you so much."

"You're welcome. You've done well; remember to use your heart."

"Oh, I will. I most certainly will."

His heart was filled with gratitude as he opened the door for her and watched her walk away into the gathering darkness.

She's changed my life he mused as he closed the door.

Commentary

It was impossible for Wayne to use his masculine side in a constructive way because his feminine side was never developed to help bring him balance. Instead he resorted to the negative masculine, which was enhanced by his military training. Sophia's influence transformed him, so that he could discover the blessing of his inner feminine.

Examples may help clarify the power of the masculine and how its energy can be used constructively in the world. Napoleon's use of the masculine was mostly positive: focused, courageous, and always leading the front lines of battle. He was very well respected by his soldiers. Do not assume that all conquerors come from the negative masculine side. Had Napoleon treated his troops and those whom he conquered badly, he would have been using the negative masculine.

World War II also has provided us with examples of both positive and negative masculine styles of leadership. Winston Churchill and Franklin Delano Roosevelt are both examples of positive leadership. They made enormously difficult decisions, were extremely focused, and even though they may have made mistakes, were daring enough to lead their countries through to victory. Hitler, on the other hand, was obviously an example of the negative masculine.

We want to tell you about a man named Gerald. He had great writing talent, with fertile ideas, enthusiasm, and a vivid imagination. He was a poet and a novelist; he wrote reams of manuscripts that were never published. When it came down to the task of getting his work published, his enthusiasm dropped to zero, and the thought of spending time sending query letters and proposals drove him into depression. Gerald's feminine side was highly developed through his inspiration and vivid imagination. Unfortunately, because of his undeveloped masculine qualities, any impulse to get his work published was sabotaged. Not only he, but also those who might have been enriched by his talent, became victims of this lack of balance between the masculine and feminine.

Gerald's story is not unusual. Many women and men possess a creative gift that will not be realized because they lack the masculine ability to "show their wares" on a very concrete level. Just recently, we went to an art fair, and in one booth we saw some exquisite modern paintings. We talked to the painter for some time. Although he has not achieved fame, he sells his paintings at similar fairs around the country and constantly tries to get his work into galleries. We have no doubt that, if he perseveres, he will achieve recognition for his highly individual work. And, even if he does not achieve remarkable success, he will always know that he tried. He struck us as someone who is balanced and whose creativity flows into any avenue that is available to him.

Exercise:

To experience the heart energy that is often lacking in people who lean more to the masculine energy side, you may want to try the heart exercise that Sophia gave Wayne in this chapter.

Find a quiet place and close your eyes. Take some deep breaths, and as you breathe, try to let go of any thoughts or feelings.

When you feel you are in a peaceful place, focus your attention on your heart center, which is in the middle of your chest. Try to experience this center. You may feel warmth or movement, or you may even see a color or symbol. Realize that whatever you experience is your way of being focused in your heart. Sit in this experience for a while, and then notice any effects it has had on the rest of your being.

The next time you meet with a friend or even a business acquaintance, connect to your heart center and link your heart with the other person's heart. Try to feel the connection and send the person warmth as you converse.

After you do this, consider what happened. What did you feel? What was the tone of your voice when you spoke? Was there a good response from the other person?

If you have a close friend, it may be helpful to tell the person about the exercise and practice it together, as Sophia and Wayne did in the story.

12
When Ego Reigns Supreme

Masculine energy is the main energy that helps a person to survive in the world, but a balance is needed so that the masculine doesn't overcome the ego and turn negative. The following tale illustrates all the negative masculine characteristics in the extreme. Our anti-hero had no opportunity to experience any of the feminine energy that would have helped him feel balance and have given him a chance to develop the positive characteristics of the masculine and feminine. With only his survival ego self, he can never even understand what he is lacking.

This is his story:

Ruel Magnus was making his way through the forest, tramping down all the young trees with his huge feet and laughing in glee when the forest animals fled in every direction to avoid his destructive hands. He loved to grab foxes or raccoons and break them in two with a sudden twist. He was a giant, at least twelve feet tall with huge, muscular arms and legs, and feet and hands three times larger than a normal man's. The worst thing about him was his huge ego, which made him feel he was the master of all men and women and made him believe that everything and everyone belonged to him. When he went into villages, he would loot and take anything he fancied, enslaving the townspeople as his servants and making them carry his possessions from town to town. The caravan of all of his goods followed him through the woods as he trampled the undergrowth, making a road for the wagons and horses.

He plundered village after village, and even though the people were warned of his coming, few would leave, as he had a reputation of chasing those who fled and killing them for trying to evade him. The men tried to shoot him with everything from arrows to bullets, but his skin was so thick and tough that this weaponry just bounced off him.

He was now in his early thirties. He had left his home of origin long ago as a small child, so he had no memories of his parents and where they lived. All he remembered was that when he was five he was living alone in the woods, already able to feed himself by killing the animals there. At that age he was already the size of a grown man. His only companion was a wolf he had adopted as a pet, which in many ways had mothered and protected him. During his adolescence, he would go into villages at night and steal clothing off clotheslines. Later, when he grew to his full height, he would have women he captured make him clothing. Sometimes he chose a woman for sex, and when he was done with her, he would let her return home. It was something that many of the servants chose in order to finally have their freedom again. Otherwise, the servants stayed with him permanently. Any that tried to leave were instantly killed.

This next village he was heading for was a small one at the edge of the forest. It was very lovely, with an old medieval castle surrounded by walls near a large lake. When Magnus saw the castle, he roared in delight, for he had never seen a building of that kind, and it became even more impressive to him when he found that some of the rooms were several stories high; he could literally stand in them, rather than crawl through them on his hands and knees. His dwellings were usually made up of sticks and leaves, with large comforters to soften the sharpness of the wood.

Deciding that the castle would be a nice place to stay for a while, he rounded up all the people in the village and chose the stronger ones to join his staff. The castle had been empty for so long that a lot of work had to be done in order to make it livable, even for Magnus. Here, for the first time, he could dismantle his caravan and display his spoils.

One day, when he was walking through the streets of a neighboring village looking for additional wares, he noticed a woman pulling a small child into a doorway. He saw a flash of dark hair, and then the child vanished behind her mother's skirts.

He bellowed, "You there, come out!" and one of his servants ran to the woman and pulled her out.

"Yes, your Lordship," said the woman as she bowed to him, the child still hiding behind her.

"Let me see your child," he demanded.

"She's just a little girl." The woman gently picked up her daughter for him to see.

The child was extraordinarily beautiful. Rendered almost speechless by her loveliness, he blurted out in a hoarse voice, "What's her name?"

"We named her Violet, because of her eyes. Thank you. She's a good child." The woman bowed again and turned to leave.

In an effort to be charming, Magnus, attempting to smile, screwed up his face in a grimace and proclaimed, "Wait, you are indeed fortunate. I have decided that Violet will have the honor of becoming my wife."

The woman was horror-stricken. "But you can't, she's only a small child. She's too young to become your wife."

"That is true. I can wait until she grows up. If she is still as beautiful as she is now, then I will marry her. As you see, with her and me, our children are bound to be handsome." He smiled a twisted smile that made him even more grotesque.

"In the meantime, you both will come and live in luxury at the castle."

Turning pale, she protested, "What about my husband? I can't leave him!"

Magnus clenched his fists and sneered, "Then you can stay with him! You are never to see her again." He called his servant. "Take the child, she comes with me," he said, then he stomped down the road, oblivious to the cries of the mother and the child, who was squirming to get away from the servant's grasp.

After several months, Violet began to accommodate to her new surroundings. Missing her parents fiercely, she spent her days in the castle gardens, making friends with the fairies whom she was able to see and hear. They became her playmates. She was a precocious child who was full of energy, and she was a natural musician. Her companions, both children and adults, loved her, but they all felt she was a bit odd.

Magnus always ate one meal a day with her, usually lunch, as his evenings were spent with women and alcohol. When he drank too much, his voice could be heard throughout the whole castle. If he was in a good mood, he was generous, but most of the time he was in a foul mood and demanded total submission to his desires. Everyone feared him, except for Violet. She hated him and stood up to him, which he liked. As the years passed, he watched her carefully, waiting for the time when she would be old enough to marry him.

She tried lying to him about her age and continued to wear children's clothing even when she was in puberty, tying cloth around her breasts to pretend they weren't developing. Her friends prayed with her that her beauty would leave her, as Magnus would never marry a plain woman, and to that purpose, she tried to make herself look worse with makeup, but no matter what she did, her beauty shone through. In fact, she became lovelier as she matured. Violet was also tall for her age, and even wearing shoes without heels couldn't hide that fact.

One day at lunch Magnus said to her, "I know you are now old enough to marry. You are not to wear children's clothes anymore, nor are you to try to flatten those beautiful breasts. I'm no fool. I've been watching you for a long time and have waited for this day. The wedding is in two weeks. I have already told the seamstress to make you suitable clothing and a wedding dress."

Violet cried, "But I'm only 14 years old. You said I had to be 18."

"You lie to me. Your mother said you were five when I took you from her. You are now 18."

"But I'm still too young. I'm not ready for marriage."

"Then get ready. You have two weeks."

Violet ran to her garden and sobbed, praying to the fairies for help. None of her fairy friends even appeared. It was as if they'd all vanished. This distressed her even more. She ran to the people who had raised her; they also wept and tried to console her. One of the women who had taken care of her said, "He's a brute, but he really loves you, so maybe he will treat you differently."

"I would rather die than have to submit to him. He's a monster. I'll run away."

"You know he'll find you, and you also know if we help you he will kill us."

"Yes, I know. What am I going to do? I would kill him, but how? People have tried poisoning him, but he just gets a stomachache. Nothing else has worked either."

The days passed quickly. Magnus planned a huge feast for the whole village and ordered fireworks to be set off right after the wedding. He wanted this to be an event that everyone would talk about for years. Magnus's clothing was well styled for his huge body. He had found an excellent tailor, William, whom he'd enslaved many years before. This man used to design men's clothing for the court and was visiting relatives when Magnus first raided the village. Now he was never allowed to leave; he was trapped into making Magnus's clothing for all these years. He longed to see his family, but Magnus never allowed any of his slaves to return home.

On this special occasion, William asked Magnus's permission to go to the city to pick up some fine brocade for the wedding suit he was making. Reluctantly, Magnus granted his request but sent several guards to accompany him. One of the guards was a young man named Ronald, who'd grown up with Violet and was in love with her. He would do anything in his power to save Violet from this marriage, but he couldn't come up with a way to kill Magnus. It was hopeless. During the journey, he sat next to William, and they talked at length about what to do. They thought of drowning Magnus. "It would take a battalion of soldiers to tie him up, and he would kill half of them while they tried," Ronald said.

"I know, but there has to be a way."

They analyzed every possibility.

William bought the brocade and contacted his family to explain what had happened, promising he would return soon.

The jacket was beautiful, the finest that Magnus had ever seen. He never paid his slaves anything, but he was so pleased that he gave William several gold coins. "You have outdone yourself. This pleases me a lot. It makes me look even more handsome than I am. Violet will be proud to have me as a husband," he boasted.

In the meantime, Violet was having her wedding dress made by a seamstress who was also very talented. The bodice had real gems sewn into the embroidery, gems that Magnus had stolen. Her engagement ring came from a very wealthy woman who had been killed in one of his raids. Violet hated wearing it, as it reminded her of her captivity and the loss of her parents. She had hoped they would be coming to her wedding, but someone told her that they had moved far away, never to be seen again. Her fairy friends were still deserting her, and she didn't know why.

The night before her wedding, she walked in the garden, beseeching the fairies to do something to help her. Her desperation drove her to the lake to kill herself, but there were guards near her, always watching her on orders from Magnus.

The next day, resigned to her fate, Violet put on her dress and makeup and made her way down to the courtyard where the ceremony was to take place. It was late afternoon, and the sun was starting to set; it was a beautiful sunset for such a sad occasion. Ronald, her friend, was waiting for her, and he whispered to her not to be afraid, there was a plan.

"Don't do anything foolish. I don't want you to be killed. I love you." The words rushed out of her mouth, and she felt her heart breaking. It was true; she did love him. He squeezed her hand. "I love you too. It will be alright, I promise you."

Guards came to take her to where Magnus was waiting with the minister. People were standing on either side of an aisle strung with flowers. As she walked down it, she saw all her fairy friends hovering over the flowers, smiling at her. She stopped for a moment and thought, "Why have you deserted me?"

She heard back, "We didn't desert you. We have been busy helping your friends plan a surprise."

"What surprise!"

"You will soon find out."

She looked up and saw Magnus standing next to the minister, waiting for her. His jacket was hideous. It was elaborate, with folds and ruffles, and it made his huge body look even larger and more ungainly. The colors were so bright that his skin looked a dismal shade of orange. She heard a whisper in her ear and knew it was a fairy, saying, "Laugh at him, and we'll make everyone else laugh!"

She suddenly couldn't help herself; she began to laugh uncontrollably. She felt like someone was tickling her. She became hysterical, feeling giddy and desperate at the same time. Death was preferable to marrying him.

"What are you laughing about?" Magnus roared.

"You look so ugly in that jacket. It's unbelievable. It's ludicrous! It makes you even more ugly than you are. It's like an enormous caricature." She laughed so loudly that everyone else started laughing too. Soon everyone was screaming with laughter, and the kids were hooting "Ugly, ugly, ugly!"

"Stop it, stop it!" Magnus's orange skin turned red with rage.

"Where is William? Get this off me!" Suddenly, ten guards ran up behind him, and as they were pulling the coat off him and he was attempting to get out of the heavy sleeves, they tugged, saying, "It's hard to get off. Please hold your arms still so we can get the sleeves off."

He stilled his arms behind him, and suddenly, thick chains were wrapped around them so fast that he didn't have time to realize what was happening. By the time he noticed this, other men were wrapping his legs in chains, and then his whole torso was encased. He yelled and started straining against them. The chains seemed magically strong and soon covered every inch of his body.

Hooked to the rear of a huge wagon, he was now screaming for help. He even called on Violet to help him, crying, "I will make you so happy. Tell them to stop!"

All the people followed him to the lake, where a boat was waiting. He was tied to the end of the boat, dragged out into the water to its deepest part, and then the line was cut. Before his metal-laden body sank to the bottom, he cried out, "How can you do this? I have been so good to you!"

The celebration lasted all evening. During it, Violet and Ronald took advantage of the minister's presence and were married. All her fairy friends were there, and Violet asked them what they had done. "We whispered to the men, telling them how to make this happen. We also whispered to you to start laughing, remember? If you hadn't, we had others who would have started. We also helped Ronald find a blacksmith to make the thickest chains possible, and we added some of our energy to them so they would stay strong. We've been very busy, which is why we couldn't find time to talk to you."

Tears of joy in her eyes, Violet could only say, "Thank you, thank you!"

That evening the fireworks were spectacular. It was a perfect night to view them, and for Violet, the display was more than special, as she could see her friends flying between the starbursts, creating even lovelier colors.

Commentary

This allegorical tale is about the negative power of an unbridled ego and the devastation it leaves in its wake. Ruel Magnus embodies every negative masculine characteristic; he is reckless and aggressive, has tunnel vision, and is authoritative, indifferent, despoiling, controlling, and so on.

From a psychological perspective, ego development is necessary for normal functioning. Think of the ego as a formation of the psyche that, in normal development, basically coalesces by age three. Ego formation provides us with a sense of our unique identity and a "jumping off place" for manifesting action, be it making a phone call, getting a job, or developing relationships. In other words, the ego operates through positive masculine energy when powered by positive intent, but it operates destructively when expressed from negative intent.

So, what is going on with our anti-hero, Ruel Magnus? He is using his ego in the most negative way. He has no internal life, except for crude, dark emotions. Functioning out of the negative masculine only, with every trace of positive feminine energy dormant, he has been whittled down to animal awareness. In vivid contrast, William's actions in the world are colored by his positive feminine qualities of compassion and intuition. To put it simply, Ruel is functioning out of his negative ego, and William out of his positive ego (see the lists of feminine and masculine traits at the end of the next chapter).

How does one assess the nature of personal desires and change limiting, negative actions into positive and fulfilling actions? Let us create a typical day. Look back at your day and pick out what you would consider the highlights of your experience. Perhaps you are walking outside and feel the warmth of the sun on you, and it feels wonderful because it's wintertime. You take a breath and consciously let yourself enjoy the energy of the sun and the awareness that spring is awaiting you. This moment becomes a gift and enriches your day.

Then, ten minutes later, you're in your car and your tire goes flat. You realize that your husband or wife was supposed to take the car in and have the tire checked because it looked a little flat a few days ago. A wipeout happens! Your moment in the sun is obliterated by an angry call on your cell phone to your spouse. Your day is ruined—for that moment.

Within an hour, you made two choices—one positive, one negative. The first choice, your acknowledgement of the sunshine, was a gift to yourself. It brought some joy into your awareness. The second choice, to call your spouse and let him or her have it, brought discord and negative emotions into your relationship. In both cases you had a choice. The first choice that you enacted was an expression of your positive ego. The second was your negative ego. Had you consciously let go of your frustration and anger, taken a big breath and then made your call, you would have avoided punching a hole in the middle of the day. Making such a choice strengthens the positive will and changes limiting, negative action into more positive and fulfilling behavior, and it thus becomes a valuable contribution to our social fabric.

Exercise:

Think of a day that was like the one described in the commentary, a day in which you were in your positive ego and something happened to put you in your negative ego. Close your eyes and go through the day, experiencing all that happened. Make some notes.

Next, link with your heart and ask yourself: How could I have stayed in my positive ego even when the difficult thing happened? Make notes on this.

Then, in your imagination, repeat that day, and this time try to stay in the positive ego by following the advice your heart gave you.

How was this experience? How did it make you feel? Really notice the difference it makes being in the positive ego all the time.

Part Three: The Inner Marriage

13
The Magic Land of Relationships

Every relationship becomes a dance between masculine and feminine energies. In our parents' and grandparents' time the dance tended to be formal, with the dancers moving in clear and proscribed patterns. This is the traditional template of relationships, and it still dominates our culture. The man is supposed to be strong, protective, authoritative, and rational; the woman, in contrast, is supposed to be passive, often childlike, and led by her feelings and intuition. In this type of relationship, men and women stand opposite each other and rarely cross the line between the masculine and feminine, but when the line is crossed, a relationship can deepen in adventuresome complexity.

This is demonstrated by Paul and Ellen in this tale:

"Paul! Where are you? What's happening?"

Ellen covered her ears and tried to shut out the sudden cacophony of carnival music. Blinding strobe lights – red, green, and white—stabbed into the evening sky. Where was Paul? They had been strolling peacefully in the small park near their home. She had gazed up at the stars, trying to find the Milky Way, and when she turned to look at Paul, he wasn't there, and instead, out of nowhere, this carnival had appeared! Again she screamed his name, "Paul, Paul!"

"Ellen! I'm here, over here." Paul ran out of the shadows. They clutched at each other.

"What happened? Where were you?" Ellen tightened her arms around him.

"I don't know. It's crazy. One minute I was with you, and then I was in the middle of this carnival."

"Where did it come from?" she asked, quivering from the abruptness of the intrusion. "Let's get out of here; this is scary!"

"Don't be scared. It's really amazing." Paul grabbed her hand. "But I wonder how they got it here. Let's check it out."

"I don't know. It's spooky." Before she could protest any further, Paul was pulling her into a street full of rides.

Directly in front of them a carousel was going round and round, small cars were bumping against padded walls, music was playing and a huge Ferris wheel was slowly turning. Overcoming her anxiety, Ellen relaxed into a childlike expectation. Paul looked at her delightedly. With her shining, hazel eyes and tousled, blond hair, she looked like a charming teenager. There was a delicacy and grace to her slight body that made everything she wore look chic – even now, in her T-shirt and beat-up jeans. Such a pretty woman, he thought. Squeezing her hand, he felt his heart expand with affection. It was impossible to believe they had been married for eight years. He kissed her impulsively.

"Oh, what fun!" she exclaimed. "This reminds me of the carnivals back home. How did this happen? There was nothing here a minute ago."

"Ah," deadpanned Paul, "I haf conjurred forr you a prrre-anniverrrsary cele-brrration. Jhoost a few days earrrly." He then bowed debonairly.

She laughed, hugging his tall, thin frame impulsively. With his red hair and freckles, he too looked young for his 35 years. Laugh lines, engraved by a boundless sense of humor, creased the corners of his piercing blue eyes. She always told him he had missed his calling as a stand-up comic.

"Wow! You're some magician. Let's ride the merry-go-round."

Approaching the carousel as it sedately turned to its organ-grinder music, they saw children perched on the rising and falling horses. The merry-go-round was brightly painted, with all types of ornaments and flowers woven through the horses' manes and saddles. Long, colored ribbons and sparkling ropes hung from the top, moving in waves as the carousel turned. As they drew closer, Ellen cried, "Look, those aren't children. They're midgets! How strange! And look what they're wearing!"

The midgets' clothing looked as if someone had taken pieces of colored cloth, cut them into small triangles and sewn them together. The result was straight, multicolored robes, worn by both men and women; the women's were distinguished only by a row of bright ribbons adorning the front of their attire. All the women had long brown hair pulled back in ponytails. Some of the men wore small brimmed hats, but most were bareheaded. Men and women alike were singing gleefully along with the carousel music, their voices high and melodious.

"Come join us," shouted one of the little people as the carousel slowly came to a halt.

Ellen and Paul glanced at each other uncertainly. Paul asked the midget, "How did you get here? There was nothing here a minute ago."

Looking around, to their surprise, they saw that the park was now full of midgets. One of the little people slid off his horse. "What's happening is a special miracle. You do believe in miracles, don't you?"

"Yes!" exclaimed Ellen, now enchanted and intrigued.

He continued, "My name is William. This is my wife, Sophia." A woman leapt agilely off her horse and stood next to him. Even smaller than the other midgets, she had beautiful, delicate features and fair skin that contrasted William's dark, swarthy complexion. Both had dark brown, almost black eyes that were full of mischief. "The others here are all related to us. We are one family," William added.

"It's a big family," laughed Sophia in a high, sweet voice. "We enjoy playing here. Come ride with us. We insist."

Before they could respond, Sophia grabbed Ellen's hand and led her to a horse. Paul quickly followed, clambering onto a horse next to hers.

As the carousel began to move again, and the music swelled and quickened, something very strange happened. William and Sophia were on the horses in front of them, and as their horses moved up, their compact little bodies elongated into tall, thin replicas of their former selves. Each time the horses descended, their bodies resumed their small shapes. When Ellen and Paul looked around, they saw that this was happening to all the little people on the carousel. Looking at each other, they then realized that the same thing was happening to them.

"Look at you," Ellen called in amazement when she saw Paul elongate into a very skinny version of himself. Then, looking down at her own body, she laughed in astonishment.

"This is weird," Paul gasped.

Both then became aware of an expansion of energy in their hearts.

"I'm feeling... so open, it's scary," Ellen said.

"That's it; that's how I'm feeling, too."

The feeling of expansion filled them with unusual clarity. Ellen immediately realized Paul was afraid of something, and when she asked him what was wrong, he said, "My heart feels you'll never really love me the way I need to be loved." He reddened, "I don't know what made me say that... but it's true."

"How do you need to be loved?"

"I need to be me—to not always have to act in charge and in perfect control. I need you to love me in times when I feel scared. I feel you won't love me if I show you my fear. I feel you want me to be the strong man to lean on." Paul looked downcast as his body returned to normal.

"Oh, I'm so glad you said that!" replied Ellen, and as her horse arched up she revealed, "I don't want you to feel you have to be strong and in charge all the time. It's wonderful to hear you being vulnerable. It makes me love you even more."

She paused, "I've never told you this before, but sometimes I really need space. I often want be alone, without any demands made on me. I feel I can't do that because it would hurt your feelings, but it has nothing to do with you. It's just that I need space to think and reflect."

"Well, I sometimes want that too, but I'm afraid if I'm not attentive all the time, you'll be mad at me." As his horse descended, Paul sighed and said, "It feels good to be saying this."

Ellen and Paul continued riding the carousel until most of their unspoken feelings about each other were expressed. As the carousel came slowly to a stop, they realized the midgets were gone. They dismounted and looked at each other.

"That was extraordinary!" Ellen put her hand up to Paul's cheek. "And wonderful." She looked around. "Where is everybody?"

The strobe lights were gone, the music had stopped and an odd quiet had settled over the park. The bright lights of the rides were still on, but there seemed to be only a few midgets strolling on the streets

They walked in silence down a small road that led away from the remaining activity. I can't believe that happened and how revealing Paul was. He's never allowed himself to be vulnerable. Ellen squeezed his hand with love.

Paul also was lost in thoughts about Ellen. He had known her for so many years, yet he'd learned so many new things about her today.

The road narrowed into a path. Smiling, they continued to walk and only stopped when the path took them onto a sandy beach. How wonderfully cool the sand looked! Ellen took her shoes off and started running toward an indigo sea.

"Wait for me!" Paul shouted, still undoing his shoelaces. He reached her after a few minutes, out of breath, and they started walking in the cold, foaming water as it rolled in with the tide. The sun was beginning to set. Its glow was casting pink and orange on the shimmering white caps. Floating clouds danced within the rays, carrying lavender and pink across the horizon. So immersed were they in the beauty of the moment that they never even questioned how a sea had suddenly appeared in the suburbs of their home. It no longer mattered; both felt they were in some shared, mysterious dream.

As they walked slowly in the surf, a long wooden pier came into view, lit up by ropes of sparkling white lights that adorned every available spot. A medium-sized motorboat was tied to the end of the pier. On the bow was a huge sign advertising a special underwater dive. A small man, another midget, was working on the motor. When he saw them, he bounded athletically onto the dock to greet them.

"Hi, folks," he said amiably. "You want to dive?"

Ellen looked at Paul eagerly. "Oh, let's! I've never been diving."

"Okay," he responded. "Why not?"

As they stepped on deck, the small man introduced himself. "I'm Ruel," he said. He had a square face, hazel eyes, and a handlebar moustache. For such a small man, his voice was surprisingly deep and oddly whispery. There was an air of bravado about him.

"I'm Ellen, and this is Paul. We'd love to go," she exclaimed.

"This is a great ride. You'll see. Why don't you sit in those chairs and we'll take off?" Ruel indicated two deck chairs on the bow of the boat.

As soon as they settled into the chairs, the engine started and the boat sped out into the glowing sea, stopping far beyond the shore. Ruel led them to the back of the boat where a diving vehicle was moored. It was about seven feet tall and bell-shaped, with large windows that wrapped around its circumference. "Let's go exploring," he said.

The door of the diving bell opened, and a small woman stood looking at them. She looked like a mischievous little girl, pretty and full of vitality.

"This is my wife, Lillith," said Ruel. "Meet Paul and Ellen." As they greeted each other, Ellen was dimly aware of discordance between Lillith's innocent appearance and a fleeting, knowing expression in her eyes.

One by one, they stepped into a small chamber just large enough for the four of them. Ruel closed the hatch, and they began their descent into the deep waters. It was very dark within the tiny compartment; only a small outside light illuminated the water.

The vehicle landed with a soft thump on the bottom of the sea. Ruel opened the door. "Don't worry," he reassured them, as they hesitated. To their surprise, no water entered the bell. They stepped outside onto a sandy bottom full of seaweed. Long strands of it twisted upward through the water and lined walkways that extended outward from the landing site. To their amazement, they could breathe normally. Paul turned to ask Ruel how this was possible, when the tiny couple began to argue.

"I never said I would go shopping with you," Ruel shouted.

"Yes you did. You promised me this morning at breakfast!" Lillith started to cry, large tears spilling down her cheeks. Her face was red, and she looked like a pathetic child.

"Here we go again!" Disgusted, Ruel said, "Alright, don't cry. I'll go with you."

Astonished, Paul turned to Ellen and declared sharply, "That's what happened this morning! You manipulated me the same way."

"What? What are you saying? I did not!" Her words burst out angrily, "you could've said no!"

"You think so! You were acting like it was the end of the world if I didn't go with you."

At that moment, Lillith jumped into the conversation, her eyes suddenly dry. "Oh, men are all alike. They're so stubborn, and bullies, besides! C'mon, walk with me. They just don't get it."

Ruel and Paul, standing next to each other, watched their women walk off together. Ruel shook his head, "There they go! There's only one way to handle them, I guess."

"What do you mean?" asked Paul, depressed by the argument.

"We have to be firm. Strong. They really like that, but they won't let on."

"I don't know," said Paul. "We should be able to talk it out. We did before. I don't know what just happened. Do you?"

"Naw! They're just acting like women. C'mon, let's go after them."

As they walked, Ruel continued with his philosophy of women. "Like I said, they want to be controlled. They act like they don't, but the truth is, they need us to lead. It drives me nuts sometimes, all the mixed messages. I really lose it."

Walking in silence, Paul felt Ruel's words almost twisting his gut. In spite of himself, he thought, He's right! She'll stop respecting me if I show I'm weak.

The two women were also busy talking as they walked down the lanes of the underworld garden. Light from glow fish and luminous plants filtered through the blue green water. Sea creatures and fish with brilliant geometric patterns swam through the plant life. "You know," Lillith was saying, "men are so dense sometimes. It's really so easy to manage them."

"Why do you need to manage them?" Ellen asked. "I mean, it's not so bad with Paul. Most of the time he's pretty great."

"Oh, I'm sure! So is Ruel." She paused. "But, you know, when they get stubborn – like what just happened to both of us," she grinned, mischievously, "there's only one way to handle them." Then she winked at Ellen as she whispered, "with subtlety. Ruel can't stand it when I cry." Then, she added, with a tinge of triumph, "he's mine!"

They walked in silence for a few minutes. Lillith continued, "You know what it's about? Their egos! They have such fragile egos, and if you don't keep massaging them, they'll just look for someone else to do it."

Beginning to feel uncomfortable and more disloyal by the minute, Ellen said, "You make it sound like a war plan. I mean, I know Paul has his stubborn moments. I'm not perfect, either, but why can't we just talk about it instead of all this intrigue?"

Lillith flashed a look at her, barely able to hide her impatience. Then she tossed her head, and said, almost in a whisper, "Because, it's the intrigue that keeps them interested. It's the mystery of not knowing what's coming around the corner. Don't you know that? How do you think you're going to keep a man if you're an open book? He'll just get bored. That's the truth! They're all alike, I assure you."

Maybe she's right, thought Ellen. Things seem really good between us, but look at all the breakups our friends have gone through, and most of the time it's about an affair, and boredom. Maybe I'm just being naïve. When she looked at Lillith, she saw the little woman grinning up at her, almost as if she'd read her thoughts. "Oh, God," Ellen said fearfully, "I hope you're wrong!"

At that moment, they heard Ruel. "It's time to get back to the bell." His voice was surprisingly loud for such a small person. As they turned back, the two couples separated, Ruel and Lillith leading the way.

Ellen and Paul walked in silence among the waving green fronds. Both felt uncomfortable, as if they had forgotten how to talk to each other. Sneaking a look at her husband, Ellen saw that his jaw was set stubbornly. She knew he was avoiding looking at her. They stopped for a moment and watched a small fish being eaten by a larger one.

"I want to go home," said Ellen dispiritedly, near tears.

"Yeah," agreed Paul. "Me too!"

Ruel, apparently hearing them, turned around and said, "Here's the bell. Let's go. We'll be on the surface in a minute."

On the way up, Lillith sat perched on Ruel's lap and nibbled playfully on his ear lobe. She winked at Ellen, as if to say, "See?"

Both Ellen and Paul felt tired when they returned to the dock. Politely, they thanked Ruel and Lillith for the ride. Paul offered them money, but the couple declined, waved, and, laughing uproariously at some private joke, sped away.

"Well," said Paul as they stood looking after the fading wake of the small boat. "There they go. What a weird scene!"

He felt awkward, like he was making small talk with someone he barely knew. What's going on? He wondered. This is awful. His stomach was in knots.

Ellen was near tears. "What happened? We were having such a good time, and then, suddenly..."

"Yeah, I know," said Paul. "C'mon," he added almost gruffly. "Let's get out of here."

As they turned their backs on the sea, they shivered from a cold breeze that had risen. They were walking in the direction of the carousel when they saw William and Sophia coming toward them on the path.

"Where were you?" asked Sophia. "We've been looking for you." Her small face looked up at them with concern. "We were afraid you were lost."

Will's smile was so welcoming that both Paul and Ellen couldn't help but smile in return. Ellen, feeling a deep relief, said, "We just had a crazy adventure. I don't understand what happened."

"Tell us," said Sophia.

Something about the little couple made Ellen and Paul feel that they wanted to confide in them. As they walked together slowly, they recounted their adventure under the sea. When Paul mentioned Ruel and Lillith's names, Sophia and Will looked at each other, frowning.

"Who are they?" asked Ellen.

"They're mischief makers," Sophia replied firmly.

They continued on in silence. Suddenly, Paul looked at the sky and said, wonderingly, "Look, after all this time, it's still dusk! The sun hasn't even set yet. Isn't that strange?"

Ellen, relieved to focus on something beyond herself, agreed.

"Why is that?" she asked Will and Sophia, who were leading them along the path.

Falling back, Will explained, "By now, you should realize that you two have wandered into a kind of 'Middle Earth,' as some of your fantasy writers would describe it. This place exists on another level of reality. You know, there are many levels of reality beyond the physical. People visit them in dreams all the time."

"Is that why we could breathe underwater? That was so bizarre," said Ellen. She suddenly felt energized with excitement at Will's revelation. "I did think I was in the middle of a dream."

"On some level, you were, and are," explained Will. "Though it's very real at the same time."

"But, why is this happening?" Paul asked. "What is this really all about?"

Sophia replied, "I think you should wait to find out. After all, you wouldn't read the end of a book before you get there. That's cheating!" she added playfully.

"Which leads us to your next and last adventure." Will, smiling broadly, stood facing them.

Ellen and Paul glanced at each other uncertainly.

"Look, it's clear you've both been through a hard time," said Sophia. "But this is the middle of the story. It's important that you resolve it."

Will added, "Remember how you learned how to talk to each other in a deeper way on the carousel? What happened with Ruel and Lillith is also an important lesson, and this new adventure will help you to understand what that lesson was, but," he paused, "it's up to you whether or not you want to continue. Why don't you talk about it and decide?"

Sophia took Will's arm and they walked a short distance away.

Paul and Ellen gazed after them and then faced each other. Ellen, frowning, asked, "What do you think?"

After a moment, Paul said, "You know, we don't really have a choice. We have to see it through."

"I know what you mean. It would be like leaving the theater before the movie is over if we go back now. Maybe it'll help us understand what happened out there," she said, nodding in the direction of the sea.

"Hey," she added with a grin. "I really love you." She stood on her toes to kiss him.

He smiled down at her and ran his fingers through her hair. "Right. We'll get through this, whatever it is. What's happening is unbelievable, but I think this next piece is really important, just like Will said. If nothing else, it's certain to be interesting."

They both turned and looked at Will and Sophia, who, clearly delighted, were already returning.

The four of them walked a little further until they came to a large meadow. A fine mist had settled over the grass. The beams of the eternally setting sun, captured by the moisture in the air, cast a golden glow. Through the mist they saw a large tower in the middle of the meadow, with two smaller towers on either side. The larger tower was shooting out rays of colored light, and the smaller ones seemed to be absorbing them.

William turned to them. "Don't be afraid. You're going to be taken into space, and you will return safe and sound, I promise you."

He led Paul to one of the small towers, and Sophia took Ellen to the other. They were each strapped into seats on small capsules that supported their backs and were open from the waist to the head. Each capsule had its own control panel.

"How can we breathe in space? Where's our oxygen?" Ellen nervously asked Sophia.

"Don't worry. It's like your last experience. You had no problem breathing underwater. It'll be the same. Believe me, we've never lost anyone yet."

The engines started simultaneously, and a surge of energy propelled the capsules up the towers and into the sky. The motion was fast but somehow, strangely relaxing. Instead of being frightened, both found themselves in a surprisingly restful state. The wind that blew against their exposed bodies was warm, increasing their feeling of safety. As they moved further into space, they saw stars, colored lights, and white shining crystals floating in the blue blackness.

They continued their ascent, drifting slowly, side by side. Enraptured by the vastness of the vault in which they were floating, neither spoke. Stars seemed to tease them by making them want to reach out to touch them. A comet streaked across the sky as if to dazzle them. Both felt as if they were on the edge of some kind of knowledge that was deeper and more profound than anything they'd ever felt.

Shattering the silence, a loud, deep voice issued from their speakers. "It's time to return. It is up to you to find the way back." Abruptly, whatever energy was propelling them stopped, and they found themselves falling into even deeper darkness.

"Oh, no!" Paul called out.

"What'll we do?" Ellen yelled. Instinctively, they reached out and grabbed each other's hands. As they pulled their capsules closer together until they were almost touching, Paul found an extra strap tied to his seat and secured Ellen's capsule to his.

"Hold on, at least this way we won't be separated." They gripped hands as the capsules drifted along in the dark vastness of space. It was impossible to know how fast they were going because they had no reference point with which to gauge their movement.

Suddenly there was a crackling sound from their radios, and a loud voice broke through the static. Although it kept cutting out, they caught a few words: "...see... should've stayed...big mistake." They looked at each other in horror.

Paul, frowning, said, "Wait a minute. That sounds like the guy who took us out on the boat. Ruel! The voice we heard before was definitely William's."

"You're right! What does he mean? Something about a mistake."

"Great!" said Paul sarcastically. "Okay, let's figure out how to get back." He peered closely at the control panel. "Look, lots of gizmos here. We've been too distracted to notice anything. Let's try them out, but carefully, okay?"

"Right," said Ellen. "Let me try this lever first. The strap's holding us together, so if you don't do anything, we'll still be together."

Paul frowned. "What do you mean, if I don't do anything? You're acting like this is my fault!"

"That's not what I meant! I meant, just don't do anything. Why are you so touchy?"

"Touchy? Why are you so bossy?"

They were glaring at each other so fiercely that they could feel a hot and repellent energy flowing between them.

"I think we should do this separately," said Ellen sullenly.

"Yeah," Paul agreed. "This is definitely not working. We're just bringing out the worst in each other."

They sat grimly in the stillness. The darkness was beginning to feel oppressive.

"You realize what just happened, don't you?" Ellen finally said.

Paul looked at her. "What?"

"The minute Ruel came on the scene, we started fighting. What's that about?"

"I don't know, but there's something very negative about him, and it seems to pull us in."

"We get mad at each other, remember? The same thing happened in the ocean. Even hearing his voice is enough to set us off."

"Damn, I still feel mad," said Paul.

"Me too," she said.

After a silence that seemed to them like an eternity, Paul said, "I have an idea. Let's just look at each other. Don't say anything."

As they started to look into each other's eyes, Paul gently reached out for her hand. "Let's feel our love for each other. We've got that."

After a moment in the vastness of the star-studded sky, he whispered, "Can you feel it?"

"Yes," she whispered back. "My heart feels... full!" Then she turned to Paul excitedly, "Remember what William said? This is a challenge for us."

"Right!" agreed Paul. "He meant it's a challenge concerning our relationship!"

"This whole adventure has been about that." She added, "This has been very educational, wouldn't you say?"

"I would say you're right, my dear," he replied playfully. "But it will all be for nothing if we don't figure out how to get back."

"Good point," she said. "Any ideas?"

"Let's look at the control panels again. Why don't you press the lever you wanted to before?"

"Okay," agreed Ellen. "Let me try this lever first. As I said before, the strap's holding us together, so if you don't do anything, we'll still be together."

"Okay, go for it!"

Ellen cautiously took hold of the lever and moved it to the left. Instantly, the capsules veered in that direction. Then she moved it to the right, the capsules responding likewise. When she moved the lever forward and backward, they went up and down.

"Well, that's easy. This should help when we get closer to earth. I'm so glad you thought to tie us together. We really have to work together to figure out which direction to go."

"This is amazing. I don't have what you have—just these two buttons," he said, pointing to his dashboard.

"Now," he added carefully, "Don't you do anything while I check these out."

"Right," she agreed.

When he pressed the first button, it slowed down their speed. The other one made them go faster.

"Amazing. I can change the speed. I vote for slow!" He pushed the first button again.

As they looked at each other, they smiled, feeling a joyful connection with each other. Ellen's eyes glistened with tears. "Wow," she said. "I love you so much!"

"And me, you," he replied, grinning happily at her.

At that moment, the darkness lightened to an azure blue, and they saw, far below, the faint lights of the towers they had left behind. Carefully, in close collaboration, they began their descent. The large tower was still shooting out colored beams to the smaller ones.

Worried, Paul scanned the scene below. "What'll we do? We can't get caught in one of those rays. There's no way to know what their energy pull is like."

Ellen thought for a minute. "Let's test it out." Removing a scarf from around her neck, she said, "I'll throw this down into a ray and see what happens."

"Great idea. We'll move close to that one over there." He pointed to a blue ray near them. Then, slowing down some more, Paul took the scarf and carefully dropped it into the ray. The scarf just floated through it.

"Good, the rays don't have any energy field at all."

"Shouldn't we try something else, just to be sure?"

"You're right. Let's use my belt." Paul quickly removed it from his pants and again moved close to a ray, this time a red one. The belt also just floated through.

"Now, what'll we do?" Paul asked, worried about how they would land.

"I can take you to the left, just above your tower, and when we untie the strap, you can go straight down into the top. Then I can move right and drop down into my tower. That should work."

Paul was silent for a moment before responding, "You know, my gut feeling is we need to do this together. We've come this far. I know it will be okay." He peered through the rays to try to see the middle tower more clearly.

"Look, there's an opening in the top of the big tower. Let's try for that."

"How do we know there's a landing place inside?" Ellen asked.

"I feel it'll be alright. If not, we can go back out."

"Okay," Ellen agreed. "I'll maneuver us. You control the speed."

They carefully moved through the rays, calling out directions to each other as they neared the opening. Relieved, they saw there was plenty of room for both their capsules. Slowly, they entered the tower and descended its shaft to the bottom, where, jubilant, they landed safely.

A crowd of midgets greeted them with cheers and applause. William appeared, smiling at them. "We're so happy you were able to come back together. It's a difficult feat for couples. Both of you had to cooperate to make the right decisions. Bravo!"

"What happens to couples who don't cooperate?" Paul asked.

"Most often, they separate at the beginning of their fall and try to do it on their own. We're watching on a computer, and when we see them doing this, we relay a signal that guides them back down. If they initially stay together, they often separate at the end and try to go to the small towers. They seldom realize that a new solution is needed and that they can work on it together. Again, bravo!" William clapped his hands.

Ellen and Paul hugged and kissed each other. When they turned back to William, he and all the others had vanished, and they found themselves back in the park, sitting on a bench under the night sky.

Commentary

The dance between the sexes has been evolving into greater complexity since World War II. When women began to take over men's jobs to support the war effort, they were forced to call on their dormant masculine energy. With the advent of the feminist movement, with women moving into traditionally male roles and with more stay-at-home dads, the dance was changing even more. No matter how traditional or complex a relationship may be, there seems to be an innate drive within it to achieve balance. It is as if the partners are on a playground seesaw: as one moves up, the other moves down. For example, when one member of the couple is connected to a strong masculine "achieving" energy, the other will often become more receptive or passive. In this way, unconsciously, partners work out a kind of balance in relation to these energies. This very natural and compensatory way of working through primary energies is beyond gender and applies to both heterosexual and same-sex couples.

However, even though a couple will unconsciously establish a balance between the two primary energies within their relationship, there is, within each individual, a deep drive to achieve such wholeness within him or herself as well. For our mythical modern couple, this yearning for wholeness is expressed as they ride the carousel. As their bodies elongate, Paul becomes more feminine in his vulnerability, while Ellen expresses her masculine need for independence and individuation.

As the couple plunges into the emotional waters of the unconscious, the masculine and feminine energies are sucked into the vortex of their psychological and social conditioning. Instead of being open and vulnerable with each other, they try to control each other in order to get their needs met – Paul by bullying and Ellen by manipulating. Here, goaded by Ruel and Lillith, they express the most negative and non-integrated aspects of the masculine and feminine energies.

Without consciousness, couples can become mired in rigid and one-dimensional roles for their whole lifetime, with each person playing out a degraded version of the masculine and feminine. When consciousness enters a relationship, it can take off like the couple's final space ride, which symbolizes their journey into the unknown.

The smaller towers represent masculine and feminine energies. The central tall tower contains both energies and discharges a flow of creative "lights." Paul and Ellen's separateness is symbolized when they are seated in their individual, smaller towers. Soon after they are propelled into the starry heavens, they find themselves traveling together. This glorious experience is like the beginning of a relationship. There are no barriers, only mystery and excitement, but at some point they must return to earth. The moment of danger, when they free-fall into darkness, represents times of deep trouble and crisis when the life journey becomes bumpy and threatens to destroy a couple. How do they return? They can jump ship by finding a safe haven in a new relationship, or they can choose to stay together and work it out. When they opt for the latter solution, they intermingle their masculine and feminine energies, and, in that interplay, creativity flowers.

As they were figuring out how to land safely, Ellen drew on her masculine energy, experimenting very rationally with the rays by throwing her scarf into one. Paul's gut feeling that they should land together in the central tower was really his intuition, a strong characteristic of the feminine.

The lesson for both of them is that, together, they constitute all of the instruments of an orchestra, and as they each learn the entire range of instruments, they more than double the richness and intensity of their music.

Exercise:

Figures 1 and 2, below, present some of the main characteristics of the masculine and feminine; these figures have emerged from the many workshops we have led on Balancing the Masculine and Feminine. In each figure, the characteristics on the left are integrated, and those on the right are common, non-integrated distortions of basic integrated characteristics. The dots that go from the first column to the second column are like spectrums that move from the most pure integrated states to the most non-integrated states. Obviously, we all fall somewhere in between the two extremes as we evolve into a greater wholeness.

In order to get a sense of your masculine and feminine profile, take time to study the two lists, one at a time. Reflect on each quality or behavior: Are you closer to the integrated or the non-integrated side of the spectrum? Place the number 1 wherever you sense you are. For example, look at the first characteristic in Figure 1, the Feminine Characteristics: "service-oriented" is the characteristic in its purest form and "pleaser" is the characteristic in its most non-integrated form. Place the number 1 where you sense you are on that spectrum at this time in your life. Or, if you feel this quality or behavior does not apply to you at all, simply leave it blank. Proceed in this way through the whole list, and then turn to the other list and work through it in a similar manner. Try not to judge yourself as you work—this is not a cosmic test, but a loose self-assessment.

When you have gone through both lists, review your findings. Are you generally less integrated on the feminine side or the masculine? Focusing on one of the lists, choose a characteristic that you would like to integrate more fully, and decide one or two ways you will begin to do that. Then, in a week or two, review that characteristic again. You may discover you have changed to some degree and can adjust your placement on the spectrum. Put a number 2 on the line to indicate where you are then. Also, if you review both complete lists after doing this, there may be positive shifts in other characteristics as well because of the progress you've made in that one area.

Continue to work with the lists. Over time, you can try to change some of your more negative qualities and review your placement on each spectrum as you evolve.

Figure 1: Integrated and non-integrated feminine characteristics

FEMININE CHARACTERISTICS

Integrated	Non-integrated
Service-oriented	Pleaser
Sensuous	Vampish
Sensitive	Hysterical
Intuitive	Flaky/Scattered
Introspective	Moody
Loyal/Devoted	Dependent
Receptive	Passive
Compassionate	Sentimental
Sharing	Gossipy
Responsive	Meddling
Nurturing	Smothering
Guiding	Manipulating
Open/Vulnerable	No Boundaries
Creator as Inspired	Dreamy Fantasizing
Patience	Stuckness
Endurance	Obsessiveness

Figure 2: Integrated and non-integrated masculine characteristics

MASCULINE CHARACTERISTICS

Integrated	Non-integrated
Courageous	Reckless
Assertive	Aggressive
Focus	Tunnel Vision
Power of Leadership	Authoritarian Power
Detached/Unattached	Isolated/Indifferent
Adventuresome	Despoiling
Organized/Structured	Rigid
Protective	Controlling
Creator as Manifestor	Materialisation
Discriminating/Discerning	Critical
Strong	Bulldozing
Cooperating	Competitive
Teaching/Disseminating	Autocratic
Productive	Workaholic
Persistent	Hanging On

14
Trapped in Reflections

We come into this world with a genetic inheritance and some traits and predispositions already in place. Much of who we then become has to do with our family of origin and the country and culture into which we are born. No matter how optimum our family of origin is, we are bound to be challenged and to find behaviors that sufficiently preserve us. Thus key aspects of our personalities are already shaped or formed before we even go out into the larger world of schools and communities.

Each behavioral and defensive aspect within us is like a separate system, a 'mini person,' or subpersonality that is uniquely suited for specific situations—with its own emotions, thoughts and body experience. It even has its own beliefs about the self and the world. These subpersonalities serve us well for many years. Then, by adulthood, or sooner, some of them will no longer work—outmoded and, curtailing our freedom, they begin to get our attention.

The following story illustrates one person's discovery of outmoded subpersonalities. It also illustrates that, male and female alike, we can get to know not only our various personality traits but also our true nature, which lies deeper than or beyond our genetic inheritance and personalities:

Cynthia reached out to read the price tag on a small oval mirror in a delicately wrought silver frame. Without warning, the lights went out, and she found herself wrapped in thick blackness. She groped her way toward the entrance of the home furnishings department of the store when, suddenly, the lights flickered back on. Relieved, she looked around, but was startled when she found herself in a completely different room. There were no furnishings, just walls covered with large, vertical, floor-to-ceiling mirrors, intricately framed in antique gold. Reflecting into one another endlessly down a long hall, they seemed to dissolve into silvery mist.

Where am I? What happened? She hurried down the hall looking for a way out and almost collided with a man who seemed to appear out of nowhere.

"Oh, I'm so sorry!" she said. He smiled at her engagingly. He was tall, slender and very blond.

"Can I help you?" he asked. "My name is Will. Are you lost?" His voice was low and strangely comforting. She found the clarity and directness in his cobalt blue gaze incredibly appealing.

"Yes, I think so. I must have gotten turned around when the lights went out. I've been coming to this store for years, and I've never seen this room."

"Why don't you take your time and look around? There are some very special mirrors here. Feel free to explore. The glass is very special, a new product that you can actually walk through. Try it out. I think you'll be intrigued. I'll be back soon."

Before she could respond, he had disappeared into what looked like one of the mirrors. Curious, she wandered over to the place he had exited, which she assumed was a cleverly disguised door. As she faced it, she saw herself -– in pieces! It was as if a knife had cut her into vertical strips. The cut-up strips began to undulate and fly past her, each into a different mirror. Shafts of brilliant, blue-white light careened from one mirror to another in the great hall.

"Help!" she yelled, as she instinctively ducked to avoid the flying pieces of herself. What's going on? I didn't break the mirror! How did that happen? Where's the salesman? Oh, god, this is nuts! I'm out of here!

As she backed away from the mirror, she glimpsed her reflection in the neighboring one. That's better, she thought. At least I'm in one piece. But when she stood before it, she saw that there was a real woman looking back at her! She could have been Cynthia's twin, just heavier. Oddly, she was wearing a longer version of the same blue chiffon scarf around her waist that Cynthia had tucked around her neck.

"Hello!" the woman said. "Would you like to come in?"

Cynthia protested, "I don't understand this. I thought this was a mirror and you were me."

"Me... you? Don't I wish it!" She glanced at Cynthia's body.

"I'm a bit confused. Could you please direct me to the exit?"

"I'm happy to help you, no problem. But, come, have some lunch with me first. I'm Lillith."

"Oh, I'm Cynthia. You know, I'd really love to, but I have to get home."

"Come on. It won't take long. I'm really hungry, and I hate eating alone. Besides, we have something in common," she said, pointing to the scarf.

"Well, all right. Actually, I forgot to eat lunch. It's very nice of you."

Lillith backed away from the opening as Cynthia tentatively stepped through the frame. She found herself in a small kitchen and dining area. It was a blue and white culinary heaven. Cookbooks filled a tall bookcase and on the shining white counter, a crockery container held an assortment of cooking utensils. Bottled spices were grouped on three shelves over the counter and fresh herbs dangled from hooks on the powder-blue wall. A bowl filled with a colorful salad mix rested on the table: bright red peppers, radishes, and cherry tomatoes were mixed with all kinds of greens. Cynthia loved salads.

Lillith quickly set two places at the table. Like Cynthia, she had large brown eyes and light brown hair. Even her features were similar, small and delicate, although Lillith's face was heavier. They were both in their early forties.

As they began to eat, Cynthia asked, "Do you work here? I just had the strangest experience. Maybe you can clear it up for me."

Looking up from her plate, Lillith asked, "What's the mystery?"

"There's a mirror out there—I don't know how to explain it, but something weird just happened."

"I hate looking in mirrors. I'm getting so fat!"

"I know what you mean, but this was different..."

"Oh, dear," Lillith interrupted as she munched on her salad. "I keep dieting all the time, and I can't seem to lose any weight."

"Well, this salad should certainly help; it's delicious. Thank you for sharing it." Cynthia's fork tackled a mound of red peppers, her favorite.

"How do you keep your figure?" Again, Lillith eyed Cynthia's body.

"I don't know. It's difficult. I'm like you, always dieting, eating salads, and trying not to binge. But if you're eating this and you're not losing weight, maybe it's your thyroid. Have you ever had it checked? That could be the problem."

Cynthia almost giggled as she heard herself speaking in such an ordinary way in this extraordinary situation. She studied Lillith more closely. She has a pretty face, but she's right, she's fat. Look at those rolls under her bra, and those tight jeans make her look dumpy. If I don't lose weight, I'm going to end up looking just like her.

"No, it's not my thyroid. I checked that," Lillith was saying. "But why are you dieting? You're so thin."

"What do you mean I'm thin? I need to take off at least ten pounds!"

Lillith frowned at her. "Are you crazy? It's people like you that really make me mad." Her face reddened as her voice grew louder. "I've been struggling for years to take off even five pounds, and I'm still fat. Look at you! God!" She looked away from Cynthia and shoveled mouthfuls of salad into her mouth.

Cynthia stood up, shocked by the force of Lillith's anger. She said, anxiously, "You said you'd show me the way out."

"Find your own way out," Lillith replied sullenly.

Seeing no exit in the room, Cynthia quickly stepped back into the hall of mirrors. What a bitch! I was just trying to help her. Now what?

Nervously approaching another mirror, she was relieved to see her own reflection. Her height was average, 5 foot, 5 inches, but her small bones, long legs, and slim body made her look taller. Brown, curly hair, cut really short, framed her oval face. Fingering the curls, Cynthia tried to flatten them. She'd always hated her curls. Any longer and they'd be a bushy mop. Automatically, she turned her body back and forth, examining herself to see if she was gaining weight. She was wearing tight jeans and a fitted blue blouse, which emphasized her small waist and narrow hips and showed a tiny bulge at the top of her thighs. I need to exercise more to get rid of this. She adjusted the light blue chiffon scarf around her neck, pleased at the way it emphasized the dark blue of her blouse. But first I've got to get out of this fun house!

She walked with caution down the hall, looking for an exit. Soon she arrived at another frame, which opened into an office. A woman was sitting at a desk, typing on a computer. Ah, thought Cynthia, she looks pretty normal. Maybe she can tell me the way out. She knocked tentatively on the frame. The woman, frowning, looked up and beckoned her in.

As Cynthia entered, she looked for a door out of the room, but was disappointed.

"Have a seat," the woman said brusquely. "My name's Pamela. I'll be right with you." She turned back to her work, ignoring Cynthia.

Cynthia sat down and studied the woman. She was very thin. Her navy-blue, tailored pantsuit and shirt made her look almost anorexic. The blue chiffon scarf hung from her jacket pocket. Her straight, light brown hair was cut in a severe style. She had angular features, and wore very little makeup; just a touch of pink lipstick lent color to her pale face. Pamela finished typing and swiveled her chair to face Cynthia. She smiled briefly, her lips knife-like. "What can I do for you?"

"Hello, I'm Cynthia. I'm sorry to interrupt you. I'm hoping you can help me."

"I can take a short break in a moment. Let me just finish this." As Pamela turned back to her typing, Cynthia looked around the room. It was clean and orderly. Neat stacks of paper sat on a long table at the side of the room. On the top of each pile was a piece of colored paper that evidently indicated the contents of the stack. The walls were covered with complex charts and graphs that looked like the floor plans of a building.

Cynthia looked out the window next to her chair and felt comforted to see the familiar street below. Traffic was stalled, and shoppers were dodging around the cars. A large yellow dog was trotting confidently along the sidewalk. As she looked up at the building across the street, she was almost blinded by the sun's reflection in the window opposite her.

Pamela finished her typing with a flourish and addressed Cynthia. "Now, what can I do for you?"

"I'm trying to get out of this place. Can you tell me where the exit is?"

"I don't know what you're talking about. I'm always here."

"You're always here? How can that be? Don't you ever go home?"

"This is my home. I don't leave because I work all the time. Just look at all the filing I still have to do today," she said, pointing to the table.

As she spoke, she seemed to flatten out and become nearly two-dimensional. Cynthia felt like she could almost see through her. My eyes must be going bad. She looks like a paper doll. Whew, this is really weird!

"But," she protested, "How can you work all day and not have any social life? You must leave this place sometimes."

"I don't know what you mean. I love my work. Doing this is much more satisfying than going out to a movie or having dinner with someone."

Suddenly, the phone rang, and Pamela became involved in a business-related conversation. A high-pitched ring startled Cynthia, then the fax machine spewed out a stream of papers. Still talking, Pamela grabbed the papers with her free hand and tossed them onto a new pile. Cynthia had a sudden vision of an octopus whose many tentacles were in constant motion.

The phone conversation sounded like it would never end. Frustrated, Cynthia realized nothing more was going to happen, and without saying goodbye, she stepped back through the frame.

Disappointed and feeling a rising panic spread through her body, she walked down the hall until she came to a mirror that reflected a pastoral scene of a meadow. The grass was like a lush green ocean, with a breeze rippling its surface into waves. Oh, great, she thought. I can get out this way. She stepped through the frame and into the grass that reached almost to her waist. Fluffy clouds were moving majestically across the pale sky. The only sounds were the humming of bees and the singing of birds in the distance. As if waking from a dream, Cynthia realized she shouldn't be in the country. Where were the stores, the familiar streets? Her stomach clenched in fear. What's happening to me? She began struggling toward what seemed like a road in the distance and almost fell over a young woman lying on the ground. Bound in what seemed like swaddling clothes, she looked like a big, helpless baby in a white cocoon.

Alarmed, Cynthia knelt at her side. "Who did this to you? Let me help you."

"No," replied the woman, looking up at her with a face that reminded her of herself as a child. The woman's eyes were wide with fright. A cloth was wrapped tightly around her, and her legs were folded in a fetal position. The blue chiffon scarf tied around her head, hiding her hair, made her look even more pitiable.

"Please go away. I like being here. I feel safe here." The woman's voice was small and reedy.

"Who are you hiding from?"

"Leave me alone. Go away. Nobody can bother me here, or make fun of me, or hurt me."

"But, why are you in those clothes? Don't you want me to pull them loose so you can walk?" Suddenly a wave of helplessness overcame Cynthia. She sank down into the enveloping softness of the tall grass. A passive calm washed over her, dulling her fears.

"Oh, I know why you're here," she said. "It feels so safe. I could stay here forever."

The woman burrowed deeper into her hiding place. She said, her voice muffled, "Find your own place. There's plenty of room out here. Don't stay near me."

What am I doing? This is crazy! Cynthia forced herself to stand up. She tried to walk, but the grass was so thick and tall, she couldn't move through it. Fighting an overwhelming lassitude, she reluctantly turned back toward the entryway. Once back in the hall, she leaned against the wall, her eyes closed. Who was that woman? Why did I want to stay? I could've just slept and slept. I must be exhausted.

"Hello! Are you all right?"

The voice was sweet and high-pitched. Cynthia's eyes opened wide to the vision of a gray, curly-haired head poking out of the next mirror.

"Oh, I'm fine. I'm just a little tired. Please, can you tell me how to get out of here? I'm really lost."

"Why don't you come in for a moment and sit down? I'll ask my husband."

"Thank you. I really appreciate it."

"My name is Cynthia," she said as she entered into a small and comfortable living room.

"I'm Veronica. Please, sit down."

The older woman was wearing a flowered housedress and sandals. The blue chiffon scarf was in the pocket of her apron. Her sweet, smiling cheeks had bright spots of red rouge on them that were almost as dark as her lipstick. Somehow she seemed like an older version of herself. She was peering at Cynthia anxiously.

"Sit here. Can I get you something? Tea? Coffee?"

Cynthia sank down on a comfortable couch piled with large, soft pillows.

"No, thank you. I really must get home."

"Are you sure I can't get you anything?" Reaching over Cynthia, she pulled a pillow from behind her back, plumped it and returned it, saying, "Isn't this better now?"

"Thank you. I'm fine." *Please, please, just talk to your husband.*

"Can't I at least get you a glass of water?"

Before Cynthia could say no, Veronica had disappeared into the kitchen. She quickly returned with a large glass of water and thrust it in Cynthia's hand, hovering over her anxiously.

"Veronica, I'm fine. Where is your husband? I really need to ask him for directions."

"Oh! Let me just check to see if he's up from his nap." She ran upstairs.

Cynthia leaned her head back against the couch and closed her eyes. I've got to get out of here. These people are so strange. They're so – one-dimensional. Obsessive, that's it.

"He's still sleeping. Oh, and so are you. I'm sorry. You must be exhausted."

Cynthia's eyes popped open as she realized she had fallen asleep. "You're right, I must be tired. Sorry."

"Oh, that's all right, dear. I don't want to wake Henry. Please wait. It will only be another 15 minutes and I'm sure he'll be up. Would you like something to eat in the meantime?" Again, she disappeared into the kitchen.

Lord, thought Cynthia. She's doing it again. I won't survive 15 minutes. She's such a pleaser!

Suddenly very uncomfortable and her cheeks hot, she called out, "Sorry, Veronica. I can't wait. You've been very nice, but I'll find my way out." As she stepped into the hall, she could hear Veronica protesting behind her back.

Cynthia looked down the hall and saw there were many more mirrors. I've seen enough. I can't stand any more of this. She walked past several mirrors, carefully avoiding looking into them. One, however, caught her eye. It was dark and slightly ominous. She cautiously peered in and saw a man in a black robe sitting at a judge's bench. The chiffon scarf was being used as a cravat around his neck. He was very thin, and his face was reamed with wrinkles. He resembled her father. As his black eyes fixed on her, he beckoned her through the window.

"Cynthia, come here."

To her surprise, she obeyed him immediately, stepping quickly into a courtroom. She stood before him. He sat up high on the bench, and she noticed a small sign there with the name Judge Ruel. The Judge leaned forward and impaled her with his eyes. I feel so small. Her stomach turned over. I feel sick.

The judge had a long list in his hands, which he began reading in a droning, stentorian voice. "You forgot to set the alarm clock and woke up late this morning." He shook his head.

"You ate too much for breakfast." He glanced at her hips.

"You should have called your mother first thing, instead of going shopping and spending more money." He sighed.

"And you should have taken a bus instead of a cab." He cast his eyes upward, as if to let God in on her infamy.

"You forgot to pay your telephone bill again."

As he continued reading, Cynthia realized she was listening to the thoughts she had been thinking about herself earlier that morning. Retreating from his harsh words, she backed out of the window and out of his sight. She slumped down onto the floor. This is terrible — do I really do this to myself? How depressing! I don't get why this is happening. All these women are like me, and this man knows my thoughts. I must be going crazy! What'll I do?

Looking up, she saw a mirror at the end of the hall. It was different from the others, very large and oval, with a simple, modern silver frame. There was something about it, a subtle quality of light, that attracted her. She stood up and slowly moved toward it. Looking in, Cynthia saw a beautiful woman. She was wearing a blue chiffon dress, the same material as the scarf. Her brown eyes sparkled with enthusiasm, and her lovely face was glowing. There was an essence, almost a light, surrounding her. This woman seemed to be an incredible transformation of her. It was as if all the fragments of the first mirror finally came together into a great wholeness. A ray of love and power emanated from her. The woman stepped out of the frame and embraced her gently.

"You're not crazy," she said. Her voice was warm and reassuring. Cynthia was almost overwhelmed with her strength and goodness.

"You've had to go through this experience to see the limited aspects of yourself. Each mirror has revealed a different part. For instance, Lillith is an exaggeration of what you feel you look like."

"I guess that's true. I always feel I'm too fat."

"It's not about being fat or thin. It's about how you feel about yourself."

"But that's how I feel. How can I change that? All the other people in the mirrors—they're all me? I'm a workaholic like Pamela. That's the truth. I'm dependent and needy, like Veronica. I smother people. Sometimes I just want to lie down and disappear, like that big baby in the meadow. I judge myself all the time. I'm a perfectionist. I always criticize everything I do. I'm always putting myself down."

Cynthia's eyes filled with tears. "That's who I am. How can I be different?"

The woman looked into her eyes. "There's more to see than the negative. Look at me; you are also me." As she looked at the woman, Cynthia's tears changed into feelings of joy, and she knew for one moment what it would be like to become her.

The woman smiled and touched her arm. Cynthia then found herself back in the home-furnishing department, looking at the price tag of a small, oval mirror with a delicately wrought silver frame.

The salesman with the cobalt eyes approached her. "Have you found what you've been looking for?"

Commentary

The hall of mirrors represents how men and women experience fragmentation today. Cynthia's discovery that there is no way out of the hall symbolizes how trapped we can feel when we believe that a particular fragmented aspect of our personality is who we really are.

She is shocked to see her image in pieces in the first mirror. These fragments, or "subpersonalities," (*Psychosynthesis* by Roberto Assagioli, M.D.) are the unconscious roles we play. They are common to all of us; you may recognize some of them in yourself.

In the second mirror, Lillith represents Cynthia's body image. Here she appears less attractive and heavier than she actually is. We often experience a split between what we see in the mirror and how we actually look. Most of us are aware that mirrors in clothing stores "slim" us, and it is amazing how we accept this distortion of ourselves.

The third mirror reflects Cynthia's workaholic subpersonality. Being a workaholic is a negative masculine characteristic that causes havoc for men and women alike. Work becomes not a joy but an addiction that, like any addiction, serves to mask feelings of disappointment, pain and emptiness. The price we pay for the denial of these feelings is the contraction and shriveling of our natural life force. What remains for a workaholic is a driven lifestyle with no time for reflection and true creativity.

The next image in the hall of mirrors is of a woman bound and hiding in tall grass. There is a secret place in many people that is self-created in order to hide from the world. Fear, arising from childhood conditioning, such as physical or emotional abuse, leads to this need to hide. If a child has been pushed aside by parents and made to feel insignificant and stupid, this place is subtler. She or he may hide through silence. To not speak is to not be noticed. Anonymity becomes a self-imposed prison.

When Cynthia meets Veronica, she confronts her own "pleaser," or care-taking, subpersonality, which is common to many of us. It is a learned response to parental neglect or strictness. The child learns very early that if he or she can please the parent, approval will follow. Although the impulse to help is an appropriate and loving response in any human being, sometimes, as in Veronica's case, the result is smothering the other person.

So, how does one distinguish between being a caretaker and having a loving impulse that comes from the heart? It is often difficult to tell. One signal is that you will tend to feel fatigued after a bout of caretaking. When you are truly coming from the heart, you will feel energized. Caretakers are famous for ignoring their own needs. Let's face it, the old maxim is true: until we love ourselves, we can't love others.

Did you recognize the judge? This is an absolutely universal subpersonality who dumps on us all day long. It is super-parental. When the judge or critic is in force, we feel, as Cynthia did, like a child. Until we become aware of this dynamic, the judge can abuse our inner child and make us feel like a pathetic loser.

The good news is that subpersonalities can be transformed into helpful qualities that enrich our lives. For the most part, they worked for us as children, helping us to survive in some cases. However, when we mature, they become liabilities that hinder our development. When we don't need them anymore in their old jobs, they respond quickly to the offer of a new position. For example, in the case of the judge/critic subpersonality, once we begin to recognize this nagging part of us and begin to heal it, it transforms into the qualities of good judgment and discernment.

As Cynthia peers into the final mirror, she sees herself clearly, undistorted by projections. Her reflection is vibrant. This image represents her potential. Here she stands in her power, having shed the impoverished self-images that curtailed her life force. She is grounded, enthusiastic, and full of life and energy. Her heart is open, her intuition is flowing and she is a channel for inspiration. She is no longer afraid to be in the world as her authentic self.

As a first step in the process of achieving balance between the masculine and feminine, we must look at ourselves as we are now with as much detachment as possible. The inner journey towards wholeness starts with personality integration. This process can continue throughout our lives, but, really, at this stage, one needs only to recognize those elements in our personalities that cause us the greatest inner conflict and do some simple, often rewarding, inner work with them.

Exercise:

The following is a list of some common subpersonalities. As you read the list, reflect on whether you might have such a subpersonality; also, be aware that you may have a different name for that part. If so, use the name you prefer:

The Critic or Judge: a part that constantly criticizes, judges, and even belittles both yourself and others.

The Pleaser: someone who is always doing things for others, not out of kindness, but out of an inner need to be loved.

The Inner Child: a part of you caught in emotions that never had a chance to be metabolized and thus, never matured.

The Saboteur: a part that will sabotage anything you need to do or finish. It works closely with the judge or critic to make you feel like a failure.

The Workaholic: someone who works all the time and feels the need to do this in order to succeed and feel worthwhile.

The Perfectionist: someone who is never satisfied with his or her work; it is never good enough, and they keep trying to improve something that is already good. Often, the critic or judge is closely allied with the perfectionist.

The Spiritual Subpersonality: a fanatic in terms of the spiritual, this part is often clothed in overblown 'goodness' and superiority. It too works with the critic in terms of issues of worthiness/unworthiness.

Write down your name for any subpersonality that you recognize. Also, in reflecting on this list, you may have thought of situations in your life where other subpersonalities seem to be at play. For example, are there some situations in your life where you feel a lack of confidence? Or, are there times you feel strong emotions, whether you express them or not, that seem overcharged for the situation? Or, are you perhaps someone who worries a lot? Take time to add anything you wish to your list. Then, choose one subpersonality to focus on first, and try the following process with it:

Recall a recent time when you felt this subpersonality was present for you and when you perhaps became it. Recall all you can about the situation. Focus on remembering the feelings you felt, how you experienced your body, and any thoughts that went through your mind. Then imagine you can really step back from that situation. Take a few deep breaths to help yourself step back into your mature adult self.

When you are ready, allow an image that embodies the subpersonality to come in. Take time to allow the image to become clearer; sense all you can about it.

Then visualize yourself with this image in a relatively neutral place, perhaps a meadow. It's pleasantly warm. See or sense the subpersonality in front of you. Notice your thoughts and feelings about it. As best you can, let yourself be curious about it. Notice the position and posture it's in; notice the expression on its face. Let it show you how it moves. Try to sense out its mood and emotions. Imagine talking with it. Ask it what it wants and what it needs.

Then, to the extent you are comfortable doing this, imagine you take a step towards the subpersonality and, for a few moments, become it. Assume its posture, its body size, and its mood.

What is it like being this part? As this part, what are your feelings? If you have thoughts, what are your thoughts? What does the world look like to you? How far can you see? What do you believe about the world and about yourself?

When you are ready, take a few deep breaths, step out of the subpersonality, and become your adult self again. Look back at the subpersonality. Do you feel any differently towards it now, after being it? Has your understanding of it changed? Can you accept that you have this subpersonality?

Ask it how old you were when it became active in your life. Continue to dialogue with this part of yourself about what happened at that time, and allow it to communicate anything it wants to you.

Finally, become aware again that you and this part of you are in a meadow. The sun is shining down on you and your subpersonality. Breathe in the sun energy, and notice how your subpersonality responds to the sun. It should either stay the same or temporarily transform into its positive aspect. If it runs from the light or shrivels up, ignore it and work with another one.

If it stays the same, tell it that you will no longer listen to it when it is negatively affecting you, but you will listen to it when it is helping you. Continue to dialogue with it, but be firm in telling it that you will only listen to it when it is in its positive form.

The next step is to "disidentify" from it, which means learning to step back from it into a more whole part of yourself so that it doesn't take over your life. For example, if Cynthia had been able to disidentify from her inner judge when she was suffering under his heavy authority, she would have recognized her judge subpersonality immediately, and she could have stepped back from it and told it to stop. She could then invite it into her life as a helper, literally asking it for help when she is faced with a decision she has to make.

It is important to remember that subpersonalities are not 'bad guys'; their way of relating and getting needs met worked well in the past. They all have a gift to offer you; generally their needs resonate with higher qualities of being, so as you work with a part to heal it, you will gradually broaden and deepen this quality within yourself and your life.

Fairly often, the potential of a subpersonality is revealed in the section of the exercise where the sun energy shines down on it, and sometimes that's all it takes for the potential to be a reality. More often, however, we have to do more work with the part before the healing is complete and the subpersonality is transformed into an integrated quality in our lives.

You can repeat the process suggested in the exercise with more of the subpersonalities you recognized. You may also wish to ask a psychotherapist to help you with this work.

15
Hope Walks Paths of Truth

Everyone is faced with obstacles in life. We can look at them as challenges from which we can learn, or we can get overwhelmed and believe they are too difficult to overcome. If we think negatively about something, the results will be negative; the opposite is also true, thinking positively attracts a positive outcome. Our attitude toward the events that happen to us forms a pattern we carry with us. Unless we consciously change our negative thinking to positive thinking, we will carry a negative pattern throughout our lives.

The following story is about changing attitudes:

Bernard stood outside his cottage, deeply inhaling the sharp, early spring air. The rising sun struggled to make an appearance but kept slipping away into the morning mist. It looked like rain, but this wouldn't stop him from taking his daily walk. Being in nature energized him. When he couldn't walk, he fell into a profound gloom.

He'd known for many years that he must live in the country. When he finally retired, he bought a small cottage near the state forest. It was the perfect setting for his needs. Long ago he'd been married, but his wife had left him because of his moodiness. The one child they had, a daughter, also found it impossible to live with him, and she'd even stopped phoning him.

While at most times he was a tired and crabby old man, when he walked in nature it was as if a kindly being entered his body and inhabited it for the length of the walk. An old friend once told him he had a split personality and suggested that he see a psychiatrist. Bernard blasted the man with foul language, and that was the end of the relationship.

When he was younger, he didn't rage as he did now. Fortunately, his work was repairing electrical equipment, so he only saw customers when they dropped off and picked up whatever needed fixing. Some of his behavior was due to ongoing pain in one leg, which he tried to ignore but to no avail. Walks actually mitigated the pain, which worsened when he sat for long periods of time.

On this particular day, Bernard decided to try a new path in the forest, one that required more climbing than usual. If it rained, it shouldn't matter, because the trees were very thick and overhung the path like a canopy. He hadn't climbed for several years, so this would be something new for him.

His walking stick was a thick oak branch he'd stripped and shaped. He was a tall man, over six feet, and solid, with muscular shoulders and arms reflecting his youthful army training. Ongoing depression and moodiness had, over time, carved deep lines around his mouth that ran downward into a permanent grimace.

But now, as he was walking upward on the path, his face was clear, and his eyes sparkling with interest. Suddenly, a deer bolted out of the trees, crossed the path and fled into the woods. It was a small doe, and Bernard stopped, quietly watching her beautiful body leap over some fallen branches. He would have loved to reach out and pat her. Just thinking about it made him smile. Why couldn't people be as nice as animals, he wondered? A thought flashed in his head that animals aren't corrupted by greed. His ex-wife had been greedy, taking everything they'd bought together. Rather than fight, he'd given her everything he had and even paid monthly support for years. It wasn't that she didn't deserve something, but she even took a picture his mother had painted, and that had been his only memento of her.

Sighing, Bernard continued his walk. Most of the time he didn't think, but just observed the tree leaves turning their faces toward the sun and rippling in the wind. He enjoyed the colors in the bark of the trees, and the shadows they cast on the ground. He loved the silence, with only the rustling of leaves and the sounds of birds as they called to each other.

The climb suddenly became steeper, and now there were some larger rocks that partially obstructed the path. He sat on one of them and drank some water. Looking upward to where the path disappeared around a bend, he hoped the trail would flatten out again. He'd have to turn back if it became too steep, but most of these paths were man-made and wouldn't be marked if they were impassable.

He thought he heard a noise and realized that someone was coming down the path. It turned out to be another hiker, a young man who stopped in front of him, breathing heavily. "Hello. This is quite a climb!" He put out his hand, "My name is Ruel. Do you need help? You look tired."

"No, thanks. I'm Bernard. Tell me what the path is like above."

"Well, unless you're a mountain climber, you shouldn't try it. Very rough terrain and slippery. It's drizzling a bit up on top."

"Really! Can't feel it here with the trees."

"Trees disappear above. Some nice views, but not worth the climb, if you ask me."

"Does it flatten out anywhere?"

Ruel thought for a minute, "Maybe just once, but not for long. My advice is to turn back now, before the rain gets worse."

"I'll go a little longer and then maybe do that. I hope I can make it. I like a challenge."

"Good luck, you'll need it." Looking Bernard over, he added, "You know, I'm a lot younger than you and in better shape, and this climb was very difficult for me. Take my advice, it's not worth having a heart attack at your age."

This really annoyed Bernard. "I like challenges, and I'm in a lot better shape than you may think!" he said with an edge of shrillness.

"Okay. Don't fall." Ruel continued down the path leaving Bernard upset, something that never happened when he walked.

But fall he did. It was as if Ruel had cursed him, because at the next turn, he slipped on a rock and took a nasty tumble on his bad leg. This made him more upset. If Ruel had been there, he would've thrown a rock at him.

By now it was raining hard. He could hear the drops hitting the treetops. The leaves were bending under the weight of the water that was already coursing down the path. Bernard turned and, with the stick, very slowly descended the path until he arrived at the clearing where he had started the climb. The rain had stopped, and the sun was shining. He wanted to go back, but by now his leg was beginning to throb, so he limped home, depressed and angry.

It took a couple of weeks before his leg felt well enough to try to hike again. Bernard decided to take a new path, one that didn't look so steep but was near a river, winding in and out of the woods. It was a beautiful day, and he started out early with the hope that he would go to the end and return after a picnic lunch. This path proved to be very pleasant. It wound through a meadow overflowing with wild flowers, and when it came to the river, it continued along the bank for several miles. The river was narrow in places, and it would widen and split into two branches at others. The path would then cross over the river on some boards and continue in the middle, with the water flowing on both sides.

In one section there were flat stones for crossing back, stones that were a little wet, so Bernard had to be very careful not to slip again. He thought about how this path had its challenges, with more ahead. It was like his life. Why had he always been challenged in relationships? Even as a child he'd had few friends. People called him bossy, and he guessed he was, but his father had been so controlling it made Bernard look like a lamb.

His thoughts turned toward his daughter, Sophia. He knew he'd been hard on her in the same way his father had been with him. Why was she so rebellious that he was always punishing her? Sophia was like this path, difficult and tricky to stay on, but also beautiful and gentle in places. She was so affectionate. When he was in a mood, she would sometimes throw her arms around him and hug him, saying, "Daddy, take me for a walk and tell me about nature." That's how these walks had begun. Maybe that's why he loved them so. Sophia was his pride and joy in those early years. It was only later, when she became a teenager, that he began to be hard on her, disciplining her too much and causing her to rebel. During the divorce she'd sided with her mother.

The path started to narrow, and he wondered if he'd made a wrong turn. It was as if it was affected by his thinking. When he thought about Sophia and the good years, the path was wide and surrounded by flowers, and then the dark thoughts brought rocks and weeds. This path was strange. He thought, Let me try just thinking about positive things and see what happens. His first thought was about Maria, his ex wife. When he met her she was twenty and he had just finished engineering school. Bernard remembered how beautiful she was, with her soft expressive eyes. She had worn her long dark hair pulled back in a ponytail until she chose to let it loose to undulate over her body as they made love. She had the enthusiasm of a child and the loving heart of a saint.

Maria was a bicyclist and he joined her on rides through the countryside, but after they married he stopped going with her. His leg had already started to act up, and the bicycle made it worse. In those first years they shared a lot, and somehow, after he stopped cycling with her, things started to go wrong. Sophia was born early on, so she became the focus for both of them, and slowly their relationship took second place. Maria wanted to finish college, but he'd insisted she stay home with Sophia. He realized later it was a mistake, as she was a bright woman and became very bored with just being a housewife. After she left him, she returned to school, got her Bachelors degree and then secured a Masters in Business Administration. Now she was working for a big firm in an executive position.

Bernard became aware that the path was again becoming rocky, along with his latest thoughts. It tired him to continue, so he found a place by the river and ate his lunch. What could he have done differently to still be with her? Maria had asked him to do couples therapy with her to try to save the marriage, but he'd refused, thinking therapy was nonsense. Now he realized it might have helped them stay together. The bitter fights at the end were all he could recall until this moment as he listened to the rushing stream. Suddenly, memories of their love were invading his thoughts. It'd been good at the beginning. He just didn't know how to do more or to share his feelings, which she'd always wanted. Sharing feelings was a woman thing, not a man thing, but maybe if he'd tried to do some of the things she wanted, they'd have made it together.

His mother was never happy with his father, who wouldn't listen either. Why'd I have to be so much like him? Why couldn't I have inherited more of my mother's gentleness? It was all about being a man and acting like a man. His father used to lecture him about being strong, and strength meant a man was always in control.

Clouds floated across the sun and he felt suddenly chilled in the shadows. Just then a figure came walking down the path. It was Lillith, his neighbor. She was an elderly woman, spare of frame, with an unpleasant flint-like demeanor.

"Hello, Bernard, fancy seeing you here."

"Lillith, how are you? I didn't know you were also a walker."

"I'm not, but today looked so nice I decided to come down to the river. I was planning to sit just where you are, but I'll just find another spot."

"Don't do that." Bernard rose, "Here, take my seat. I've been here long enough, and I want to finish this trail and return before dark."

"You'll never do that! It's a long trail, and it sometimes goes down into the mud, but I'll take your seat if you're leaving."

"How much longer is it?"

"At least a couple of hours and then going back will be another four hours. Can't do it. Don't be foolish."

"Well, I have a flashlight, and I'm feeling that I can make it to the end and back."

"Watch out for the snakes. There can be some big water snakes in the muddy sections. Not good when it's getting dark."

"I'll do that. Thanks." Bernard resumed his walk. In an hour the path did swerve closer to wet regions of the river, and his feet were sloshing in mud and low water. Sure enough, just as Lillith had warned, a black snake went sliding by him. His stomach revolted. He hated snakes. Black ones were not poisonous but still, just very unpleasant. Should he turn back? Fear spread through his body. There might be more snakes that he couldn't see as the sun went behind clouds. What if he stepped on one? An inner voice said, Stop it. You're a big strong man. Finish the trail. You can do it. Look at the beauty of the water and the mud.

Bernard looked around and realized that it was indeed very beautiful. The dim light was playing on the water and reflected in the mud, creating light and dark shadows amid the green of the surrounding plant life. He also saw that the trail curved up again, away from the wet area, and that the muddy stretch was really quite small. In no time, he was on dry land, walking up the trail as it ended overlooking the river with a view of hazy blue hills in the distance. Breathless, he stood looking in every direction. His heart was full of joy. He'd finished the trail, and what a wonderful experience that was. He cried out, Thank you, thank you, to that inner voice that he had listened to. I wish I'd listened to you more. If I had, then Maria and Sophia would still be with me.

The voice said, They are with you, here in your heart.

And he knew that was true.

The next day he decided to try the steep path again, the one he'd fallen on. His leg was feeling fine, and the weather was sunny and warm. In his heart he felt the need to prove to himself that he could do it. Truth was, the idea of falling again and being alone did bother him. What would happen if he broke something? He could die on the mountainside. Maybe he should wait and try to find a companion to do this trail with him? Thoughts kept trying to stop him, but he felt a resolve and determination settling in. "I'm a good hiker. I'll be careful. I need to be strong. I can do it."

The trail seemed easier this time. Even the rocks held firm and he had no trouble climbing them.

At one point he had to decide whether to go left or right. It looked like the path went both ways. He walked a short distance each way and spent time examining the terrain to determine how the land was laid out. On the left, it looked like more rock formations were tumbling down the side, and on the right it looked like the path sloped down a ways. Going down and up didn't bother him, but he also noticed that this path, in the distance, seemed to be overgrown, so he might have to work his way through some thick brush, whereas on the left he might have to climb over some rocks that had slid down. How loose were they? Well, if they proved to be loose he could always turn back and take the right-hand path. Following his judgment call, he took the left path. When he came to the rocky area it proved to be clear enough, and only a few rocks were loose. He was glad he'd decided to go this way. Both paths ended up on the same trail again.

Three quarters of the way up he met another man coming down who stopped to talk. "My name's William. Are you going all the way to the top?"

"Yes, I hope so." Bernard thought, Don't tell me this is another one who is going to tell me I can't do it!

Instead, William said, "Well, you've been through the worst part. It's easy going from here, and the views are splendid at the top. Well worth the climb."

"Another man named Ruel told me just the opposite last time I tried to climb to the top."

"I know him. He's very negative about everything. Doesn't have a positive bone in his body. I assure you, it's not a difficult climb from here. Which way did you go when the path split?"

"I went to the left over the rocks, and it proved fine."

"You made a good choice. The Park should close the right path. It can get very slippery as it goes down into a marsh.

"Thank you for telling me about the rest of the path. I planned to do it whether it was difficult or not."

"Keep up the positive thinking. It makes a big difference." He waved goodbye.

It does make a difference, Bernard thought. I've been like Ruel my whole life, but being more positive makes me feel so much happier. Look at Lillith. She also was so negative and wrong about the path. I would've missed an exciting experience if I'd followed her advice.

William was right. The rest of the path was a much easier climb, and the summit was spectacular. The view was of mountains and hills in every direction, with purple and rust rock formations and evergreen pinewoods darkening the mountainsides. Below, in the valleys, were broad expanses of green terrain, farms and pastures, and clusters of houses that formed the surrounding towns. He sat down and allowed the beauty to fill his being. It made him feel ten years younger.

On the way down the mountain, he thought, It'll take a lot of courage, but why am I waiting for Sophia to call me? Why can't I call her and invite her up for a weekend of hiking? The worst thing that could happen would be that she'd refuse, but she just might want to come!

Commentary

In this allegory, each path represents different obstacles in life and the qualities that we need to overcome them. Bernard's first challenge is the steepness of the first path. Ruel, who paints a bleak picture of the steep climb, creates such a disastrous scenario in Bernard's mind that, through the power of suggestion, Bernard takes a painful tumble. This episode and the other events throughout the tale illustrate the power of the imagination: We manifest what we envision. Our attitudes toward life events shape our experiences to a great degree. If we "see through a glass darkly," then all is dark. This does not mean that we must become a Pollyanna—one regarded as being foolishly or blindly optimistic. Rather, we need to step back to a more neutral zone of our consciousness; we need the ability to view life as an adventure that teaches us how to extract joy from that which is inherently joyful, such as being in nature, listening to beautiful music or being with a dear friend. On the other side, when life presents us with difficult and often desperate challenges, we must embrace the attitude of a mountain climber: consciously taking one step at a time with the knowledge that the mountaintop awaits.

Psychologically, it is the quality of hope that spurs us on through life. Each morning, Bernard awakens with the hope that his climb that day will offer him the joy that he seeks. When Ruel comes on the scene and activates Bernard's dark side, which views life so negatively, Bernard falls and injures his leg.

Bernard's next adventure takes him into thinking about his marriage to Maria and about his daughter Sophia, who is dear to him. He realizes how much he has lost, not only his daughter but his marriage, because of his inability to share his feelings.

The so-called 'manly' man is incapable of sharing his feelings, an inability that is the downfall of many a relationship. If he shares any feelings, they tend to be negative ones. Fortunately, pockets of deeper understanding are beginning to happen with men's groups that are forming in some areas of the country, but this activity is very minimally developed. One can only hope that the trend will continue to spread in the future.

When Lillith shows up, she, of course, represents the negative feminine aspect of Bernard that can see only ugliness within beauty. He becomes frozen with fear when he sees the snake. It is his inner voice that prompts him to see the beauty within the mud. This is the voice of his Higher Self, that aspect of each of us that is represented by the characters Sophia and William as they close the gap between the feminine and positive masculine energies that we are seeking to embrace and express in our lives.

This tale illustrates several basic psychological principles: the power of thought, either positive or negative, to change our reality; the power of imagination for good or ill; the power of noticing, and of choosing; and the recognition of creative and joyous experiences that woman and man may, and often does, have, along with the painful and tragic ones. They are those experiences that are aptly called "peak experiences," such as self-realization, fulfillment, achievement, illumination, peace and joy.

Certainly Bernard experiences fulfillment, achievement, peace and joy as he stands on top of the mountain peak—a powerful symbol of the heights of human endeavors. These qualities are available to all of us to integrate into our life experiences.

Exercise:

Look at the basic psychological principles stated above. They are:

The power of thought, either positive or negative, to change our inner reality;

The power of imagination for good or ill;

The power of noticing, and of choosing;

The recognition of positive, creative, and joyous experiences, which all of us may have along with the painful and tragic ones.

Think about each statement in terms of yourself. Then ask yourself the following questions:

Are my thoughts usually positive?

Do I imagine good things happening?

Do I often notice things and choose the positive?

Do I regularly recognize and acknowledge positive, creative, and joyous experiences?

Rate yourself from one to ten, ten being the highest, in terms of being positive.

If your rating is under 5, then you are more into the negative. Take each of the under-five items and ask yourself:

What does my negative attitude stem from?

How can I change this to make it more positive?

What is my first step for doing this?

Judith Bach, Ph.D. & Nanette Hucknall

16
Playground Planet

It's normal for people to want to find a partner who has those qualities that are lacking in themselves. Their search is sometimes called the search for one's "twin soul." This is because, when there is an imbalance of the masculine and feminine energies within, people look to fulfill that balance through a partner, instead of developing those qualities themselves. This story portrays how such an imbalance can cause interpersonal difficulties in a relationship. On a visit to the playground planet, three couples explore what it would be like not to depend on each other to provide missing qualities, but instead to try cultivating those qualities within themselves.

Here is their story:

When the three couples booked their flights together, they never dreamt how this vacation would change their lives. Without a doubt, the experience was far more than just a fun vacation, which was all they expected. Friends who had been to the Planet Ulysses always recommended it highly as something different from the norm, but the couples thought this was just because they needed to take a space ship to go there. The flight in itself was mind-boggling. A new invention in the pressurized cabin allowed their bodies to remain upright, and the take-off was spectacular, although a bit frightening. The technology was such that a space ride was safer than driving a car, but the roar of the booster rockets was unnerving.

Erika and Carlos, Larraine and Basil and Evelyn and Justin had been friends since their college days, and now, in their thirties, they were resolved to liven up their marriages by taking this "way-out" vacation together. The planet Ulysses was supposed to be a vacation paradise. It catered to couples, and its rule was no children allowed, just couples between the ages of thirty and fifty.

The trip took three and a half days, traveling out of the solar system and into a neighboring one at a speed so fast that, as the space ship swept by star clusters, they looked like sparkling crystals spewing jets of luminous color across the darkened sky. It was a breathtaking experience! They all agreed it was an incredible way to begin a vacation.

Their arrival on the planet was unusual. The surface was mostly water dotted with islands, so they landed in a capsule that dropped into the sea where a ship awaited them. The main resort was on a large island and was surrounded by smaller islands that offered different activities.

One island was geared to such sports as tennis, swimming, track, and volleyball. Larraine and Basil had decided that they would spend most of their days on that island. They both were athletic and spent time at home working out in the gym. Larraine was a tall, muscular woman. Basil thought she was beautiful, but her habitually serious demeanor often made her look older than her 35 years. He was almost her twin in coloring, with similar eyes and brown hair. He was a corporate manager, whereas Larraine taught high school French. Seen together, they were a striking pair.

Of the three couples, they seemed the happiest. Although they were very affectionate with one another and never quarreled or disagreed in public, at home they lived very separate lives, sharing very little. Even when they ate dinner they often read reports from work or magazines and books. Although they had many common interests, neither felt comfortable expressing feelings, so there was a sense of isolation between them. Even their lovemaking was routine and lacked intimacy.

Erika and Carlos chose another island, one that offered games requiring mental agility. Both were physicists and loved the challenge of such activity. Unlike Larraine and Basil, this couple was totally different in appearance and personality. Erika was multifaceted, with a very high intelligence that sometimes made it difficult for others to understand her. She was pleasantly pretty with no distinguishing features. She rarely wore makeup, but when she did, it enhanced her hazel eyes. Carlos tended toward sloppiness, his shirttails often hanging out, and his longish black hair uncombed. He repeatedly left stacks of paper strewn around the house, a constant frustration for orderly Erika. They'd finally agreed that he could be as messy as he wanted, but only in his study. What drove Erika crazy was his capacity to dress up when he wanted to; he could groom himself to a polished aloofness that became a magnet to other women. Erika was fully aware that he loved their interest.

They fought constantly. One issue was that Erika wanted to start a family, while Carlos felt that they weren't ready financially. Although he claimed he wanted children, it was not an imperative for him, and he unconsciously resisted the responsibility that came with being a father.

A third island was devoted to visual effects. It appealed to couples in the arts, as the beauty of its environment was meant to stimulate creativity. This was Evelyn's choice, but not Justin's. Aesthetics meant more to her than to him. She was an artist, whereas he was an architect; he loved structures but wasn't particularly interested in nature. Evelyn was quiet and reserved. Not obviously attractive, her beauty was displayed when she moved and smiled. Small in size, she was overpowered by Justin, who was over six feet, strong, and quick in everything he did. He was very handsome, with dark hair and eyes and a strong, athletic body. His preference was to go to the sports island with Basil and Larraine, and he was very reluctant to spend most of his time gazing at beauty. Evelyn finally convinced him by saying, "Why spend all this money just to play the same sports you can do at home?"

Their marriage was going through a difficult stage. Both felt bored and wanted more excitement in their lives. They'd even talked about separating for a while and dating other people. They were taking this vacation mainly because it sounded stimulating. Separation was still a possibility when they returned.

There were other islands the couples could have chosen, but they'd finally settled on these three. The requirement was that they had to spend at least 70 percent of their time on one island. In the evenings they would return to the main resort and share their experiences over a gourmet banquet. When they had asked friends who'd been to the planet about their experiences, they'd said they weren't allowed to talk about it. They would only say that it was well worth the price.

The resort was very beautiful. There was a main modern building with several dining areas and an outdoor swimming pool that wound through gardens and ended in a lovely waterfall. Every couple had their own private bungalow and garden with an entrance to the pool. The lush foliage with vivid flowers was breathtaking; some were species unknown to the couples. What they found incredible was the absence of insects on the planet. The climate was tropical but not too hot.

The first evening, they all ate together on a patio by the pool. The flight had been so easy that no one felt tired. Instead, there was an air of excitement and anticipation for the adventure to begin.

"What time do you have to leave for your island tomorrow?" Carlos asked Basil.

"Nine. How about you?"

"We depart earlier, eight. I'm surprised we go at different times."

"We leave at ten, which I thought was quite late," Justin said.

"Maybe they have only one boat," Erika added.

"I doubt that, but it's a good question to ask."

"Maybe it has to do with the activities. Aesthetics may need less time to absorb," Carlos observed.

"True, and it gives us more time in the morning to swim. I like that," said Justin.

They asked the waiter when he came by, and he supported Carlos' theory that the schedule related to the activities on the various islands.

The next day was again clear and sunny. Carlos and Erika departed early, while the sun was rising over the water. Their voyage lasted almost an hour, as the Island of Mental Pursuit was the furthest away. Six other couples were on the boat, all of them scientists. The island was small, with the foliage of trees sheltering the play areas. Each couple was given a scorecard to write down the results of the games. While some of the play areas could accommodate several players, others were small and only one couple could participate at a time.

The games were either board games or puzzles, many of which had word patterns to figure out. All were difficult, and after completing just two of them, Erika needed a break. Along with another couple they'd been playing with, she and Carlos found a lounge where coffee, tea and other refreshments were served all day long. Carlos wanted to continue as quickly as possible, whereas Erika felt she needed more time. That's when they had their first argument.

She protested, "We've been playing for almost two hours, and it's really fatiguing."

"I know, but we need to get through all the games today, otherwise we'll be behind the others."

"So what if we are? This is a vacation, not a competition."

"It's both. I want us to win this."

"I don't care who wins. I just want to have fun."

Their voices became louder until an attendant came up to them and asked them to be quiet.

They played the next game with another couple. It was a board game that required strong concentration. They were allowed to fill in the squares only if a key word hidden within the pattern of surrounding words was discerned. The process required intuition, not just mental savvy. Erika did very well with this game, much better than any of the others. Carlos was the worst, which upset him. The next game was more to his liking. It was a scientific crossword puzzle laid out on the ground with big squares and cut out letters. Erika was supposed to play with him, but he took over and basically did it on his own, which really annoyed her.

By lunchtime they were barely speaking to each other, and some of the other couples appeared to be going through the same tension. The women started gravitating toward one another and the men did the same, an interesting phenomenon, as the games after lunch required all the players. There were to be two teams, and without planning it at all, the women became one team and the men the other. The men won the first game, as they went into action mode, whereas the women took more time talking about the best ways to solve the problem. After the results were posted, the women won most of the games due to team cooperation. The men argued more and made less of an effort to work as a team.

All were exhausted at the end of the day when William, the guide, went over the games and explained the proper ways to resolve them.

"These games aren't just planned for your scientific minds; they also require the use of your intuition, which is why the women did better than the men. Yet, in some cases, the women were penalized because they took too long to come to a decision. This is due to overanalyzing and over planning rather than deciding on one direction and following it. Because of this, even though their understanding was, in the end, better than the men's, the scores for both groups are almost the same. What needs to happen tomorrow is more of a balance. The women need to use more of their masculine side, which is more action oriented, and the men need to use their intuition and think about the problems more deeply, rather than jumping into action right away. These games are about finding the right balance."

He paused and smiled at all of them with an edge of irony in his grin, "I hope you all had fun today."

No one replied, but when the couples boarded the boat they all mumbled discontentedly to each other.

In the meantime, Larraine and Basil went off to the Sports Island with about ten other couples. The island was bare, with almost no foliage and mainly just large playing fields. Some of the games required one couple and others the whole group. The morning was spent playing ball games that were very different from any games they knew at home. What they thought was a tennis court ended up being for a game in which a large ball was bounced up to the net and bounced back. The ball had to be thrown a certain way otherwise it wouldn't bounce. After many tries Basil figured out the pattern, whereas Larraine was still stumped. She wanted Basil to show her how to do it, but he refused. "You have to figure out the pattern yourself, otherwise it would be cheating."

"How can it be cheating? We're doing this together, not separately."

"When it's only you and me, it's separate. That's how I see it." He continued to move his ball back and forth until he had finished the allotted time.

Feeling really frustrated, Larraine finally figured out the pattern and only completed half of Basil's total before the time was up.

Most of the morning was spent in highly physical games. Larraine was better at some of the more physically demanding ones because she worked out every day. Basil played volleyball and baseball with his company, but only once a week after work.

By lunchtime, Basil was very tired and grumpy. "I don't like these games at all. I thought we would be playing games that we knew from the States."

"I did too, but some of them are very intriguing, especially because the equipment is so unusual."

The other couples they had met were also grumbling about the difficulty of the games. Most people ate in silence, and then lay down for a quick nap before the activities commenced again.

The afternoon was spent playing group games, several of which required two teams. The women separated themselves from the men, and the games became a competition between the sexes. There was one game in which the players had to find their way through a huge maze. The women divided up every time they approached two possible ways to go. When one group came to a dead end, they would whistle, and the group that was still moving would stop and whistle back until the other group found their way back to them. Since all members of each group had to get through the maze at the same time, this was a good plan.

The men just kept together in one group and then would argue when a choice had to be made. If they came to a dead end, they all returned and took the other direction. When there were three directions to take they would be confused as to which one they'd already taken. The women came out way ahead on this one, but in a ball game that required height and agility, the men outstripped the women. One man suggested that maybe they should split back into couples, as the game wasn't very equal, but the women protested and, in the end, were badly defeated.

At the close of this day, a guide, Sophia, appeared and asked, "Why did you split into gender groups? These games are about using the best of the masculine and feminine energies." She continued, "It's not just physical prowess that matters. These activities are about finding the best approach to using your abilities. The women did better in some games, and the men in others, but all of you would have done better if you had stayed in mixed groups and assessed which gender would have been best to lead each game. Maybe tomorrow you will find more balance."

Evelyn and Justin left late in the morning for the Island of Beauty. They were surprised that there were only three couples on the boat and wondered if they'd made the right island decision. When the boat landed, it glided under an archway of roses that was so breathtakingly beautiful that they were pleased at their choice.

The roses extended beyond the harbor to paths that led through gardens full of exotic flowers that the couple had never seen before. Some paths converged into circles with fountains in the middle. The water flowing through the fountains was always of a different color; it somehow picked up the predominant colors of the plants surrounding them. Benches and swings were everywhere. It was a fairyland of beauty. They weren't allowed to photograph the plants and flowers, but they could stop and draw them, which they did. They had brought paper and watercolors with them and spent the morning drawing and painting. The other couples did the same, except for one or two people who weren't artists; they would just sit and gaze into the blossoms. The people who weren't painting became impatient with their spouses, demanding that they go on, as the painting was taking too long. Justin, in particular, was annoyed at Evelyn's need to paint everything.

"It's enough! Some people are way ahead of us, and we have the whole island to explore."

"Okay, but this is so lovely."

"It's all lovely, but let's go! I'm bored. This is very pretty, but it's becoming too much. We should have gone to one of the other islands. I want to change tomorrow."

"How can you say that? Everything here is so inspiring, try writing about it. You brought a notebook, didn't you?"

"Yes, but what am I going to write about? Writing about a flower and a garden is boring. Everything here is visual."

"Why don't you write about us?"

"There's nothing to inspire me about us. We're also pretty boring."

She shot back, "Maybe if you were more inspired you could improve this relationship, particularly the sex!" She went back to her flower painting.

Oh boy, what a vacation this is, he thought. He decided to lie down on a bench and have a nap. As soon as he closed his eyes, he found himself back in the gardens. They looked the same, but he realized that all the flowers were surrounded by what looked like fairies. They danced among the leaves and blossoms and made sounds like violins playing. He approached one of them and asked her name.

"I have no name, but if you want to give me one, that would be nice."

"Alright, how about the name Allison?"

"That sounds nice. What is your name?"

"Justin, I'm Justin."

"And what is your wife's name?" She pointed to Evelyn, who was busy making a watercolor of a large type of lily.

"How do you know she's my wife?"

"I heard you arguing before. Husbands and wives often argue here."

"Well, you're right. Her name is Evelyn. Would you like to meet her?"

"This is your dream. For me to meet her, she would also have to take a nap. Only then is that possible."

"I'll tell her that when I wake up. Can you tell me what you and your friends are doing in the garden?"

"We are part of the flowers. We take care of them and help them grow."

"How very interesting. So you are only on this planet?"

"Oh, no, we are on your planet also, but you can't see us. We are a part of everything that lives, whether it's a tree, a flower, or even you, a human. We are nature spirits, and everything alive is part of nature."

"But I don't see any of you as part of me."

"Well, just look and you will see us."

Justin looked down and was astonished to see small, fairy-like beings flowing in and out of his body. In fact, he was so startled that he woke up. He was back on the bench but couldn't see the fairies anymore.

Running to Evelyn, he told her what had happened and insisted that she lie down and take a nap so she could see what he saw.

"Oh, how wonderful! Let me try." She lay down, exclaiming, "I'm afraid I'm too excited to go to sleep."

"Just relax, close your eyes and…"

He grinned as she fell into a deep sleep. Sitting near her, propped against a tree, he took out his notepad and wrote about what had happened. Feeling groggy, he then stretched out on the grass, fell asleep again and saw Evelyn talking to Allison. He tried talking to them, and they actually heard him, so they continued the conversation as a threesome. Evelyn was asking questions about the flowers, which didn't interest him at all. Impatient, he interrupted a couple of times to ask his questions, which centered more on their work. Evelyn then objected, and they got into an argument. Suddenly all the fairies vanished, and they were the only ones remaining in the dream. They both woke up at the same time and continued the argument.

"You're always so selfish! You interrupted me when I was asking questions."

"Your questions were stupid. I wanted to know important things, like how they do their work."

"You don't think it's important to know why the flowers are so big here?"

"No, I don't think it matters in the least how big they are or how colorful."

On and on they argued until it was time to take the boat home. All the couples, when boarding, seemed at odds with one another. Some had experienced the fairies also, but they experienced them differently than Evelyn and Justin. One person felt them but didn't see them.

William was on the boat with them. He told them, "You were in a very special place, but your energy has hurt some of the vibrations there, and the nature spirits have requested that you not argue anymore in their presence. It was too disturbing."

That evening, when the three couples shared stories, they all felt better somehow. Their experiences had faded so that it was difficult to remember what actually happened. They all recalled there had been disagreements, yet none of them could express exactly what they were about. They also felt it necessary to return, but didn't understand why. Somehow it was about "balance."

The next day went differently. Erika and Carlos argued only once, and when the teams were formed, they were mixed, so the results were better. The same held true on the Sports Island. There was more cooperation between the men and women on the teams. On the Beauty Island, people started to share their experiences with the fairies, and they developed questions they could ask about their kingdom. Evelyn and Justin came up with a plan to improve their experiences without upsetting each other.

Throughout the week, they all increasingly forgot about themselves and became more focused on and present for the experiences they were having. As a result, they came back from the islands relaxed and joyful. When it was their turn to try another island, they did so with regret, but since the same groups of people were still together, they found the new experiences very easy and fulfilling. Erika and Carlos, who had no desire to experience the Beauty Island, were elated with what they saw there, as were Larraine and Basil. None of them had believed in nature spirits, and they had felt that Evelyn and Justin were fantasizing when they spoke of them. They came back totally changed and far more open to everything. Evelyn, who hated all sports except swimming, hadn't realized how good it felt to move her body. She and Justin also had a lot of resistance to playing mental games, but once they were involved in them, they realized how good it felt to mentally figure things out rather than always just feeling them out. Erika and Carlos, who viewed everything analytically, rather than experiencing life from their hearts, and who never exercised their bodies, began to realize what they were lacking.

Their last few days were spent in the main lounge, discussing relationships. Everything was going very well until a new couple, Lilith and Ruel, arrived one evening. Both had been to Playground Planet before. They sat with the three couples and told them what had happened to them once they left.

"Of course, we were feeling very blissful with the experience, but as soon as we went home, everything collapsed," Ruel explained.

"What do you mean, collapsed?" Justin asked.

"We went right back to the same old behavior. Ruel became controlling again; in fact, even worse," Lillith said.

"And of course Lillith became her old bitchy self. The island experience lasted for one day."

"So why did you come back?" asked Larraine.

Ruel looked around, and then whispered, "We're planning to carefully watch how William and Sophia run the place and then sue them."

Lillith, leaning forward, added in a low voice, "Haven't you noticed how you've forgotten all about what's not working in your relationship? That's part of the plan. They make you forget—it's probably something they put in the food—and they make you feel that everything is hunky dory now, when, in fact, it's not. The reality check comes when you're back home; all your memories of discontent will return. I'm doing this with Ruel, but we plan to split up after the law suit."

"That's awful, but it must be true! I can't remember very much about our relationship before coming here," Carlos observed.

"Well, you will, believe me, and it will be worse than before."

Evelyn protested, "But our other friends seem so happy now!"

"They might say that, but it's a cover-up. They probably were brain-washed by the fairies to say that in order to entice more people to come here. Don't let them do that with any of you. They tried with us."

On that happy note, they got up and left, leaving the six in a state of shock.

"You mean all of this was for nothing? We're not going to be able to communicate anymore when we get home?" Erika looked at Carlos worriedly.

"I wouldn't want to go back to that," he said. "We've really learned to open up to each other—and to you all!"

At that moment, William and Sophia entered the room and approached the group's table.

"We saw you talking to Ruel and Lillith. What did they tell you?"

The six of them looked at each other. No one wanted to say what happened.

"I'll bet they said you hadn't changed, and that you'll return to your old quarreling selves," William said, frowning. "They've never been through this experience, so they can't tell you anything that's happened. We've never allowed them to participate. They are very negative and purposely try to destroy this good work. They come suddenly at night to try to make people believe they haven't changed, and then they leave."

"But why do you let them come? Why do you let them stay here?" asked Justin.

"We just work here. It's good work and we love it, but the people who own this place have a policy that anyone can come who can pay the price. We've talked to them about Ruel and Lillith, but their philosophy is that those two together add up to so much nastiness that the contrast actually makes this place seem even more wonderful. Part of our job is to keep an eye on them and do what we're doing right now."

Sophia added, "Sometimes they succeed in making couples go back to their old ways, but mainly the changes people have experienced are so powerful that their negativity has no influence."

"But we don't even remember our past. They said you purposely make us forget. Is that true?" Basil asked.

William responded, "Yes, it's true that in this experience you hardly remember your old patterns of relating to each other, because at first it's best to see each other with new eyes. Once you've experienced that, it's much easier to let go of old patterns. Now, this evening you'll begin to remember all of it, including the process you just went through. Be aware of how you have all changed. Now you can see the past and understand more about why it didn't work for you. Before, you men were mainly acting out of the positive and negative sides of masculine energy, and you women were mainly acting out of the positive and negative sides of feminine energy. All of you were imbalanced in some way. When you fought with each other, it stemmed from the negative aspects of the masculine and feminine energies. Here, you have been experiencing how much more productive and creative it is for all of you to work out of the positive aspects of both the masculine and feminine, and to completely let go of the negative aspects of each."

"I know that's true, but how can I remember to do it?" asked Erika.

"You'll remember, because you've already started the process. You've all developed much more balance." Sophia looked at each person. "Whenever there's balance between the positive masculine and feminine, there's cooperation. When there's balance, most work can be done joyfully, and when there is balance, relationships are about genuine sharing and about helping one another. We hope all of you will choose to hold on to the changes you have gone through, rather than falling back into the old patterns that were destroying your marriages."

Sophia and William stood up, said their farewells and, arms wrapped around each other, left the room.

"I agree with William and Sophia. I know I've changed, and I know I want my relationship with my wife to grow in love." Carlos leaned over and kissed Erika.

They all started hugging each other and agreed that Playground Planet was not about playing but about becoming balanced.

"But know that if you are balanced, then you truly can play!" Larraine said, and they all laughed.

Commentary

This story portrays the interpersonal difficulties that arise when each individual within a relationship lacks balance between his or her own masculine and feminine qualities. Within such relationships there exists an inherent opposition. He is active; she is passive. He is rational; she is intuitive. Or, it can be just the opposite: he may be intuitive and she rational, or, he may be passive and she active. There is the old saying that "opposites attract." Yes, they do, in the sense that people often cleave together as couples because each individual desires to become complete through the other.

For a time, this completion works on a very practical level. "I'll take out the garbage," says he. "I'll do the cooking," says she, or vice-versa. Many of the clichés that exist in relationships are the result of a lack of balance between the masculine and feminine.

However, as time goes by, the humdrum nature of such arrangements often takes over the relationship until both partners are glassy-eyed with boredom. Weeks, months, and years go by with such couples, and what might have been an interesting adventure often turns into a conflict, if only to make life more interesting. The truth is, those who are drawn together to complete each other—because, inherently, there is a deep need in everyone for completion—more often than not are living only half a life.

Now imagine, as on the Playground Planet, that you are evenly balanced in positive masculine and feminine qualities. If you are currently in a relationship, imagine that this is true of your partner also and that you are connecting from this place of completion. What would that be like? You might not only feel a powerful sense of completion, but together, you could experience the most interesting and adventuresome aspects of what life has to offer and be in a relationship that constantly renews itself.

For those of you who are single, you will be able to experience your life in a rich and satisfying way because you will be fully partnering yourselves with your inner masculine and feminine qualities.

You, the reader, may be wondering about the relationship between the subject of this book and the introduction of nature spirits in two of the stories. We are all part of nature, and we believe that humans have a responsibility for the general atmosphere that surrounds us. We believe that there is life within everything that grows, a vitality that exists in all of nature, including us. When we clash with each other, that vital life, symbolized by the fairies, is affected, and it dims the beauty around us and within us. Negativity then gains the upper hand and all of us suffer.

The ability to experience the life of nature is the gift of feminine perception. To render the beauty of nature into a painting is the masculine at work. To deeply experience the beauty of a sunset, of a magnificent canyon or of a flower is the feminine at work. To compose a poem about these experiences is the masculine. Both masculine and feminine energies are essential in creative work.

Try doing the exercise suggested in this commentary.

Exercise:

Imagine that you are evenly balanced in positive masculine and feminine qualities. Give yourself time to let the experience be as deep as possible. If you are currently in a relationship, imagine that your partner too is balanced in positive masculine and feminine qualities, and that you are connecting from this place of completion. Ask yourself:

What would that be like?

How would that feel?

Play a scenario in your mind about how your interactions would be.

Finally, reflect on your relationship as it is now, and on what needs to happen on both your parts in order to connect from this place of completion. Then ask yourself: What needs to happen to have our relationship renew itself?

If you are single, remember you will be able to experience your life in a rich and satisfying way because you will be fully partnering yourself with your inner masculine and feminine. Take time to imagine that you truly are balanced in positive masculine and feminine qualities, that you have the richness of both within you. Ask yourself:

What would that be like?

How would I be different?

How would that feel?

Then imagine moving through a typical daily scenario.

Finally, reflect on yourself as you are now, and then ask yourself:

What needs to happen for me to be balanced in this way?

17
The House of Chaos

Thoughts have a great impact on oneself and others. Our thinking patterns really affect our lives. Even though thoughts are within our minds, their vibrations travel outwards, thus affecting not only ourselves but also our homes, those about whom we are thinking, and our environment. The effects may be subtle, but they are strong and pervasive: negative thoughts will have a negative impact and positive thoughts a positive one.

The following tale traces one couple's struggle with negative thinking, and shows how they improve their communication:

The grey and dreary day reflected Lauren's mood when she sat down to confront Joseph, her husband. "Why do you always stare at attractive women?" she said. "It really upsets me."

"What's wrong with looking? It's harmless." He grinned. "You're jealous?"

"It may be harmless, but it could lead to something more."

She really wanted to say, "Jealous? Why would I be jealous? I'm just as attractive as they are!" And she was. Her blond hair, worn in a French knot with a loose curl tumbling down her cheek, blue eyes, and oval face added up to a very beautiful woman. When she smiled, which was seldom of late, her whole face lit up.

Joseph, on the other hand, came across solemn in his facial expressions and tone of voice. His seriousness conveyed an impression of sternness, which, though not true, made people wary of him. He had dark hair and eyes and a droopy mustache that always needed trimming, which accentuated his large features. He had a sense of humor tinged with an edge of sarcasm. Before they were married the previous year, many of Lauren's friends had tried to talk her out of it. They felt he would dampen her wonderful bounciness, and that did seem to be happening. Their disagreements had become more intense and their periods of not talking to each other more pronounced.

They had been living in a small apartment, which was a major problem, as there was no room to get away from each other. Just recently they had bought a large house, which they were in the process of decorating. Besides their dispositions, their tastes were also very different. Joseph preferred dark colors on the walls and brown leather furniture, while Lauren wanted bright pastels and lots of white. There had been a mixture of their tastes in the apartment, but their differences became a problem now that they were faced with more rooms to decorate.

Another difficulty was that they both felt a strange energy in the house and feared it might be haunted. The previous owner, a very elderly woman, had died there. Weird shadows had begun to appear on the walls and in the air. During an argument over what color to paint the living room, they saw a large oval-shaped shadow float by, drifting near the ceiling. Another time, in the kitchen, when Lauren was talking about buying a complicated wine bottle opener, something Joseph didn't want, what looked like black pebbles flew through the air. Joseph had the experience of seeing a square, black mass in front of him when he was stomping down the hallway, angry with Lauren because she'd invited guests to dinner while the house was still being painted.

Lauren's current insinuation that Joseph might be unfaithful set the wrong tone for compromise.

"Can we change the subject? You know this is going nowhere. Holy cow, look!" He pointed to the corner of the room. Two shadows were moving back and forth, changing shape. This time they looked more like human forms.

Lauren recoiled, "Oh, no, they're ghosts! What'll we do?"

Joseph bravely called out, "Who are you?'

One of the shadows replied in a sibilant whisper, "We are you and her!"

"What do you mean, you're us?"

"Just that! Every time you think a negative thought, you make one of us. Just now your sarcasm made me. Your wife made the other one when she said you stare at women."

The shapes then started forming into weird creatures. Joseph's shape had distorted mouths smiling sarcastically all over its head, while Lauren's became puffed up, and crossed its arms in an angry stance.

"You mean you're our thoughts?" Lauren asked.

"Yes, just the negative ones; at the rate you're both going, this house is filling up quickly."

Two more shadows appeared at the other end of the room. "Those were your thoughts yesterday, Lauren, when you decided to do something without checking with Joseph. The other one is yours, Joseph, when you did the same." Both forms were small and snake-like.

Suddenly, the room was full of all kinds of weird shapes and beings. A big open mouth flowed by with steam coming out of it. "That's from when you were shouting at each other yesterday." The square shape that Joseph had encountered in the hallway reappeared and turned into a rigid block of cement with a small head protruding from the top. The black pebbles formed a woman's body with a pocked face, and a whispery voice said, "Lauren, I am your manipulative thoughts."

On and on the weird creatures came and went until Lauren and Joseph were exhausted. They both closed their eyes to stop seeing them.

Joseph finally addressed the first creature. "Now that we've seen all of you, please go away and tell the others to go, too."

"I can't do that. Only you can."

"How can we do that?"

"I don't know. I'm just one of your thoughts."

"Let's get out of here," Joseph grabbed Lauren's hand, and they hurried out of the house. Walking to the park, they sat down on a bench to rest.

"What are we going to do?" Lauren asked, her head in her hands. "This is horrible!"

"I don't know."

Just then a couple they knew came walking by.

"Lillith, Ruel, hello!" Joseph called out.

After the greetings were over, they all decided to go for a coffee at a nearby café. Lillith and Ruel were in their late thirties. Both worked in the computer world, designing software. They were dressed in matching jeans and colorful T-shirts. Petite, with lovely features, Lillith had blue eyes and shoulder length blond hair. Ruel was also small in stature, but he was rugged, with a handsome face, long sandy-colored hair and a mischievous smile.

Lauren and Joseph had met them recently at a party. Even though they didn't know them very well, Lauren decided to ask them for their advice and told them their strange tale.

"How intriguing," Lillith laughed.

"It may be intriguing but it's far from being funny." Lauren replied.

"Excuse me, but maybe that's the way to handle it. Everyone fights and has bad moments, but no one is plagued by their thoughts. I would laugh at them and not take them seriously. That should dissipate them."

"Yes, I agree," Ruel said, "The more you make fun of them, the faster they'll leave."

"Well, it's worth a try. Thank you," Joseph responded, feeling hopeful.

When they returned home the house was quiet, but as soon as they entered the living room, it filled up quickly with the creatures.

"We think you're really funny. Just look at you!" Lauren and Joseph started laughing, falsely at first, and then they were caught up with an edge of hysteria. They laughed and laughed until they noticed that the creatures were not leaving. In fact, with each laugh, they were all becoming bigger and bigger.

"Oops, I don't think this is a good idea," gasped Joseph, reaching out to Lauren. As soon as they stopped laughing, the creatures stopped growing.

They went into the kitchen and found it was also full of the weird shadows.

"What are we going to do?" Lauren wailed.

"Why don't we ask Sophia and William? They might know. They're psychologists." Joseph picked up the phone and called their friends right away. After he explained the problem, William said, "That sounds really disturbing. We'll be right over."

Lauren and Joseph had met Sophia and William at a couples workshop when they were all just dating, and they'd become good friends right away. William was the serious type, like Joseph, and they had a lot in common, mainly politics and art. Sophia was more gregarious and full of fun. Her main pleasure was to go dancing. She was tall, slim and athletically-built, with a plain but interesting face that made people stop and look twice at her. This was because her high cheekbones gave her an oriental look that was quite exotic. William, on the other hand, seemed smaller than her with his stocky build. He had brown hair and intense blue eyes.

When Lauren and Joseph took them into the living room, it was full of the shapes, but Sophia and William couldn't see them.

"How come?" asked Lauren.

"They're your thoughts, so that makes sense to me," Sophia explained. "But, because they are your thoughts, only you can get rid of them."

"But how?" Joseph asked.

"Well, normally, if you want to get rid of negative thoughts, you simply have to say no to them. I would confront each one and tell it you recognize it and don't want it to be here or in your mind anymore," William suggested.

"Let's try it. I know that square one is mine." Joseph confronted the form. He said he understood what it represented and he was choosing not to be stubborn anymore, so it could leave. It vanished instantly.

"Oh, thank you! That's great! Let me do that." Lauren picked a shape that represented her need to always be right and tried to do the same, but it didn't vanish.

"Why doesn't it leave?"

"What do you think it represents?" asked Sophia.

"Oh, you know sometimes—well, maybe more than sometimes—I get into thinking I'm always right about things. It's really a bad habit, I know! But why won't it leave?"

"Do you think that maybe this form isn't your desire to be right, but is something else instead?" Sophia asked.

Lauren asked the shape what it represented, but it didn't answer her.

Joseph interjected, "I don't think that belongs to you. It's mine…"

"I'm sure it's mine!" Lauren insisted; suddenly, another shape formed near her.

"Oh dear, I think this one is my wanting to be right all the time," Lauren exclaimed. She then tried the process again: "I will stop trying to be right all the time! I really will." This time it worked, and the shape disappeared.

"This is going to be hard work. We have to know what the thought is first and then who it belongs to." Joseph was looking gloomy.

"I've an idea," said Sophia. "Why don't you come to dinner? It'll be leftovers, but we have plenty. Stay with us tonight, and we'll try to think of all the negative aspects of the feminine and masculine energies that you've expressed here. Then, tomorrow, you can help each other recognize them."

They thankfully accepted the offer. After dinner, Lauren and Joseph started to make their lists, asking for help from Sophia and William.

"When you say feminine and masculine energies, are you talking about being a woman and a man?" Lauren asked Sophia.

"No, these are traits within both of you. For example, a negative feminine trait is manipulation, which is something a woman or a man can do."

"Oh yes! Joseph can be very manipulative."

"Let's not make any new thought forms here, please," William laughed. "But it's true, both women and men can be manipulative. Also, a woman can be as aggressive as a man sometimes. That's a negative masculine attribute. Why don't you list some of your feelings and actions? Then we'll try to identify them."

It took all evening, but they finally came up with a list they could try out in the morning. They realized that to really make this work, they needed to cooperate and work closely together. "Be loving! You need to send out positive thoughts," Sophia had suggested, and they knew she was right even though they weren't feeling very loving.

When they returned to their house the next morning, the dark forms surrounded them.

"Sweetheart, would you like some coffee?" Lauren cooed to Joseph, and the shapes pulled away, giving them some space.

"Yes, but let me help you." They both went into the kitchen, which was now void of shapes.

"I have an idea," said Lauren. "Let's contact the first shape that explained it all to us. It was your sarcasm, remember? It knew what the others represented."

"Good idea. I think I can recognize it. Shall we take turns in destroying these?"

"Yes, it does take energy, so we shouldn't overdo it, but it's really important to get rid of enough of them so they're not smothering us."

Going into the living room, Joseph recognized his sarcastic form, but when he asked it to identify the other forms, it said, "No way! I saw what you did to those two yesterday. I'm staying around."

"But if you don't help me, I'll destroy you. Help me and I won't."

"I don't trust that. Besides, you still need me, as I'm the only one who will talk to you. The reason I'm so strong is because sarcastic thoughts are a big part of you."

"We'll see about that," Joseph destroyed the form.

"Why did you do that?" asked Lauren. "I really like your sarcastic wit, except when it's directed at me."

"Well, this character was!" Feeling abashed, he said, "Sorry about that. I'll try not to do it again."

Looking at their list, they could identify some of the forms by their shapes. They realized that critical and judgmental thoughts always looked like judges. When they both had the same thought form and their process didn't work, they would switch, him dealing with hers and her dealing with his.

By lunchtime, more than half were gone. The rest were trying to loom around them, but they held them back by expressing loving words to each other.

By late afternoon they had destroyed most of the forms except for ten. These ten were a problem. First of all, they were very sly and did everything to avoid being targeted. They were also small, and difficult to identify. They didn't have any obvious features, like the screaming mouth.

Joseph and Lauren went back to the kitchen to figure out how to uncover the identities of the last group of forms, and just then, Sophia and William dropped by. Hearing about their dilemma, William suggested, "Why don't you look at some of your feelings that aren't so obvious? For instance, do either one of you ever think about splitting up? Do you think about old loves? Or do you fantasize about something that you haven't told each other?"

Both Lauren and Joseph started to say no, but then both stopped, looking a little guilty.

"Maybe these smaller thought forms are hidden because you've hidden them from each other," Sophia offered.

"I guess that may be true," said Lauren, frowning. "But I think it's important to keep some thoughts to oneself. I think a little bit of privacy is important in a marriage."

"I agree! I sometimes have stupid thoughts that I certainly don't want to share," Joseph added.

"Well, you don't have to share those thoughts, just recognize them and see if the form responds to it," Sophia explained.

"I think all ten must be mine then," Joseph said.

"Really! You don't think I could have some hidden thoughts?" Lauren asked.

"Well yes, but I have a lot."

"A lot?" A quizzical look passed over Lauren's face.

"Well, I imagine these ten are the strongest ones." William smiled warmly, and Sophia nodded and said, "I think you need some private time from us, and maybe from each other."

After they left, Lauren turned to Joseph and asked him, "Have you ever thought of leaving me?"

"When we fight, I do. Don't you?"

"Yes, of course, but do you think about it often?"

"I thought this was going to be private."

"Well, why don't we see if there are two out there that hold those thoughts?"

They went into the living room where the remaining shapes were gathered and examined them carefully. There weren't any two that looked alike.

Lauren said, "Obviously, one of us has been thinking of splitting up more than the other."

"It's got to be mine. Let me pick it out."

Joseph looked at them all and found one that was cut in pieces. "It's got to be this one." He did the process, thinking, I know you're my thought of wanting to leave Lauren, and I want to let go of you, but it remained unchanged.

"Well, that's not mine." He began examining the others.

"Let me try that one," said Lauren. "It might be mine." When she did the process with the same form, it vanished.

Joseph was shocked. "You want to leave me more than I want to leave you?"

"I guess so. It's not been fun for a long time."

"You'd never do it. You don't even have the courage of a puppy dog!"

That thought immediately produced the sarcastic form again.

"See?" said the form. "I told you I would be back soon."

"Well, leave, just leave!" said Joseph wearily. He repeated the process to vanquish it, naming it as sarcasm and consciously letting it go.

Lauren laughed, "Wow, this could be fun. Maybe I won't leave after all. Finding out who wins this match should be interesting."

Another form appeared, just like sarcasm but much smaller.

Joseph started to laugh. "I think that one belongs to you."

"Okay!" Annoyed, Lauren blasted it away. "Let's go back to the kitchen and find another one."

"I don't need to." Joseph looked at the forms, picked one that had a twisting, muscular body and no arms, and easily made it vanish.

"What one was that?" Lauren asked.

"I'm not saying."

Lauren thought about it. "Does it represent a way of life?"

"Not saying."

"I think it concerns who you would like to be. It's all about the body." Lauren thought some more. "Ah! I know. It's about being a surfing bum. You used to love it. The twisting body looks like someone on a surfboard, and its lack of arms is about not having to work. You use your hands a lot in your work. You're always on the computer. Why couldn't you tell me you still want to surf?"

"You've made remarks about what a silly sport it is, that it's only for kids. How could I tell you how much I loved it?"

"I'm sorry. I didn't know you still wanted to do it. On our next vacation to Hawaii I'll come along and watch."

Joseph's smile was genuine. "I'm glad you guessed it! Now, you choose one."

Lauren studied the forms and finally picked a small one of a squat, fat woman and vanquished it.

"Wait! I want to see that one again." Joseph tried to stop her but was too late. "Don't tell me you want to gain weight. You look great." She shook her head.

"You think you're fat? You always say you could lose a couple of pounds."

Again, Lauren shook her head.

"Come on," he urged. "Tell me."

"No, it's really private."

"Okay, I'll think about it. Now it's my turn, and I choose that one!" He pointed to a geometric form that looked like reversed triangles forming a six-pointed star, zapping it.

"You want to convert to Judaism?"

"Six-pointed stars don't always have to relate to Judaism. There are other meanings."

"Well, I don't know any of them."

"Good, then you won't guess it."

There were still six forms left, and Lauren said, "I'm tired. Let's figure those out in the morning."

The next day they took a brisk walk after breakfast and again bumped into Lillith and Ruel.

"Did they leave?"

Joseph said, "Mostly, but not because of the laughter. We tried that, but it made them bigger. Some friends gave us another method."

"What was the method?" asked Lillith.

They explained the process.

Ruel commented, "Well, that might work temporarily, but I bet they will all come back. Your best bet is to sell that house."

"I hope you're wrong. We love the house!" said Lauren.

"Think about it. If you don't, you'll keep making thought forms that'll plague you." Ruel smiled his crooked smile.

"Thanks for your advice." Lauren squeezed Joseph's hand.

When they continued their walk, Joseph said, "You know, I think those two aren't friends. Their advice has a lot of false overtones."

"You're right. I don't like them. They seem very negative, and I certainly hope they're not right about making new thought forms, but you know, maybe it will happen again."

"It won't happen if we try to catch ourselves, especially if we share things more instead of just thinking them. Let's try to do that from now on."

When they returned home, they went back to the kitchen to think of new tactics for learning the identities of the remaining six forms. They were having a difficult time of it, when the phone rang. It was William.

"How are you doing with the forms?" he asked.

"Not good! We have six left, and we can't figure out their identities. We have our lists, but none of them seem to fit what's on the list."

"Have you seen each other's lists?"

"No, we want to keep it private."

"Well, if you both worked on the lists together, maybe swapping the lists would bring some new insight."

"But I have a couple of things on my list I don't want Lauren to know, and I think she has the same."

"Talk to each other about it. Maybe start with the items you don't mind sharing."

"Okay. Thanks, we'll try that."

They redid their lists, leaving out the thoughts they didn't want to share with each other, and then they read the remaining items together. Taking one at time, they examined the forms and discovered some hidden features they hadn't noticed before. They were able to get rid of four that way.

Lauren said, "Only two left, and neither one of us seems to know what caused them."

"Let's look at the hidden ones we're holding. Maybe now we can each work with them individually," suggested Joseph.

Nothing happened. The two that remained were very close in makeup. One looked like an elf, with a pointed hat, wrinkled skin and crabby-looking features. The other, which was also elf-like, had a frowning mouth and huge cold eyes. They kept away from each another and hid in corners a lot.

Joseph suggested, "You know, maybe we can just leave these here. We don't see them often; they hide a lot. Let's just forget about them."

"I can't! There's something about them that really bothers me. I feel they could be influencing us even when we can't see them."

"Then we need to share the remaining things on our lists."

They looked at each other for a moment and then anxiously exchanged lists.

"You feel I have a mean streak in me that someday may be violent?" Joseph was astonished.

"Yes. Sometimes your tone of voice really scares me."

Joseph tried to conceal his harsh feelings as he said, "Getting angry is different from being violent."

He went on, "And you! You have down here that sometimes you hate me and would like to hit me!"

"That's true," she said. "There are times when you are so mean that I really hate you."

He looked at the forms. "Well, they sure look like they fit these thoughts! I know I tried to get rid of both these forms, but neither one disappeared."

"I did too. I tried with all my other private thoughts and nothing worked."

When the phone rang again, it was Sophia. Joseph put her on speakerphone, and they told her what was happening.

"Have you ever thought the same thoughts at the same time?" she asked.

"When we fight we probably feel the same way and have the same thoughts," said Lauren.

"So, it may be that these forms belong to both of you. Come up with similar thoughts now, but make them more positive ones this time. Then do the process together."

They followed her suggestion and the last forms vanished.

"Whew!" said Joseph as he and Lauren collapsed on the couch together.

"Me too! I'm wiped out! Let's celebrate and make a plan to keep the house clean of negative powerful thoughts so we don't have to do this again."

"That's for sure! I'll get the champagne and we'll have a toast."

When they settled back on the couch, Joseph said, "Some of the thoughts that you finally had to share were about leaving me. Do you still want that?"

"I don't know. You had similar thoughts. How about you, do you want that?"

"I don't know either," he admitted. "There are times when I love you with all my heart and times when I want to be alone and not see you at all. I guess I need more space. That's why I wanted this big house. I thought it would give me that, but it hasn't. We seem to fight more here than before."

"I agree. I want to be with you most of the time, but I also get tired of having to interact with you, or anyone for that matter. It's nice now to have my own office so I can listen to my music and enjoy some of the things that I can't share with you mainly because they don't suit your taste."

"When you go off alone," he said, "I think you're hiding something from me."

"I think the same when you close the door to your office and don't come out for hours."

The conversation continued along these lines until Joseph said, "Lauren, let's be honest with each other. Giving each other space is good, and not arguing over the decorating is good, but the bottom line is, should we try to make this marriage work or call it quits? What do you want?"

She thought for a long time. "I know I don't want any of those thought forms back. I also know I love you, but I question whether we can keep from getting angry at each other. Why don't we go for help to a marriage therapist and talk about the forms we didn't want to share?"

"I'm willing to do that," he said. "In fact it's a good idea. If we can bridge our differences, we can build a good marriage. If not, we'll know it's time to end it." He yawned, stretched and then said, "I'd like to know what the thought form was that you wouldn't share. You know, the small fat one."

She frowned and thought for a moment. "Okay, I know we decided not to have children, but once in a while I have a longing to have a child, and I see myself being pregnant. And you, what about the six-pointed form?"

"I know you don't believe in religion, nor are you spiritual, but once in a while I want to know more about mysticism, and the six-pointed star has a mystical past. I read about these things privately, and I sometimes feel upset that I can't share my thoughts with you."

Lauren said, "Why don't we talk about all this in our therapy?"

"Yes, let's," he replied, reaching for her hand. "You know, I think seeing those thought forms was really important. Thanks to Sophia and Will, maybe one day we can have a relationship like theirs!"

Commentary

Although this chapter reads like a fantasy, there is an underlying truth in the events that take place in our couple's house. Our thought patterns are very powerful, more powerful than we can imagine. We've all walked into houses and apartments that, if we take the time to notice it, affect our moods and make us feel welcome, warm and perhaps joyful, or are oppressive and energy-draining.

Joseph and Lauren's relationship, which is inscribed in the rooms of their house by the negative energy of their thoughts, keeps pulling them down. Each day, they are creating a stronger cycle of simmering anger and frustration. Once they realize that they are both responsible for what they have created for themselves, they become empowered to try to either change their relationship or end their marriage.

Many people are learning to consciously try not to pollute the planet, but we rarely think about how we are polluting the atmosphere through negative thinking. In 1952, Norman Vincent Peale wrote a book on "The Power of Positive Thinking." If we think positive thoughts, we often will attract more positive outcomes. This chapter was about the power of negative thinking and its effect on relationships.

There is no guarantee that the relationship between Joseph and Lauren will work out. They may not endure as a couple, but if they do break up, they will have learned to be more conscious of the impact their thought patterns have on themselves and on others.

As we look at the world today, it is hard to imagine how this planet is going to survive the hatred, violence and general negativity that surrounds it. If we could all see the atmospheric pollution that emerges from our negative thinking, we would be horrified.

Years ago, in New York City, the level of noise pollution was diminished by a law banning horn honking arising from impatience; anyone who violated that ban was fined. That helped a great deal. However, it's time we start thinking about the effects of thought pollution on the future of this planet.

A couple of chapters in this book address the aliveness of nature. With weather changes, such as global warming and the advent of "severe weather," which are happening daily around the world, it feels like nature is reflecting planetary chaos and the negativity of human thought.

There have been many experiments conducted with plants over the years that have indicated how interconnected we are with nature. Someone once had a singing teacher who would sing to his plants every morning. He claimed it helped them grow with great profusion. Since then, there have been many studies that indicate the power of sending love from the heart to houseplants. Try it yourself. You may be astonished by the results.

Exercise:

To become more aware of your negative thinking and how it affects you and those close to you, try this exercise. Remember to look at yourself and your thinking patterns with no judgment.

Find a quiet place to sit, then close your eyes and take some deep breaths. As you breathe, let go of all thoughts and feelings, relaxing your body until you feel you are calm and centered. Link with your heart, and ask yourself the following questions:

What kind of negative thoughts do I have about myself and about others? List some of your main thoughts, then see if you can group them into patterns, for example: judging, being sarcastic, complaining, nagging, or needing to be right. Choose one of these patterns to focus on first. Get a sense of when you tend to fall into this negative thinking: in what kinds of situations, about what, and about whom?

Ask yourself the following questions:

How does this negative thinking affect me? And, how does it affect others?

What emotions and moods are stirred?

What kinds of feelings and moods would I prefer to have and to see around me?

If negative thinking is more prevalent than you would like, ask:

Where does this pattern come from? Try to get some sense of that.

Then ask: How can I begin to change this?

Finally, ask: Is there anything else I need to know about this pattern? If the answer is yes, try to understand more about the pattern so you can change it.

If you have a pattern of negative thinking, it is very important to understand where it originated from and to notice when you do it. Doing the nightly review (Chapter 5) can be very helpful both for deepening your awareness and for changing the pattern. Also, try to take each negative thought you have and change it into a positive one. Changing negative thinking makes a big difference in one's life.

18
Metamorphosis on Planet Xanophlex

Often in a relationship, the man contains more feminine qualities and the woman more masculine. This imbalance of the masculine and feminine energies can lead to misunderstandings and miscommunication. The opposite—when the woman is overly feminine and the man overly masculine—is also an imbalance.

To make an imbalanced relationship more harmonious, the partners need to recognize how they are using their inner qualities and then be willing to make some changes.

The following tale illustrates such a situation and one couple's process:

As the shuttle landed, Linda breathed a sigh of relief. She was a bit nervous landing on Planet Xanophlex. The shuttle from the space ship had to descend through high, steep mountains, which were glorious to see but very treacherous. She and her husband Joel had been here once already, and, so far, it was their favorite planet to visit. Joel was interested in the architecture, whereas she loved the terrain; the grass grew in circles and turned various colors with each new spiral. There was so much to see that they decided to return rather than explore another planet.

Planet Xanophlex was inhabited by a race of people similar to humans in many ways, except that all the men were very oriental looking, with straight, black hair and bangs, and all the women appeared to be more Scandinavian, with straight, blond hair, bangs, and facial features that were gaunt and sculpted. Both sexes were very handsome. Linda had never seen anyone here who was not good-looking.

There were many cities here, but the buildings were entirely different from those on Earth. Nearly all the buildings, whether they were large office structures or small homes, were built out of a very porous and multicolored substance that resembled concrete. The finish was highly glazed, making the buildings look a lot like pottery, yet the material was strong enough to construct buildings as high as fifty stories. On a sunny day, the colors sparkled and glowed, making entire towns or cities look like undulating rainbows.

When the couple first saw the buildings, they thought the sameness of the architecture would become boring after a short time, but, instead, it had affected them in a most profound manner. The colors felt healing, and somehow they both felt relaxed in a way they hadn't for many years. This feeling had stayed with them throughout their previous visit and even accompanied them home for a week or two.

They had spent most of their time back then seeing the cities, but this time they planned to go inland to the forests and smaller towns. Few travelers went beyond the big cities because the main sights were there and reaching the interior took a long trip through the mountains. Linda and Joel could make such a journey because both had taken a six-month sabbatical from the college where they were professors. They did that so there would be plenty of time to explore the planet because they really loved it.

After spending a week revisiting some of their favorite places in the major city, they rented a vehicle to take them inland. The vehicle was similar to an automobile, except it flew several feet off the ground. It was perfect for the interior of the planet, as it could move over fields, lakes and even small villages. There were some roads made for land vehicles, which were used mainly for transporting goods; cities and larger towns had a combination of both types of transportation. Driving their rented vehicle was quite an adventure! They had to be careful at first to avoid hitting trees. It reminded them of the flying car in the Harry Potter series.

They had gone to a travel agent who drew out a plan for them, but the agent had explained that it was better to just follow the signs and go where they felt like going. The agent had been in the interior only once and said it was a unique experience, best done without planning, and they would know why when they arrived. They were told that some of the towns had inns, which always had vacancies, and there were also bed and breakfast places, so they didn't have to worry about accommodations. The climate was warm, and if they decided to camp in the forest, they only needed sleeping bags. There were no bugs or animals on the planet. Since they were in their early forties, and loved camping out, that was a good choice for them.

Linda was strong for her size and competitive in most things. Tall and fair-haired, with smoky grey eyes, she looked like a student, though when she lectured there was no doubt about who she was. She taught first-year English with a vigor and enthusiasm that inspired others. Everyone taking Linda's course knew her reputation for heavy homework, strict grading and expectations that everyone do their best. She was a tough teacher but one who was respected, not only by her students, but also by her colleagues and the Department Chair.

Joel was the complete opposite. The only thing they had in common was that he was an athlete who was also strong. They had met in the school gym five years earlier. They'd been married for three years, and generally, it had been good, with just a few ups and down. He was tall and dark, with eyes that turned almost black when he was angry. Joel taught second-year physics at the college. He was brilliant but never showed it. In fact, he was so nonchalant that one wondered how he could possibly teach such a difficult subject. His teaching style was also very open and relaxed. Students loved taking his courses mainly because he wasn't strict or demanding. Joel taught the subject in a manner that was so simple that everyone could learn the most complex formulas.

He was, naturally, very well liked by his students, and totally not understood by his academic colleagues. Many of Linda and Joel's arguments had been about teaching methods until they decided it was better to avoid the subject.

The trip into the interior took them five days. They stopped each night, and they noticed that the towns got smaller and smaller as they headed further inland. Finally, on the fifth night, they lodged in a small village on the edge of a huge forest and decided to stay there a few days to explore the trails.

The inn was run by a couple, Lillith and Ruel, who told them to take provisions for several days, as they might want to go to the red woods, which were quite a ways inside. Linda and Joel had heard in the city that these woods were very unusual, and when Linda asked why, Lillith replied, "I don't want to spoil your experience by telling you, but we do suggest you go there."

They started out the next morning, leisurely hiking through the forest. The trail was wide and easy to walk. The trees looked like a type of pine, but they were very different from the pine trees on Earth—they were just as tall, but the branches, instead of flowing downward, moved upward as if wanting to embrace the sun. At first they were just strange looking, but soon, Joel and Linda felt an exuberance that seemed to emanate from the branches.

"I wish I could feel this way at home," Linda commented.

"I often feel this way. Not as much as I do here, of course, but Linda, if you weren't so serious all the time you could feel this way too."

"I have to be serious for both of us."

"No, you don't."

Just then, shockingly, a branch swooped down and smacked both of them.

"Whoa, did you see that? I swear the tree did that on purpose!" Linda glared at the tree, whose branch was now moving back to its upward position.

"I feel like it's telling us not to argue. Thank you, tree." Joel bowed to it.

"Silly!" said Linda.

They continued to walk quietly.

That night, sleeping under the trees was delightful. There was a full moon, and oddly enough, the tree branches moved downward onto the ground, becoming a soft blanket on which to put their sleeping bags. The pine smell was strong, and the aroma lulled them to sleep.

They continued hiking the next couple of days until they saw a clearing, with a ring of tall red trees in the middle.

"That man Ruel said they were red, but I've never seen a red like this," Linda exclaimed, in awe of the brilliance of the bright, wine-red bark that resembled glistening glass. The branches were also red, with leaves that would make autumn on Earth look like a faded watercolor painting.

"My god, they're incredible!" Joel grabbed his camera, but it wouldn't open. "This worked in the forest. Why not now?"

No matter how hard he tried, he couldn't open it. "You know, my sense is the trees don't want their picture taken." He stopped trying to open the case.

"That's nonsense. Give it to me." Linda took the camera, but she too couldn't budge the case.

"Forget it," she said. "Let's go closer." She led the way to the group of trees.

"Stop!" said Joel. "Don't go closer. Don't you hear it? It's saying to stay away!" They saw what looked like a mouth open on the side of one of the trees.

Ignoring Joel, Linda moved forward. "A talking tree. How wonderful!"

"Don't do that! It's telling you to not come closer."

"Why not? Tree, tell me why not! I want to talk to you."

Suddenly, they both heard the tree say, "You can talk to me from where you are. Do not come closer."

"You still haven't told me why not." Linda took another step toward it.

"You are a strong, willful person, and you want things your own way. Listen for once. I am giving you a genuine warning. Listen to me!"

Her face reddening, Linda spat out, "You have a nerve telling me what to do! If I want to walk near you I will." She started moving forward again.

Joel grabbed her just in time as a large branch broke from the tree and nearly landed on her head.

"You tried to kill me! If I had an axe I would cut you down." Linda was furious.

At that moment, all the trees began to move toward her and Joel in a menacing manner.

He kept dragging her backwards. "Are you crazy? Stop aggravating them, or they will uproot and come after us."

"Yes we will!" they all cried in unison.

The main tree said, "You are more masculine than the man that is holding you. You need to learn what the feminine is. Be more like him."

Shocked, Linda said, "How do you know what I am?"

"We know everything. We are thousands of years old and we know about you and him. Man," a branch pointed to Joel, "You are gentle, but you need to be stronger and more aggressive. Take charge of her. She needs to be beaten until she is more submissive. That's masculine."

"Beat her? I don't beat women." Joel was also getting angry.

"Try it. Most women like being overpowered." The trees laughed.

"Let's get out of here," said Joel as he grabbed Linda's hand. They ran back down the path until they were under the protection of the pine trees, where they felt safe enough to sit down to rest.

"What awful trees," panted Linda. "I don't understand why Lillith and Ruel sent us there. She said she didn't want to spoil the experience for us. Why did she say that?"

"I don't know, but I certainly will ask them."

"Let me ask. I personally want to confront her."

Joel thought for a minute. "You know, there is some truth in what the tree said. You often act more masculine than me, and I usually give in to you and don't take the lead in things. I feel it's up to me to talk to those two. Those trees could have killed us, and I feel the need to confront both of them. It's a man's job."

"Bull shit! In today's world a woman can confront too."

Joel sighed, "Come on, let's not argue. The branches are coming down again." Sure enough, they had started to move downwards.

Later, back in the village, they went immediately to see Lillith and Ruel, but, instead of them, an unfamiliar woman was there. "Where are Lillith and Ruel?" they asked.

"They went home. They were running the place while I was away. My name is Marion."

After they introduced themselves and told her the story of the red trees, she looked horrified.

"I told them to never let our guests go too far in the forest! Those trees were evil magicians who were transformed into trees thousands of years ago by the lords of the planet. They still do harm. The trees attack people by psychically sensing their weaknesses. In some cases, when people get too near them, they try to kill them. Sometimes they've been successful. I am so sorry! I can't imagine why Lillith and Ruel told you to go there. I don't know them very well. They answered an ad I ran for someone to take over the inn while I was on vacation."

"And I thought this planet was only positive." Linda felt sad suddenly.

"It is, it really is. Only the red trees are negative, and as I said, everyone in town here will warn people about them."

The next day, they decided to leave the forest region and continue to explore more of the interior. They traveled westward, where the food was grown, and stopped in towns that sprawled over hills and down valleys surrounded by lovely rivers and lakes. One place was a bed and breakfast on the shores of a rich purple lake. They stayed there a week, enjoying taking rides in a boat that moved by voice direction only, without any apparent motor.

For the first time, they started to talk about themselves on a deeper level. Although they knew each other's background in general, they now delved into their family histories in great detail. Joel was an only child, with a father whose personality was very rigid. He had rebelled against him constantly and decided at a young age never to be like him. While telling Linda some of the stories, he realized for the first time that she had several of the same rigid attitudes as his father.

He finally said to her, "I married my father and I didn't know it! In a lot of ways you remind me of him."

"Thanks a lot! But I like your father. He's respected in his profession, and he's been very successful in his career. In fact, I wish you were more like him."

"Thank God I'm not!"

Linda had the same kind of father. He was a doctor and very wealthy. She'd always looked up to him as her idol. Her mother was very unfocused and flighty. Linda never wanted to be like her. The stories of her childhood were full of disdain toward her mother and admiration of her father.

Joel said, "I like your mother. She may be flighty at times, but she's very affectionate and warm-hearted. My sense is she would do anything for anyone."

"Yes, too much so. People take advantage of her, and she doesn't care."

"Well, that's because it doesn't bother her. I'd like to be like that."

Linda laughed a bit sarcastically. "I can't believe I married my mother!"

"So, what are we going to do about it?" Joel asked.

"Let's enjoy this planet for now. We can decide what to do when we get home."

The vibration of the planet was becoming stronger as they moved further and further westward. The inhabitants started to change in appearance. No longer were the men dark and Chinese-looking and the women blond and Scandinavian in appearance. A mix of the two became more the norm. There were men with blond hair and blue eyes and women with dark hair and dark eyes. The features on both were very exotic, a mix between Asian and European in both the men and the women.

In one village, they found a small cottage to rent and decided to stay for two months. It was a charming town situated on a beautiful, deep turquoise lake. A stream running by the cottage led to the lake, and they had the use of a boat large enough for several people. Linda and Joel made several friends and began to have boat parties in the evening at sunset. One of their favorite couples was William and Sophia, local farmers who grew vegetables unique in texture and in flavor. They gave

Linda and Joel lessons on how to cook them, a process very different from what they were accustomed to on Earth.

Linda and Joel noticed right away that Sophia and William had a beautiful and harmonious relationship. Their lives and actions were not typically male and female. For example, they had two young children and both parents took care of them, changing roles frequently. William would sometimes feed them, bathe them, and put them to bed while Sophia was doing the accounting, and other times the routine would be reversed. There seemed to be no set rules in their behavior. Sophia was sometimes direct and assertive and William reflective and intuitive, and at other times William would be more assertive and she more reflective. Neither was overly masculine or feminine, rather they seemed to have a balance of both.

One evening, after a pleasant dinner together, they all sat on the patio enjoying the evening air. The moon was full and luminous against a black sky with bright stars, which seemed much larger on this planet, almost like a Van Gogh painting. Linda brought up the subject of the couple's relationship

"We've noticed your relationship is a very good one and wondered how you made that happen."

Sophia looked at William, "Well, it took a lot of effort and understanding to work out a balanced way of living. Both of us wanted children, but I didn't want to be the sole parent taking care of them."

"Yes, it was important for me also to be able to take care of them and be a part of their lives," William added, "and Sophia needed to develop her masculine side. When we first met, she was 100 percent feminine. She was really lovely, but she kept things to herself."

"And William was very masculine, getting things done quickly, without thinking about the best way to do them. Now we both spend time planning, for example, we talk about the rotation of the crops and how to harvest them."

Sophia smiled and added, "We've noticed, Linda, that you're more assertive than Joel, almost the opposite of our relationship."

"Yes, I take after my father more than my mother. We both realized on this trip that we married our parents. Joel is like my mother in many ways, and I'm like Joel's father. Not a great combination, I'm afraid."

"Would you prefer having more balance in your relationship?" William asked.

"I don't know. The two of you are different and have your own business. We both work full time and teach subjects that are very different. We also have no children. What would that look like for us?" Linda replied.

"What would you like it to look like?" William turned to Joel for the answer.

"I would like Linda to act more feminine. She always takes the lead in everything, whether it's a discussion or it's preparing dinner. I'd like her to be more like Sophia."

"I would like you to be more like William. You need some of the strong masculinity that comes from him naturally," Linda said.

"Wait, you just said you couldn't be like us because we were so different and our life style was so different!" Sophia laughed.

"I guess I did," Linda admitted. "So how are we going to make changes, and what kinds?"

"First of all, do you share your thoughts with each other and do you share what you are really thinking about each other?" William asked.

"No, I couldn't do that. It would cause a fight, and we have enough of those as it is," Joel responded.

Sophia looked at William. "Shall we take them to the castle?"

"Good idea," William said, turning to Linda and Joel. "But only if you are willing to view each other's thoughts. The castle is a sounding board for people's thinking."

"What good will that do?" Linda asked.

Sophia said, "Generally, it helps couples look at some of the hidden feelings that they never express. It helped us to be more honest with each other and to work through some of the problems we were having at the time."

"How does it work?" Joel looked a little anxious.

"It's hard to explain. It's a magical place that was built centuries ago. Only people in this village know about it. It's a two-hour hike from here. We'll show you the way and leave you alone there."

Linda, also worried, asked, "What if other people are there or come in when we're there? Can they read our thoughts too?"

"Won't happen," said William. "When people enter, the gate closes until they're ready to leave, then it opens again. Usually you won't be in there more than an hour."

"Okay, I'm willing to go. Maybe it will help or maybe not, but we need to try something." Linda looked at Joel, who reluctantly nodded.

The next morning they all set off through hills and small valleys. The path was easy to follow until they came to a mountain. It looked difficult to climb, but as they started up it, the path seemed to level off and the climb was quite easy. Down they went again into another valley, and they saw a castle surrounded by shade trees next to a fast-running stream.

"It's lovely. Was it ever lived in?" Joel asked.

Sophia shook her head. "No one knows, but no one would want to live in it because of what happens there."

It wasn't a large castle, but it had the requisite tall walls and turrets at the top. The material was the same as that used in all the other buildings, but somehow it seemed more solid. Thick stones had been cut to form the walls and main body of the building. When they arrived at the entrance, the doors swung open. Joel and

Linda waved goodbye and walked through them. Immediately the doors swung back and locked, causing them to feel nervous about the whole venture.

Why did we do this? Joel wondered, and his thought instantly went into Linda's mind.

You could have said no, she thought back immediately.

"Wow! This is really amazing!" he said. Then he thought. If I can hear your thoughts and you mine, why not just think them to each other?

You're right. What should we talk–I mean–think about?

Well, he thought, I guess we can think about our relationship. I think it's interesting that both those negative tree monsters and Sophia, who is very positive, said you are more masculine than me. This is a big problem between us.

Immediately Linda thought, You're my big problem!

"Why can't you take any criticism even when it's important?" Joel loudly voiced his response.

"You make it seem like it's all my fault. How about you? You're so lackadaisical and laid back. I'd like to see you with more balls."

We have enough in the family with yours! Joel immediately thought.

"Look," said Linda. "Let's not have a fight. What needs to happen here?"

"Why don't we talk about the positive things in our relationship? Let's do that first and then look at the negative things that need changing."

"Good idea," she said.

They walked through the rooms to a balcony that overlooked the stream. There were two chairs conveniently placed there.

"I brought a paper and pen to write things down." Linda pulled them out of her handbag.

"Why not just talk? We can make notes later."

They talked about the good times they had shared: How they enjoyed all the athletic things that they did together, that the sex was certainly good and that it was nice to have the same school holidays. They each then thought about more fun things that they still could do. At first it was strange to speak every thought they had. They compared the positive aspects of their relationship, and then it came time to reveal everything they needed and weren't getting from one another. That took the longest and was the hardest. Many thoughts came in that weren't voiced but were still heard by the other person.

Why don't you compliment me more? Linda thought.

Maybe because you are always complimenting yourself. Besides, do you ever compliment me?

Men don't need compliments.

Who says?

That's the way it's always been. Women always receive more compliments than men. Men shouldn't need them.

That's old-fashioned thinking, and why do you feel you have to always cook dinner? I love to cook, and I'm good at it.

But women do the cooking and besides it looks too feminine for you do it.

So you're basically saying I'm too feminine?

Yes, I guess I am. I worry about you being gay.

What, you think I'm gay? You just said we had great sex together, and now you are implying I'm gay simply because I love cooking? I don't call you gay when you act aggressive toward me!

You're right. How are we going to change? There's a lot of old laundry here that looks impossible.

First, I think we both need to admit that we need to make changes in our lives. Then I feel it's important to pick the top thing and help each other.

When it seemed like they had come to an agreement, they heard the doors start to open. Sophia and William were waiting for them outside.

"That was an incredible experience," said Joel.

Linda added, "We've got a lot of work to do."

"I know," affirmed Sophia. "But the main thing is wanting to do it. First, let's find a good spot and have a picnic." She pointed to a basket she was carrying.

Linda and Joel extended their stay for a couple more months, and worked on the two things that bothered them the most, Linda's aggressiveness and Joel's carefree manner. Both changed a little bit, not enough for them to see but enough to feel they were making some headway.

Finally, their vacation was up and they had to return home. William and Sophia promised to come visit them the following summer. They had been to Earth a couple of times but felt it a strange place to visit. They found the people in the big cities cold and unfriendly, but now, with Joel and Linda as friends, they would be able to meet their other friends and maybe come to a deeper understanding of Earth people.

Back home again, the reality of earth once more became Linda and Joel's reality. They started fighting over little things and regressed to their old habits. One day, embroiled in a negative, "Why did you do that?" argument, Joel finally said, "We can't make this work. Let's end it once and for all."

Shocked, Linda couldn't respond at first. Then she said, "Our problem is we stopped working on ourselves the way we were doing on Planet Xanophlex."

"Don't you see it's impossible to do here? There, the whole feeling of the planet was calm, which helped in making changes. Here, you still boss me around, and I won't respond to you, which makes you frustrated. It's not possible to change on earth. The vibrations aren't conducive to change."

"That's a lie. Lots of people change. Let's do some therapy. That could help."

Joel shook his head. "We've tried that and it didn't work. We are too different to make this work. Besides, I listened to you about not having children, and I've changed my mind. I want them now and you're too old."

"What a horrible thing to say to me!" Linda ran into her home office and slammed the door.

Sophia and William received the letter a month later. "We are separated and getting a divorce. We just couldn't make it work, but we both still want to have you here as our guests. You can spend a few days with me and then with Joel. We do look forward to seeing you both again. Love, Linda."

Sophia looked at William, "That's too bad. Sometimes we win and other times we don't. Lilith and Ruel will be happy."

"Yes, but we still will see them, and the divorce isn't final yet." William smiled at her with much love.

Commentary

Sometimes relationships just don't work. The significant axis of this chapter is the comparison between the two relationships of William and Sophia and Linda and Joel. Linda's hard-edged approach to life is basically an expression of the negative masculine. Joel tends to use the feminine. Even though the two share the same profession, teaching, they are completely opposite in their approaches. The image they project as a couple is of two people leashed together yet straining in opposite directions. They find it difficult to speak in the same emotional language. While acknowledging to each other that their sexual relationship is good, in other realms they are polar opposites.

The dramatic difference between the two relationships is demonstrated by the easy and harmonious togetherness of Sophia and Will. They do not live by roles and rules; they work together within a harmonious flow of energy instead of a rigid structure of "he takes out the garbage and she cooks the meals." Having succeeded in individually accomplishing an integration of the masculine and feminine qualities within themselves, they have accomplished the ideal love relationship, and, at the same time, they are models of a positive relationship with their children.

Ruel and Lillith show up, albeit briefly, in their negative masculine and feminine roles. Even on this mythical planet there is negativity, personified by the red trees. Granted it is isolated, and minimal in comparison with the negativity that exists on Earth, but the fact that it exists at all is a significant factor in the planet's evolution. There is a lesson here: even in such a paradise, a certain amount of contrast, what Jung would call the "shadow" side of life, is necessary to propel growth that can lead to harmony.

When the foursome arrives at the castle, Sophia's ironic comment that no one would want to actually live there speaks to the point that such unvarnished frankness would be too intense for most of us to endure on a twenty four-hour basis.

Even on this relatively calm and positive planet, Xanophlex, couples must work on their issues, as Sophia and William do. There was a dear teacher who used to talk about the "sacred mountain" as the one that we can aspire to climb. It is the magnet that draws us forward in consciousness.

Exercise:

For this exercise on relationships and the balance between the masculine and feminine energies, you will need to review the charts on the feminine and masculine qualities in Chapter 13.

Think of a close relationship you have been in in the past or are in now. Study the two charts of masculine and feminine characteristics, and focus on the attributes, both positive and negative, of you and the person you were or are close to. You may want to list these. Then consider how they work well together and how they clash. Take time to really examine your interactions and your roles.

Then, if it is a current relationship, ask yourself: What do I need to do to help make this relationship more balanced?

If it is a past relationship, ask: What would have made this relationship work better?

19
The Wisdom Seekers

This chapter is about coming to a deeper understanding of who you are. We all have a lower nature that tries to misguide us. When we listen to it or simply get caught up in its negativity, we forget that we also have positive aspects in our being and a positive side to who we are.

The following story is about two people's journey with these issues, and it also illustrates how working with an inner child is often vital for reaching deep inner wholeness:

It was early evening. The sun was setting over the mountains, with a deep orange and lavender transforming the barren mountains into shining purple tones. Norma and Louis wrapped their arms around each other against the chill of the evening air.

"Isn't it spectacular?" Norma whispered. "I wish we had sunsets like this at home."

"We do, but we have to drive to see them. I'm going to start a fire." He walked to a pile of wood by their campsite and returned with an armful.

"'I'll be sorry to leave this site. The mountains have been really beautiful," she said with regret.

"You'll love the park, too, and I think the pine trees will help our meditations. They're supposed to have high vibrations."

"I've only seen pine trees once in my life, when our family drove north to Oregon from San Francisco, where we were visiting relatives."

"Me too. That's why it'll be a treat for both of us. Florida has beautiful nature too, but no woods like we're going to see."

The drive to Arizona had been a long one. Seeing the Grand Canyon was great, but they planned to head to a new park in Montana that was supposed to be one of the loveliest in the country.

Norma smiled when she watched Louis making the fire. She thought, not much experience in doing that either. Louis was middle-aged and short, 5ft. 5 inches, with a broad handsome face. His brown hair was combed to hide some of the baldness that was beginning to show. He was a mix of casualness and seriousness, which often contradicted his positions on many issues.

Norma's smile conveyed much love and understanding. She was his size, maybe an inch taller, with sandy hair that became blonder in the sun. Her complexion was flawless, with a pink undertone that gave her skin a luminous quality. It was her most attractive feature. They were both in their early forties.

After he'd started a fire, Louis returned to sit by her in silence as the orange sky faded into darkness and the sun disappeared behind the mountains.

"I hope we see more of those on our trip," Norma said.

"We're bound to when we hit some of the flat lands north of here."

Camping was their favorite way to vacation. They felt that going into the rugged parts of the west was a spiritual challenge. It was a time when they meditated and linked with nature spirits, and it was also a time to bridge any differences between them. Both had corporate jobs and worked long hours, so being together for a month's camping trip was something they looked forward to each year, and this year they'd extended their vacation to six weeks. This was to be a special trip, and, besides hiking, they had decided to spend time reading and talking about different spiritual teachings, such as Buddhism, Taoism, and Yoga, mainly Eastern teachings. It was an interest they had picked up in the last couple of years.

When they arrived at the park several days later, they both suddenly felt as if something was wrong. They saw the entrance and the sign and instantly turned to each other and said, "Let's not go in there." Both felt a genuine fear.

"If we both feel this way, maybe we should reconsider," Norma observed.

"Why don't we pull over to the side of the road and meditate about it."

The meditation was a long one. When it ended, Louis said, "I think there's something unexpected awaiting us there. Let's try it. If we don't like it we can leave early."

"I agree," Norma said. "My intuition tells me that I'm going to see things I don't want to see, but it is important to see them anyway. So let's brave it."

As they started to drive toward the gates, a woman waved at them. They stopped and she came over to them.

"Are you planning to go to the camp through there?"

"Yes, we have reservations."

"My name is Lillith, and I feel I should warn you about the place. Experiencing the energy there caused my husband and me to split up. He's already left me, and I'm waiting for a friend to pick me up. Don't do it if you want to stay married."

The couple looked at each other, puzzled. Then Louis, who was driving, asked, "What do you mean? What happened?"

"They take you through hell, and I mean hell, and then tell you that you can't talk about it to each other. Of course we didn't follow that rule. They basically don't want you to talk because then you can compare their treatment. It's really destructive. Don't go in. If you do, remember I warned you. Oh, there's my ride!" She went running off toward a car that was heading toward them.

They watched her leave and then looked at each other.

"That's got to be why we were feeling afraid before. What should we do?" Louis asked.

"Well, you know me! I'm always up to a challenge. Look, we've paid for it, and we can always leave early. Let's risk it. Besides, now I'm really curious about the place."

When they drove through the gates they suddenly felt that they couldn't turn back even if they wanted to. The road was narrow, barely two lanes, and they drove for several miles through thick pinewoods. They saw no one.

"I thought this was a popular place. Where are the cars?" Norma asked.

"It's also a very large place, so maybe the cars are on other roads."

"Or maybe the marketing is false and there's not much to see here. If it's just woods and nothing else, even though they're lovely trees, I'm going to get bored here."

"Once we start hiking and meditating it might change," Louis said, "and the animals are supposed to be very different."

"Okay, don't listen to me. I'm just a bit off right now."

Finally they saw the sign for their campgrounds. They had made reservations several months earlier. They pulled up to another gate and gave their name to a guard. He sent them on to the office, where they were given a key and a packet of materials and directed to the road that would take them to their accommodations. It was sunset when they arrived at their log cabin situated by a lake, and when they saw it, both felt a lot better. The lake was like glass, calm and serene in the light of dusk.

"What a nice place to meditate." Norma walked down to the shore and sat down on the grass.

Louis joined her. "This really is perfect."

The cabin was cozy and warm. It had the basics, a stove, refrigerator, bath, and overstuffed couch. Looking around outside, they saw other cabins, but they were several yards apart with trees hiding each of them from each other. It couldn't be more private.

That night they looked over the maps of the trails and the enclosed grounds where the animals were. There were also two sealed folders, one with Norma's name on it and one with Louis' on it.

Louis handed Norma her envelope. "I wonder what these are."

As they opened them, the cabin became very silent. Suddenly the birds had stopped singing and the wind had died down. It was very eerie.

They read in silence. Both were absorbed by the information.

"Does yours say you can't talk to me about what happens?" Norma asked.

"Yes, I gather yours says the same." His voice was low.

"What should we do? Mine says this experience will be a spiritual journey, but one that we can't share during the time we are here. Does yours say that?" She was frowning as she looked into Louis' eyes with intensity.

"Yes. The ad for this place did say the experience would be a spiritual one and those who were coming should desire that, otherwise they wouldn't enjoy being here, but it said nothing like this. The days are all laid out for us specifically. Sometimes we can be together and generally talk, but we can't speak about what happens when we're alone. We're not allowed to share until we go home, and we have to sign this agreement and swear we will uphold it."

"I know. It also says that most of the time here we'll be alone, and on some of the trails we'll have to stay in other cabins alone and not return here. This is our vacation together, how can we do this?" Norma tried not to cry.

"That's why we felt the way we did at the gate. They call it a journey, and I feel it's going to be a difficult one. We don't have to agree. We can turn back." Louis put his arms around Norma and kissed her.

"I don't know. Let's meditate on it."

They sat on the couch and fell asleep during their meditation. They awoke with a start. "I saw a man in a white robe who told me I should be courageous and try to do the journey," Norma said.

"I also saw a man dressed in a white robe who told me the journey would teach me a lot about myself, and that I need to do it."

When they compared the images they were certain it was the same man in both their dreams.

The next day, on the first hike, they went together. The trail would take them to where some of the animals were impounded. They met some people on the way, but no one talked, nor did they want to. It was a difficult climb through rocky terrain and thick woods. Finally they arrived at a clearing with wire fences enclosing very large areas. Each area had rocks, and water and trees. It was nothing like any zoo they had seen before. The animals had much vaster space to roam in. The path went for several miles though these fenced-in sections. The animals mainly remained hidden. Just once in a while they would spot a pride of lions, or a small herd of antelope. At one place they saw a very large zebra in the distance, and when he saw them, he trotted over to the fence.

"Good afternoon." The zebra spoke perfect English.

They were so astonished they couldn't even reply. Finally, Louis said, "How is it possible that you can talk?"

"All animals talk in their own way. Humans can't hear them, but here, in this park, you can hear words even though I don't speak words. The vibration of the park makes it possible."

"That's amazing! Tell us about yourself. Are you alone here?"

"Sometimes yes, sometimes no. I have a mate, but she's often busy and ignores me for days at a time."

"Doesn't that upset you?" asked Norma.

"Heavens, no. I also like being alone. It gives me time to think about things, and when we are together we have more to share."

"Well, we both work long hours, so when we're together we really want to be with each other," Norma replied.

"You mean you're always talking when you are with each other?"

"Well, yes, I guess we do talk a lot, but we don't see each other until late in the day," Louis explained.

"But sometimes the best communication is silent. When I am with my mate we often don't say anything for hours. It's just nice being in each other's presence. Then, when we talk, it's meaningful."

"No chitchat? That would be interesting." Louis looked at Norma.

"Do you have any baby zebras?" Norma ignored the look.

"Yes, we have one who is six months old. He's very cute. He's back there with his mother."

"Does she take care of him all the time?"

"No, we share. Some days she acts like his mother and other days I do. When we want, sometimes we both take care of him. We both have feminine and masculine energies, just like you."

"We don't have that. Norma is feminine and I am masculine."

"That's your sex. That isn't what I mean. Both genders have feminine and masculine energies. Maybe you just haven't named yours, but we contain both." The zebra nodded his head and gave a little snort.

He then continued, "For example, you both have intuition, though Norma probably calls it that and you call it gut instinct. There are so many words for the same thing, aren't there? "I am sure you are assertive in your job, and you, too, Norma, but maybe you call it being direct. I can go on and on, but basically, you both have intuition. Most people do, but sometimes people don't develop or accept these energies, which is a shame.

"Now, I need to go give my son some nurturing." The zebra gave them a zebra grin and trotted back to the woods.

"Wasn't that strange?" Norma still had her mouth open.

"And so wise. What he said makes sense, but I never thought about it before. Maybe we need to look at our relationship and notice what doesn't work for us. For me, it's the constant chatter when we are together."

"I thought you liked that, and you certainly do a lot of talking too, but I agree, it's nice to be together, but maybe it's nice to be alone. I've never tried it, but we'll find out, won't we?"

"Yes, tomorrow is our first alone time."

That evening they couldn't get enough of each other. They made love several times and held each other in anticipation of what it would feel like not to be held. In the morning they went their separate ways. Norma's trail wound again over rocky terrain, and she stopped several times to meditate. Her meditations were filled with scenes from her childhood, scenes she had forgotten in which she felt unheard and unloved. It upset her to see them. Why now? Why did she need to go back into the past? She had let it go a long time ago. The robed man appeared again in her meditation and told her that she needed to heal those repressed feelings; otherwise they would block her spiritual journey.

"Why, can you tell me why? I'm forty-two, why do I need to drag up the past?"

"Because the past is still the present. You still have trouble expressing yourself or expressing how you really feel. You still need attention from Louis or you don't feel loved. Those old patterns are still with you. Look at them, and let them go."

"But how do I do that? How do I let them go?"

"There is wisdom within you. Link with your heart and ask for guidance."

She did this and felt an answer: "Talk to the child within. Love her, and ask her to talk to you; when you get home, go to a therapist who can help guide you in this work."

It was a fatiguing day, mainly because of all the emotions that were surfacing; emotions she didn't know were there. When she arrived at the small cabin in the woods, which was her destination, she fell into the bed and slept for a couple of hours. She awakened in the dark, feeling very much alone. There was food there, and water to drink, but no bathroom, only an outhouse. It was cold and damp when she went to it. She was worried about animals and forced herself not to think negatively. The outhouse was clean and hygienic, which was a relief. It probably had one of those new green toilet systems she had heard about.

The cabin didn't have electricity, just gas lamps. They made her nervous, but when she lit them she felt better. When she tried to read the book she had brought with her, the light was too dim. She decided to eat some dinner and was thinking of meditating again when she heard a scratching sound at the door.

It has to be an animal, she thought, and cried out, "Go away, get away from this cabin!"

"No, I need to talk to you. Let me in."

Another talking animal, damn! "No, you can't come in. What kind of animal are you?"

"One you have never seen before."

"Then I don't want to see you now. Go away."

"I was sent to tell you what you need to work on tonight. Please open the door. I won't go away until we have talked."

"We can talk this way. What do you have to tell me?"

"It's important that you see me—only then will I tell you."

"Alright." Reluctantly, Norma opened the door. Standing there was the strangest creature she had ever seen. It was very large, with black fur that resembled a bear, but its face was somewhat human-looking, with eyes and a mouth; its nose was so small that it looked more like two holes in its face. Long strands of black hair ran from its cheeks down its chin. Its only redeeming feature was its eyes, which were a perfect match to hers. There were sneakers on its feet and gloves on its human-like hands.

It was the ugliest being she had ever seen. Yet, oddly, there was something about it that was almost beautiful.

"Who are you, and what are you?" The creature walked into the room and sat down in a chair.

"I am you and not you," it replied.

"How can that be?"

"My body and hair represent the dark side of your nature. Right now that is overwhelming the beautiful side of you, which is reflected in my eyes. To change and become 100 percent beautiful is a long process, but one that is possible. Your fear makes me ugly and big. Eliminate the fear and you will see the characteristics that you need to transmute in order to become beautiful."

"How do I do that?"

"Ask for guidance from the beautiful part of you. It is your Higher Self, and it can help you with the process. Just link with your heart and imagine it as a wise being. I am speaking to you from that part now, but in a minute the darkness will drown me out." With those words the beast's eyes clouded over and he became mean and ugly, almost roaring. "Listen only to me. I am the one who rules you."

Norma shuddered and felt fear invading her being, but an inner voice said, "Remember to not give in to any fear. The creature cannot hurt you."

She rose from her chair and, pointing at the beast, cried, "Get out. Get out of my cabin. I demand that you leave!"

It roared again, but docilely left.

That beast is obviously my lower nature, Norma thought. My higher nature said I needed to see the beast's characteristics and transmute them, but how do I do that?

The answer flashed in her head. Taking her notebook, she began writing down all the things that were negative about her personality. Prioritizing them in terms of what seemed the strongest and the most negative, she ended up with a solid list. Exhausted by then, she went to bed and had a very significant dream. In the dream the same man dressed in a white robe appeared to her. She asked him how to change the first item on her list, which was her need to be in control, especially in her marriage.

He told her several things, but the main one was to step back from situations and see them in a detached manner. "Try doing things the way your husband wants to do them. Listen more to his needs, and realize that some of your needs come from not being heard as a child." He also told her to write a running account on how she was doing every night before retiring, to remind herself to be more alert to her behavior during the day, and to not judge herself when she fell into the old pattern of wanting to do things her way.

Her instructions for the next day were to return to the original cabin.

Louis, in the meantime, was going through a similar experience. He, too, was dealing with a hurt inner child, and he also faced an ugly creature, one that was more snake-like than furry. His lower nature had a lot of deviousness in it. His main characteristic to work on was the way he manipulated Norma into doing things. She was so demanding that he sometimes found the only way to do things his way was to be somewhat underhanded about it. When he meditated, he saw a lovely woman who told him to practice being more direct, but in a more casual way, to simply state his needs in a warm, undemanding manner.

He too returned to the original cabin the next day and found Norma already there, waiting for him. "I really wish we could share our experience, but we did promise to follow the rules," he said to her.

"Well, we can change the rules if we want to. I don't see anything wrong with that." Seeing Louis frown, she caught herself and added, "But we also want to stay and not get kicked out, so I guess we have to follow their rules."

"I agree! We'll have plenty of time to talk when we leave here. Why not plan something today that we both would like to do together? I'd like to walk around the lake and meditate there. How about you?"

"I guess that's okay, but why not do some climbing…" She stopped. "No, that's fine. I'd like to do that too."

They carefully worked on changing their behavior. Norma slipped a few times, but often caught herself. She tried to do everything Louis' way, but she started feeling very frustrated. Then she remembered to hold her inner child and reassure her.

Louis continued to work on being direct. Once or twice he sounded demanding, and he apologized to Norma for the tone in his voice. It was difficult to change. A few times he followed Norma's directions just because it was easier, a routine that was very ingrained in their relationship.

The next day, when both were feeling frustrated and irritated, they were hiking in silence, not wanting to talk or even be together. They came upon a clearing where a boy around ten years old was whittling a piece of wood. He was attractive, with dark hair and deep, probing eyes.

"What are you making?" asked Louis.

"A statue of a fawn." He stood up and shook hands with them both, introducing himself as Ruel.

"The wood is beautiful," Norma observed. "It should make a lovely fawn." The shape was just being formed.

Ruel looked at them both and asked, "Are you together?"

"Yes, we're married," Louis responded.

"Really, you don't act like you know each other very well."

"How would you know that?" Norma's voice became a bit harsh.

"I know a lot more than most people, and I'd say you're not very compatible. You wear the pants of the family," he pointed to Norma. "You, on the other hand, always give in to her demands. Why do you stay together?"

"We're going through changes. We love each other."

"You're both too old to really change. If I were your age I wouldn't bother. It's best to find someone else who will be more compatible with your personality."

"How dare you..." but before Louis could finish his sentence, Ruel had run off.

"What a strange boy, but what he said was true. Maybe we should realize that we're too old to change. I'm getting tired of all the effort we're putting into this relationship. This is supposed to be a vacation," Norma complained.

"I know how you feel," said Louis. "I'm tired too, but let's give it a little more time."

They continued to walk, both thinking about Ruel's remarks and feeling more and more depressed. They came to the edge of the lake. A young couple was seated on a bench, holding hands and talking quietly. They turned when they heard Louis and Norma and greeted them cheerfully. "I'm William, and this is my wife, Sophia."

They pulled up some chairs for them to sit in.

Sophia said, "I know none of us can talk about our adventures here, but, in general, how are you feeling about this place?"

"I don't know at this point. We're both feeling like it's not worth the effort. In fact, we just met a young boy who seemed to know what we're going though."

William gave Sophia a knowing look. "You must be talking about Ruel. He tries to separate people. He tried it with us. We basically have a sound relationship. We came here last year and learned a lot about each other and ourselves. We assure you, when you get home you'll see how much you've changed. There may be more work to do, but it's well worth it. It has deepened our love for each other and made us more spiritual."

"Yes, we originally chose this place because it was advertised as a spiritual journey, but honestly, it's been much more psychological than spiritual," Louis said.

"That's true," said Sophia, "but the psychological aspect is a very important part of the spiritual. Meditating is great, but it won't necessarily rid you of negative characteristics. Unless you change those characteristics, you will get stuck on the spiritual journey."

She smiled at William. "We plan to come back here often. We learn more about ourselves each time, and that helps us to develop and become how we want to be with each other."

"But you're much younger than us. Ruel thinks it's too late for us to change, and maybe he's right," said Norma.

William said, "It's never too late. I'll bet if you think about the last few days you'll see you're both starting to change. Even if it's ever so slight, it makes a difference. Don't give up!"

After meeting William and Sophia, they felt much better and started to notice the beauty around them again. With all the psychology weighing heavily on their minds, they both had stopped feeling the wonder of their surroundings. The lake was calm and a deep, violet blue, and banks of wild flowers were growing down to its edges. There were boats lined up on the beach, so they decided to take one out. The lake was large, and at the other end was a marsh where violets grew and birds built their nests. As they rowed, a heron flew over them and landed on a nearby rock. When the bird's long, slender neck rose to its full height, it turned its head to look at them with an air of majesty. Then it stabbed its beak into the water, came up with a large fish and flew off with its catch to feed its young.

They stayed for three days, exploring the beauty of nature that was all around them. Then another letter arrived. This time they were to separate for four days. The maps had detailed directions taking them over some very rough terrain.

"I worry about you being able to do this," Louis said to Norma.

"I was just worrying about you, too," Norma replied. "Your knees aren't the best."

"Maybe we should say no to this one."

"No way!" she insisted. "You know I won't give up on anything."

"But Norma! You just complained about your back bothering you. Don't be silly. We can say no and ask for an easier hike."

"That's not allowed! That would end our stay," she insisted, her face set in a stubborn frown.

Louis protested. "I think I read in the instructions that we are allowed to say no if we physically can't do something."

"You can stay. I'm not."

Louis shook his head. "Alright, but promise me you will turn back if it's too much for you to do."

"It will be fine."

But it wasn't. Norma's trail almost immediately became a steep climb upward. Within two hours she was feeling exhausted and sat down to rest. I could do this when I was in my twenties, but it sure is hard now, she thought. Even though she worked out in the gym at home, this kind of climbing was working muscles that she hadn't used in years.

Stubbornly, she continued up the side of the mountain. When she rested and had lunch, she realized that her pace was slowing down and she would never make the cabin before nightfall. She would have to go back down or spend the night on the side of the mountain, but she didn't have any warm gear with her, and the nights were very cold so she couldn't do that. Her only choice was to go back down. Going downhill she could make the main cabin before it got dark.

The idea of defeat really bothered her. As she thought, I don't care if I get cold. I have to go on, a new thought came in: What part of me said that? She immediately recognized that it was the dark creature who wanted her to freeze on the mountain. I'm not going to listen to that part. It's stupid to keep going when I know I can't make it. Damn it, I'm going back. With new resolve, she turned and started the climb downward.

In the meantime, the same thing was happening to Louis. His climb was just as steep, and his knees began to feel it almost right away. He lasted a much shorter time, deciding that he had to go back. He then thought about what he would say to Norma. She would think him weak, and if she made it and he didn't, she would never let him forget it. He was tempted to lie and just tell her that he'd had no trouble and had returned only an hour or two ahead of her after she returned, but lying seemed really wrong to him. What part of him made him think to do that? He realized it was the snake-like creature influencing him, and he chose to say no to it. He would tell her the truth.

They both arrived at the cabin as the sun was setting behind the mountains.

Laughing, they hugged each other and didn't talk about defeat, but rather about how smart they were not to push themselves physically. Inside, the fire was lit, and a lovely dinner was laid out. The letter said, "We hoped you would make wise decisions and return here. Congratulations."

There was also another letter, which they opened later, with a plan for the following day. This was also a four-day trip but on flat trails and with the times of hiking, resting and eating planned in a way they could easily manage.

The new adventure was a continuation of the psychological tests and made them probe more deeply into their inner selves and see more of the true aspects of their characters. Louis' main test was to develop more of his positive masculine attributes, whereas Norma's challenge was to be more in touch with the positive feminine. Both continued to have experiences with their dark side, and both began to see more of their higher nature, learning how to better work with it.

Each time they returned to be together, their time was spent evaluating how they had always interacted, and both slowly started to reverse some of the conditioning they had fallen into. Louis tried to be more direct and assertive, changing the negative feminine traits he had developed into more masculine traits. Norma had to do the opposite. She tried softening her aggressive manner and using more of the feminine; she still acted in a direct manner but with less controlling tones in her behavior and voice. They both took time to read and meditate, and they went on walks together, sharing the beauty around them. They met several couples like William and Sophia who had come back several times to deepen their experience. The more they spoke to these couples, the more they found hope in their process. They also met people who only stayed a night or two and then left, angry to have paid so much and not have received what they expected. Louis and Norma felt lucky to have been able to go beyond their fears and come to a better understanding of themselves and each other.

The last night they were there was spent together in quiet contemplation.

"Tomorrow we can talk to each other about our experience, but you know, I think I know what yours has been like, and I feel that, whatever it was like, what's happened to us has strengthened our marriage." Norma squeezed Louis' hand.

"I think I know about yours also," he replied. "It was good to not know during this time. It certainly helped me be more tuned in to you, and I also feel that from you."

"Amazing, isn't it? I look forward to coming back so I can get to know you better." She laughed lightheartedly for the first time in years.

Commentary

How would you like to combine self-learning with adventures such as Norma and Louis had? All you need to do is to use your imagination and go on an inner journey. Better yet, do it with your partner. If you haven't a partner, pick a close friend to travel with. Plot out your inner space together, following the story. Meet your "lower self"—the monster at the door that wanted to come in. Be courageous as you coolly assess your "lower nature"—remembering that we all have one—and write down its negative personality aspects that need changing. Be careful not to let yourself become overwhelmed. Be the fearless traveler who is in charge. Pick one aspect of your lower nature to work on, noticing when it rears its ugly head, and write about it without self-condemnation. The more you do this, the more you master your lower nature. Share your experiences with your partner or buddy. When you have conquered one aspect, move to the next one on your list.

Remember your inner child, that part of you that may have lacked the parental attention and caring that it needed. When we acknowledge and love this child, we experience a greater sense of wholeness. All that is needed is a daily internal loving connection.

After a while, you will find that you have changed and become the person you wanted to be. Remember—and this is most important—do NOT punish yourself or berate yourself for having whatever negative characteristics you discover. Be grateful that you have found them and that you can free yourself of them. By doing this, you move closer and closer to fully becoming your Higher Self, which is your positive nature.

Exercise:

You may wish to use the exercise outlined in the Commentary above, or, try the following: Remembering not to be self-critical, reflect on your negative personality aspects and make a list. Prioritize those characteristics that you feel need changing. Work with only one at a time.

Begin to do a nightly review (Exercise in Chapter 5) of the aspect you decide to work on first. From an objective, non-judgmental place, look back on the day and notice if at any point you were using this negative trait. If so, make a note of the circumstances. Then, in the morning, ask yourself to notice when you tend to go into this negative aspect.

Over time, you will notice if certain situations and/or certain types of people and behavior tend to trigger this negative characteristic in you, and you will also notice whether or not your inner child is in any way involved. Then you can strategize ways to stop your habitual reaction, including comforting your inner child if that's needed and changing your reaction to a response you prefer. Congratulate yourself each time you manage not to fall into the old habit but instead practice the new response.

Remember, this work takes time, but even overcoming just one or two negative aspects of yourself will make a difference in your relationships. All negative aspects can be changed.

Believe that.

Judith Bach, Ph.D. & Nanette Hucknall

20
The Dance of Opposites

When each partner in a relationship has a fairly good balance of the positive masculine and feminine energies, then, together, the couple can bring out the best of both energies. When such a combination exists, creativity abounds. This combination works for them because they fully respect each other's creativity and intuition.

Our story is an example of how powerful this kind of relationship can be:

When Ossie looked at the report she felt a wave of anxiety. It needed a lot more work, and the time for submission was coming up. The project needed funding, and the only possible source was the Office of Alternative Energy. If they rejected it, another year would be lost until she could try again.

Getting up from her desk, she went into her kitchen and poured herself a very large cup of coffee. It was going to be a long day and night, and she was already developing a headache.

Nuclear power was becoming the main source of energy at a time when there weren't sufficient safeguards established for the waste. Every country was low in oil production, and scientists were frantically trying to develop alternative energy sources. Wind and solar energy had been installed around the planet, but weather conditions limited their usefulness.

Ossie was convinced that her product would make all the difference, but she needed large amounts of funding for research. Even though her proposal was brilliant, there wasn't any possible way to prove it would work at this stage. Making liquid petroleum from dead leaves wouldn't sound plausible to any scientists. How could she explain that the idea had been given to her in a dream that had described all the exact details on how to do it? The equipment needed to turn the leaves into liquid was very complicated. The machine had to be built out of copper and be large enough to produce results. No one would give her the money for this until it could be proven scientifically. The dream didn't tell her how to provide the proof.

The drawings of the machinery had been made, but what needed a lot of work was the wording for how the machine would process the leaves and turn them into an energy source. They had to be dead autumn leaves that had fallen from the trees. It didn't matter what trees they were. The dead matter of the leaves, combined with water and several chemicals, produced liquid energy. It hadn't worked when she had experimented making it on a small scale. Larger machinery operating at high speeds was required to achieve the right results.

Ossie needed a grant of a least half a million dollars in order to even start the research. Discouraged, she sat quietly, thinking of how to present this project to the board. She had an appointment with them at the end of the week. A PhD, Ossie had good credentials. She had her own lab by the time she was 35 and had been working on cancer research when she had her dream. Even though her record was outstanding in her research field, with many grants to support her, the alternative energy field was new for her, and it was way off the beaten track. She realized that her staff felt she was acting a little nuts.

Working long hours with little time for social life hadn't helped. Having just turned forty, Ossie was still very attractive. She was born to an African American family of scientists. Her skin was a soft brown color, and she wore her curly hair clipped tight around her face. Most striking was her long, slim body; she was almost six feet tall and beautifully proportioned. When she was younger she had modeled in order to make money toward her tuition. The agency tried to convince her to continue and go into acting, but science was in her genes.

The scientific community in Washington DC was a tight-knit group. Presenting this proposal was putting her reputation on the line, and several close friends had tried to convince Ossie to wait until she had more definite data to submit. She still had time to cancel her appointment.

Now she sat quietly and concentrated on the project. What could she do to convince them to give it a shot? She scrupulously examined every thought and then placed each one in her heart to process it even further. She felt this was using both sides of her nature, the masculine and feminine. She employed her masculine side– her mental agility–while focused on the planning stages, whereas her feminine side was tuned in to creative inspiration as she reflected on the ideas that rose from that source. She needed both now.

Ossie was also aware that there was balance in nature and in this project. If she could only show how such balance operated to produce energy! Dead leaves no longer had elementals (earth, water, air, fire) in them. Even though they are dead matter, when ground up in water and certain chemicals, the leaves would change. The elementals in the water and chemicals could absorb the dead matter and create a new substance by birthing and forming new elementals. The dream had indicated that there were chemicals that could do that, but it didn't name them. That was to be a major part of the research.

Suddenly, Merlin, her Border collie puppy, came bouncing into the kitchen and knocked his water dish over. She saw that there was a dead leaf, probably from his paw, floating on the surface of the spilled water. She thought about how oil floated on the surface of water. So what was in this leaf that was similar to oil? Nothing really.

She continued to think and mentally placed the thoughts in her heart, still processing everything that way. At the end of an hour she was ready to write. She took out the original proposal and began working on it, expanding the concepts and introducing some new ones. She was just halfway through when the phone rang. Ossie answered it and heard the voice of her brother on the other end. "Ossie, come out with us this evening. I know you've been working all day and you need a break."

"Darius, I would love to but I can't. I'm on a roll now with the proposal. I can't stop."

"Just come out for a drink then. It will loosen your thinking. I promise it won't be more than a couple of hours."

"Okay, but let's go in the neighborhood, and let's make it an hour." Reluctantly, she closed down her computer and changed from jeans into a nice outfit.

They went to a local restaurant and sat in the bar. Darius and Maria, his wife, would stay and eat there. Ossie was close to them both, mainly because they were all scientists and could talk the lingo together. Darius taught science at the University, and Maria worked in a lab there, also doing cancer research. Both felt Ossie's project was too far out and had tried to talk her out of presenting it until she had better data. The first thing Ossie said when she saw them was, "Let's not discuss my project or I'll go home."

With that established, they talked about the family and politics. Washington was a very interesting town to live in, and they were part of the academic community there. A few of their fellow academics were friends with some top senators, and they shared the Washington gossip.

"Did you find out if John had any connections with the review board I'll be seeing next week?" Ossie hoped for an affirmative.

"I asked a few people, John being one of them, and yes, he and Ann, his wife, both know Isaac Newman, the president of the board. I asked them to put in a good word for you, and they said they would make a couple of calls. I think John also knows another board member, but that's still not going to get your project funded if it's…."

Ossie interrupted him, "Okay, let's change the subject. Thank you for the help."

An hour later, she looked at her watch and got up to leave. Turning to go, she bumped into a man coming by their table.

"I'm so sorry," he said, and he bent down to pick up the purse he'd knocked out of her hand.

"It was my fault too." She smiled up at him. He was very attractive—tall, dark-haired, dark-skinned, in his forties, and most of all, when he smiled back, he looked like a teenager who had done something wrong and couldn't hide it.

"Can I at least buy you a drink as compensation?"

"Well, I don't think so. I really have to work, but… Yes, I would love a drink." She followed him to a vacant table.

"Look at her, and she didn't even introduce us," Maria said to Darius.

"She doesn't know him herself. How could she? But I'm shocked that she would accept. I guess it was an instant attraction for her to forgo her work."

As they sat down, they introduced themselves. His name was William Walters, and he mentioned he was an engineer. Soon they were in a deep discussion about her project. He thought it fascinating.

What am I doing? I shouldn't be telling him this much, but she kept on. She even made a couple of drawings on her napkin of what she thought the machinery should look like. He picked up the drawings, studied them and then redid them, making some engineering corrections.

"The machines don't have to be as big as you think. You could cut the size in half, or even smaller, and it would still work for the experimental stage. You mainly have to develop the right combination of chemicals, and that can be done on a small scale."

"If you're right, that would make it much easier to fund." Then they talked about why she felt the machines had to be large, and he explained why they didn't need to be.

Finally, she said, "You know, I think you're right. I'm going to look at this again and draw it up differently. How can I thank you enough? You've been a great help. If it goes through I will hire you to build these for me."

"You can thank me by having dinner with me next week after your meeting. Besides, I want to hear all about it."

They exchanged cards and Ossie returned home to revamp the proposal.

Working day and night, she completed the final draft a day before the meeting. She made copies and hand-delivered them to the Office of Alternative Energy office so they could review the proposal beforehand.

The next morning was a cold winter day in Washington. As Ossie grabbed a cab to go downtown, snow showers started. Her whole body chilled, and she hoped it wasn't a bad omen.

The Office of Alternative Energy was in a government building on Independence Ave. When she arrived at the appointed time, the receptionist looked at the appointment book and didn't find her name listed.

Ossie gave her the letter with the appointment stated in it. The receptionist excused herself and went into the boardroom, coming back shortly after.

"Yes, they can see you today, after lunch. Come back at three o'clock. But where are your proposals? The board should have gotten them ahead of time."

"I brought them yesterday morning, right to this desk. There was another woman here. She said she would personally give them to each reviewer on the board."

"That must have been Lillith, she's a temp. You should never have given them to her. She probably dumped them. Give me your copy and I'll have more made right away."

Ossie was feeling very concerned, "Fine, but I'll wait and get it back from you as it's my only copy."

It was ten in the morning and five hours before the meeting. The snow was coming down fast now, and she didn't want to go home in case it would be too difficult to get a cab later on. What to do? The National Gallery of Art was only a few blocks away, so she decided to go there. Braving the winds of Constitution Avenue, she arrived only to discover it was closed. A sign on the door said it would be closed a couple of days for repairs.

"Damn!" she said. Huddled by the door of the Museum, she opened her purse to check how much cash she had brought with her. As she pulled out her wallet, a card fell out. She saw that it was William's card and the address was fairly close by. Why not see if he had a free office for her to wait in? She used her cell, and he answered. She explained what had happened.

"Yes, come over right away. I would love to see you."

She arrived, breathless and freezing, and in just a few minutes he had her settled in a big chair and drinking steaming coffee.

"Oh, what a relief. Everything is going wrong." She told him about the mistakes that had been made.

"Sometimes when things are blocked it can be good news. Can I look at the proposal?"

Ossie handed it to him, and while he was studying it, she closed her eyes and sank further into the soft cushions.

"You need to explain how these machines process the leaves and chemicals. It's not clear."

"That's because I don't know how it can be done. I haven't a clue."

"Well, I do." He thought for a minute. "Let me come with you and explain it."

"You can do that?"

"Of course. Why don't you take a nap? You're tired, and I'll work on this. I'll wake you at one, and we can order lunch."

Ossie went to sleep immediately and had a dream. In the dream she saw the machines more clearly. They were much smaller than before, and she even saw bottles of chemicals, enough to get a couple of names. Waking up, she wrote them down quickly. When William came to wake her, she told him what had happened.

"That's great. I think you should tell them about your dreams."

"They'll think I'm cuckoo."

"Maybe not. I think it's the best chance you have. They'll want data, and the best data you have is recurring dreams about the project. My feeling is you should tell them."

"I know the scientific community. They won't buy it."

"They are more astute and intuitive then you know. Believe me, tell them."

"I'll have to play it by ear."

They arrived promptly at 3 p.m. The meeting was in full session, and when they walked in at least one member visually showed surprise at seeing William. She was an older woman, in her sixties; very elegant with an aristocratic charm that was apparent in the way she dressed.

"William, what are you doing here?"

"I'm here to explain some of this project, mainly the equipment, for my friend, Dr. Parsons. I didn't know you were on this board, though it makes sense knowing your background."

He looked around the room at the other members of the board, saying, "I hope it's not going to be a problem since Mrs. Walters is my mother."

Isaac Newman, the President, stood up and shook their hands as he said, "I don't think it's a problem. The equipment certainly isn't explained adequately in the grant proposal." He then introduced them to the other members of the board.

One in particular gave Ossie a chill. His name was Ruel Sullivan. He was a short, elderly man with gray hair and a beard. When she shook his hand, he gave her a sullen look that bordered on contempt. He made her so nervous that she toppled a glass of water and grabbed her copy of the proposal just in time. Suddenly she was a little girl who was always clumsy and making messes.

Quickly, she called upon her Higher Self and asked it to take over and calm her anxiety. They were all watching her, waiting for her explanation of the project.

"I'm a scientist. I think many of you know about the cancer research that has built my reputation in this community." She smiled and continued, "and some of you may think it weird, knowing my background, that I would be presenting this project for funding." She looked directly at Ruel.

"We live in a society that is suffering from a lack of resources, mainly because we have abused and misused them throughout the years. My proposal will create a form of energy that will cost very little to produce. It involves gathering dead leaves and utilizing their fiber to produce a vast source of liquid fuel that can run our cars, heat our homes and replace gas and oil, which is dwindling in production."

"But how do we know this will work?" asked Isaac. "This proposal doesn't give us any data."

"I can supply the data in a year, but first I need the money to develop and invent the equipment for the research."

"None of us can tell by this proposal how your leaves and chemicals will work. In fact, it's quite outrageous to even present this to us." Ruel said, his voice cold.

William stood up. "I agree. It is outrageous, and this planet needs a new form of fuel, which is also outrageous."

He continued, "Let me show you how these machines will work." He took out some large drawings, taped them on a board on the wall and then, very carefully, explained the technology of the equipment and how it would work to pulverize the leaves without making them lose any of their substance. It was a brilliant presentation that impressed everyone, especially Ossie.

"That does explain the process very well, but how do we know what the product will be? It could be liquid paste as far as we know," laughed Ruel.

Ossie retorted, "Or it could be liquid fuel. Isn't it worth the research to have such a breakthrough?"

Another man murmured, "It could be a pipe dream and a waste of money."

William looked at Ossie meaningfully, and she knew that the look meant: "They're not buying it, so there's nothing to lose."

"Okay, I didn't want to tell you this, but I have to. This is not just a silly notion I came up with. Some say that Einstein came up with his whole theory of relativity in a dream state. He would think about it and fall asleep holding ball bearings in his hands. When he did fall asleep, the ball bearings would roll out and wake him in a semi-sleep state. That's where he received his ideas, and that's how his theory of relativity came into being. I am not comparing myself to Einstein, but I saw this machine functioning and making liquid fuel in a dream, and today I dreamt the same dream and even saw the names of a couple of the chemicals. This idea was given to me so I could research it and help us in the energy crisis. I know it's true, and you may think I'm nuts, but I'm not."

The room fell into silence. Then, Sophia Walters spoke, "My dear, I for one do not think you are crazy. In fact, I believe you are a genius—maybe not an Einstein, you're much prettier— but you are genuine. I believe in dreams, and I think some of my colleagues here do, too. This world is too complicated; we must realize that there is much that is unknown to us. Making fuel from leaves or any other part of nature is most possible. All our drugs come from plants, and somewhere, someone had to have the intuition to listen and to experiment with them."

Ruel scowled, but the others all nodded in agreement. "I think it's time to take a vote," Isaac said. Turning to Ossie and William, he asked them to wait outside the room.

They sat quietly together in the hall, not talking. William picked up her hand and held it, which felt very comforting.

Finally, after what seemed an eternity, the conference door opened, and Isaac came toward them. "Congratulations, we will give you the grant, but the next time you submit you must show us more data and more results."

The others, except for Ruel, followed him with good wishes. After much hand-shaking, Ossie and William left the office. She was in such a daze that William had to put his arm around her to keep her from falling.

"Let's celebrate," he said. "No more work today. We can start tomorrow if that's all right with you."

"More than all right!" Ossie reached up and kissed him lightly.

Commentary

The story's two main characters, Ossie and William, perform the "dance of opposites." Each already has a fairly good balance of the positive masculine and feminine, and together, they create a new, deeper balance of these energies, weaving back and forth between the two opposite states of being. When such a combination exists, creativity abounds. The reason this combination works for them is because they fully respect each other's intuition, creativity and application.

Ossie's inspiration emanates from deep within her unconscious and is expressed as dreams. This energy, purely feminine, begins to turn into the masculine when she describes her dreams to William and he offers solutions to her that help her manifest her inspiration. The whole process is continually replicated in our breathing in and breathing out. This is just one simple example of the completely natural pairing of these two energies. When we breathe in, the feminine is active; when we expel breath, the masculine is in play.

Humanity's evolutionary challenge is to learn how to balance these energies as this couple does. If we look at the world today through the lens of such balance, we have a long way to go. Here are some examples: During this epoch of terrorism, which is spreading around the world, the negative masculine is behind the acts of violence. At the same time, there is a beam of light in those countries that are training such terrorists because women, who have been relegated to their homes and hidden away, are now coming to the forefront and becoming leaders. To translate that into this book's language, there is a protesting transformation going on from the negative feminine to the positive masculine. This is also true in certain areas on the African continent where women-run businesses and enterprises are springing up like green plants in the desert.

At this point in our history, the best we can do is create a balanced way of being for ourselves, so that we live more fully with a rich inner life (the feminine) and a productive outer life (the masculine).

Exercise:

For this exercise, you will need to refer to the charts in Chapter 13. This exercise is about improving the balance of the masculine and feminine within you. If you are in a relationship or partnership of any kind, it is also about understanding your interactions with each other.

Study the two charts of Chapter 13 and how you graded yourself on the charts. Then make lists of your positive masculine and feminine characteristics and of your negative ones; add any traits that are not in the charts. Notice which positive aspects are weak, or not well developed in you, and which ones are strong. Are there any that are perhaps too strong? As you study your lists, really try to get a sense of the balance of your masculine and feminine characteristics.

Reflect on how you can use the feminine in its positive aspects and how you can use the masculine in its positive aspects. In order to do this, are there any specific qualities of the positive feminine and positive masculine that you need to develop more fully? Do you need to be conscious of where and how you use these negative traits to change these habits?

Really think about how you'd like to improve your inner balance of the two energies, and then decide on a first step you can take toward that. Do a nightly review (Exercise in Chapter 5) to keep track of how you are doing, both within yourself and in your interactions.

If you are currently in a close relationship: Take time to reflect on your partner's characteristics as well as your own, also reflect on how the two of you relate. Then ask yourself: How can I balance my feminine and masculine to make our relationship work more positively?

If you aren't in a relationship this is about looking at your inner balance and seeing what you need to work on to make balance happen.

21
The Potential of the Feminine and Masculine

Our last chapter is about broadening the concept of balancing the feminine and masculine by taking it into a community and showing how it can become a model for good governance.

This type of model can expand into all branches of government, and hopefully, in the future, will become a prototype for social structures, organizations, and, ultimately, national and international relationships:

The roar of the wood-sawing engines drowned out all the other sounds. Sophia felt overwhelmed, not only by the noise but also by the destruction of the woods. The huge machines were cutting down trees like they were matchsticks. She pressed down hard on the gas pedal to speed up her car. Behind her, the other cars and trucks followed, moving as quickly as possible over the road leading to the demolition crew.

Leaping out of her car, she ran to the foreman, waving the court order that would make them halt the work. The foreman signaled to his crew to stop the engines while he read the order. Several townspeople joined Sophia, waiting for his response.

Shaking his head, he said, "You can't do this! This is private land, and the owner can do anything he wants with it. There are no logging restrictions, we checked that."

"What you're doing isn't logging. Logging is allowed. This is clear-cutting of the forest. Logging leaves trees and new growth." Sophia pointed at the bare ground where the trees had been removed, and all that remained was uprooted dirt and stumps.

She added, firmly, "Remove your crew and don't return unless you have permission from the court. If you or any of your men come back, you'll all be under arrest."

"Does Mr. Hutchins know about this?"

"He does now. Someone is handing him a notice as we speak." Just as she said this, the foreman's cell phone rang.

"Yes, they just stopped us. What should I do?"

After he hung up, he turned back to her. "We'll see you in court. It better be soon cause we have a hundred acres to clear."

That evening there was a special town meeting, which most people in the community attended.

Sophia stood up to speak. She was the mayor of the town Ariel, a beautiful New England town known for its lakes, mountains and woodlands. It was considered to be a place where travelers could camp and enjoy the beauty of nature at its finest. Sophia had been the mayor for over a year and was very much loved by her constituents and community. She was in her early 30's and small, with long brown hair and hazel eyes. Her enthusiasm and warmth made people feel included and accepted. She listened to others with focused intent, which was why she was so well liked by all who met her.

"My friends, we have a monumental issue around the well-being of our beautiful environment. A developer, Clay Hutchins, just bought over a hundred acres of our lovely woodlands and is mass destroying every tree on it. His company plans to build hundreds of houses side by side, and that will bring not only second homers to the town but also many permanent residents. If he does this, it will overcrowd our small town. It will ruin our lakes and trails if we have too many people using them, and it will definitely overcrowd our school. "

"I thought we had regulations that require two acres to a homestead," called out a man in the back of the large meeting room.

"That's true for Ariel, but his acres are divided between our town and Osborn, which has no regulations."

"How'd that happen?" asked Harry, a newcomer in town.

"It's complicated. Osborn is a very small village. It's really two farms and a gas station."

"Oh, I thought it was part of Ariel."

Tony, a handyman, grinned and said, "Nope, Osborn may be tiny, but it seceded from Arial a hundred years ago. Had some kind of dispute with us they couldn't work out."

"What can we do then?" asked an elderly woman.

"That's why I called this meeting, Maureen. We must find a way to convince Mr. Hutchins to change his development plans.

"If he leaves some of the trees, and makes each building lot two or three acres, then it won't be as bad, but if he continues to cut everything down and follows his current plan, it would ruin the environment, not to mention what it will do to the animals that reside there. The acreage also has a natural lake that supplies water to the wildlife. He wants to clean out the lake and put in docks for the more expensive homes."

Rebecca Morris raised her hand. "But how can we convince him not to make these changes? We're talking about a lot of money here. He's not going to want to give that up."

Sophia replied, "I think it's important for all of us to come up with ideas about the best way to approach this issue. I suggest that we divide up into groups and do some heart storming and brain storming."

"I know what brainstorming is, but what's heart storming?" asked Jerry Baum.

Sophia placed her hand over the center of her chest. "Heart storming is about connecting with your heart and using your intuition to come up with new ideas and solutions. Then you take those ideas and brainstorm ways to implement them. It's a balance of the feminine and masculine sides within each of us, whether we're male or female."

"This town has done a lot of that before with our projects. We just didn't have a name for it," said Sophia's husband, William.

She smiled at him, "Yes, that's true, and that's why this community is so harmonious and balanced."

Ever the pessimist, Ruel Jones commented, "That might be fine in our community projects, but I see this as a strictly legal and political issue. Trying to change a developer's plans is futile. Maybe we should just figure out how to contain this new group of people."

Sophia replied, "That will be our last resort if we can't come up with a better plan, but right now, let's assume we have the means to make him change his plan. Even if he builds fewer houses, we'll still have to strategize ways to assimilate the new additions. The issue now is to convince him and his company to cut back on his plans."

"Impossible!" mumbled Lillith, Ruel's wife.

Sophia ignored her remark and quickly glanced at William. She continued, "I propose we do this differently, like when we've worked as teams on specific projects. Those were small teams. We have almost a hundred people here, and it's important that everyone take part in designing this plan. I'd like you to break into teams that represent all the aspects of this community. Many of you are professionals who commute to Albany or Springfield, and some of you work more locally. We need diversity on this project, so I've made a chart of teams that I believe represent the interests of this community."

She uncovered a large pad of paper that was resting on an easel:

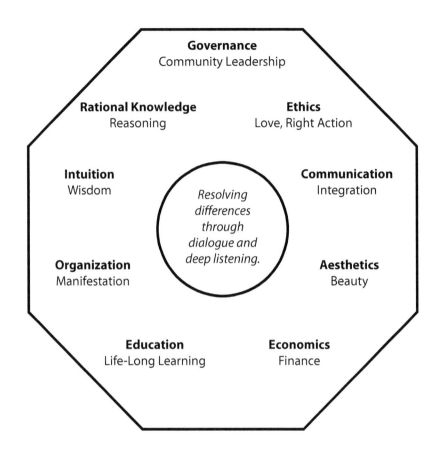

"I've been thinking about this model for some time," she said. "The situation we're facing now provides us with a perfect opportunity to see how it works. It's really about creatively designing a solution, not 'problem solving.' As a town, we have an opportunity to communicate from the perspectives of the major interest groups in the community in order to resolve issues such as the one we're facing now. We can approach this in a most creative way."

"Let's begin with what we already have: Governance! The Governance Team will contain a representative from each of our Town Boards – the Select Board, the Planning Board, the Conservation Commission, and the Department of Health. They'll work together to create guidelines, so when the final plan is put together, it will move through each individual Board more swiftly than usual. This will certainly be an incentive for Mr. Hutchins and, hopefully, will change his attitude to a more cooperative one. At the same time, it will help the people buying these homes by easing their path to living here. They'll feel welcomed into becoming a part of our growing community."

Sophia paused to look around, "All the rest of the teams will be composed of you! If you want to be part of the process, pick a team you'd like to work with. For some of you it will be obvious. For example, Ethics, if you're interested in social and ecological issues, the job of this team would be to come up with a plan that would inspire Mr. Hutchins to look more deeply at the environmental issues involved with his project."

A couple of women started whispering in the back, but stopped when Sophia looked at them. She smiled and continued, "The function of the Communication Team would be to do some research about Mr. Hutchins: his way of life, his personal interests, anything that would help us know him better. This information will be given to the other teams to help them develop their processes."

"This is really too far out," protested Ruel.

"It works, believe me. I've seen it implemented," Sophia shot back. "The Rational Knowledge Team will need to research Hutchins' company and its goals, with the idea of convincing him to change his plans and conveying to him how both he and our community could benefit."

Millie, the gas station owner, haltingly raised her hand. "Excuse me, Sophia, but why is it called the Rational Knowledge Team?"

"By 'rational knowledge' I mean information gathering, such as our situation now. In general, rational knowledge is the counterpart to intuitive knowing, and when these two modes work together, it's a powerful combination."

"As some of you know, organizations, businesses and governments have made difficult decisions with such techniques as brainstorming. That's one way – and, don't misunderstand me, it's basically a good way, but it's unbalanced. Up until very recently, decision-makers have been using only half of their faculties. That half is what I'm calling rational thinking, and, don't misunderstand me — it's important. Once we have a plan, that team will be able to implement it. Without our rational minds, nothing would get done, but now there's a new wave of decision-making coming to the fore that includes using our intuitive faculties."

Sophia looked thoughtful as she said, "Well, actually, it's not really a new wave, but a very old wave. Spend time with our Native American brothers and sisters and see how they make decisions! It's purely intuitive and right brained. A truly balanced approach to the decision-making process involves uniting both approaches. Our intuition is easily as powerful as our capacity for rational thinking. That's true for both men and women!"

A young woman, Nancy, asked, "Doesn't this have something to do with our masculine and feminine sides?"

"Yes, it does, Nancy. That's exactly right. Most people consider rational thinking to be strictly masculine, and it is! The intuition is the feminine, but the truth is that some men are more intuitive thinkers. Einstein was a good example. Also, some women are more rational thinkers. Ideally, we all should have an even balance of both. So, it really makes sense to include both aspects in our team model."

Lillith burst out laughing. "I'm sorry," she said, "but this is off the charts! What on earth is that about? An Intuition Team? How droll!"

The moderator pounded his gavel. "You're out of order, Lillith!"

Unfazed, Sophia said smoothly, "Let's continue with the Intuition Team. I'd like to propose that Mary lead that team, as she's led a lot of workshops around developing the intuition. Any of you who are interested in learning how to work with your intuition might want to join her."

"We have four teams to go," she continued. "The Aesthetic Team!" Her smile was engaging. "You know, this town is charming, and the landscape is beautiful around here, enough to keep an artist busy for a lifetime. Beauty is our greatest commodity. The Aesthetic Team's job will be to convince Mr. Hutchins that preserving the beauty of the area will help him sell his high level homes. So, anyone interested in working with that team, whether you're artists or you love being out in nature, please volunteer."

Checking her notes, she continued, "What's next? Education!" Looking around the room, she asked, "Is Steve here? Oh, there you are. Steve, now that you're retired from teaching, would you be willing to take on the Education Team?"

He grinned, "I thought you'd never ask. Of course!"

She looked at the chart. "Great! We're moving right along. Ah, the Organization Team. The job of this team will be to take a broad overview of the whole process and to structure the order of the presentations to Mr. Hutchins. There may additional costs concerning our involvement in changing Hutchins' project including court costs that we need to know about."

"Now," Sophia said. "Finally, we need an Economics Team to balance the money we may need to come up with in addition to what we have in reserve. Anyone interested?" No one volunteered.

"How about you, Rick?"

Leaning against the wall in the back of the room, he asked, "Doesn't the Governance Team take care of that?"

She replied, "Not really. This team would also work with the needs of families who may be having a hard time financially and need a tax abatement and check parts of the town that need repairs and upgrading."

With a frown, Rick said, "I must say, I don't feel good about all this. What about our local businesses, my dairy farm, Harry's vegetable stand, the sheep farm! How about the fact that we could profit from all the people who would be moving here with Hutchin's original plan? There would be more people buying our products. I think we should add a category for people who will profit from the original project."

Ruel nodded. "That's a good point." Looking at Sophia, he said, "You're asking us all to agree that Hutchins' housing development will not be good for the town. Rick's right, he'd profit from it."

"Maybe and maybe not," she replied, addressing Rick again. "The stores Mr. Hutchins is planning to put into the development would take away from your business, Rick. In fact, you could research everything he plans to do and how it would affect local businesses, either negatively or positively. For example, how the additional people will pollute the atmosphere with gasoline fumes from more automobiles."

"I hadn't thought about that," he mumbled. "Too much pollution could ruin my crops."

After a frowning moment, and with an embarrassed grin, he said, "Okay, I'll take on the Economics Team."

Sophia smiled, "That's it! Each team that doesn't already have a leader will choose someone to represent it. In the week before we meet with Hutchins, all the leaders will meet, and we'll come up with an overall plan to present to him."

Lillith said with a scowl, "You really think Hutchins will go for this? All he'll need to do is dismiss our efforts!"

Sophia replied smoothly, "We have to be prepared for any or all of his reactions. The Communication Team will need to address what his reactions might be and decide the best way to respond to whatever happens."

"How much time do we have?" asked Hal, the General Store owner.

Sophia said, "Mr. Hutchins is trying to get a court hearing as soon as possible, but we asked for at least a month to prepare. First it's important to present the plan to him, and hopefully, if he agrees, we won't have to take it into the court system, but in case we can't convince him, we'll still have to prepare for a court hearing."

"So we need to have this plan ready for Hutchins in three weeks? That's impossible!" Ruel was shaking his head.

"Not really," she responded. "Granted, we're all busy, so we'll have to spend some evenings and weekends working on this." She looked around at the faces and saw a mix of expressions. "I know it's difficult, but this is about saving our lovely town and preserving the beautiful environment around us. Think about what would happen if we doubled our population from this one development!"

By the meeting's end, the teams had been organized and they had selected their leaders. Each group scheduled two or three meetings a week for two weeks, to be followed by the group leaders' meeting on the third week, where they would plan the presentation for Hutchins.

It was a busy time with the deadline facing them. Residents who had never been particularly active in town affairs became involved in teams of their choosing. Meetings were held in peoples' homes, in the firehouse and in the church meeting room.

Even those few who were fearful of change, and who were often oppositional, were caught up in the wave of communal responsibility and joined teams.

The two weeks seemed to fly by. The general store and post office at the crossroads of the town doubled with activity and energy. At the beginning of the third week, Sophia and Will met with the group leaders at their home to prepare for the meeting with Mr. Hutchins. Will had set up the easel with Sophia's diagram, which now included the leaders' names.

The group leaders were seated in a circle in the living room when Sophia turned to Mary, a petite, grey-haired woman in her late fifties. "Mary, do you mind going first? What came out of your collective intuitions about this issue?"

"The first thing we did was meditate on the question, 'what's the best way to deal with Mr. Hutchins and his project?'"

Placing her hand on the middle of her chest, she said, "We put this question into our hearts and focused on it. Each person came up with a piece of the puzzle, and when we put it all together, we ended up with a very simple strategy. When we meet with him on Saturday, we must all come from our hearts and truly welcome him. It should not be a pretense, but we should welcome him like good-hearted neighbors, like we welcome each other. This will help us appeal to his better nature. First, I'm sure he'll be surprised, but it will be a positive surprise. He thinks he's coming to battle us."

"Good," said Sophia. "Anything else?"

"Oh, yes! When we probed a little deeper, most of us got the sense that he's actually thinking about moving here."

"Well, that changes the landscape!" commented Will.

"Of course, we need to get some information about his family from you, Germaine, and validate that it's true. If it is true..."

Germaine, a real estate agent and leader of the Rational Knowledge Team, interrupted her with, "You're absolutely right, Mary. In fact, just yesterday he called and made an appointment with me. He wants to look at some land while he's here."

She then looked apologetically at Mary, saying, "Sorry, you're not finished."

"Mostly, just one more thing. The last question we meditated on was, 'if it is true that he'll be moving here, what is the best way to deal with him?' Bottom line, our strong impression was that we must be very confident and firm, and we must appeal to the fact that he may likely be a neighbor and part of our community."

"That's good. Thanks, Mary."

Sophia turned to Germaine, " Please continue your report. Does he have a family?"

"Married, with four kids. We spent some time going over the possible obstacles we will face with him. From researching other projects of his, we found out that he's spread all over the country. We actually found some articles written about him, some positive and some negative. It's not going to be easy. Our sense is that there could be severe bumps along the way. With the research we did, he comes across as really stubborn and somewhat autocratic. Legally, he can do anything he wants with the Osborn land. That puts us in somewhat of a bind. He could build the Empire State Building there and nobody could stop him."

"Well, let's hope not," grimaced Sophia. "Yuki? Please tell us what your Ethics Team came up with."

Yuki, an elderly Japanese woman, nodded. "This is a very big issue. Ethics is a path. I like to think of it that way. As people who live in a community, we have learned to treat each other ethically — with respect! But when people come and cut down our trees like they were doing, it is disrespectful, to us and to nature!

"This community lives on ethical principles. I've lived here for many years. When I first came, people looked at me suspiciously. I was different, so they were wary. As I've grown, the town has grown. Now I would never live anywhere else. We have built ethics into our daily lives. We help each other — like the 'barn raising' last year. So many people turned out to help.

"Now, we feel that when Mr. Hutchins comes we must start to create a respectful relationship with him. We must be strong but respectful. We should treat him as we would treat anyone who wants to live here."

"Thank you, Yuki," said Sophia. "Who'd like to report next? Bruce?"

A middle-aged man with white hair nodded. He was on the town's Select Board, and he was the team leader for Governance.

"Here's what we've come up with in our conversations. Because the Osborn part of this project has escaped any zoning regulations, it's our majority opinion that we should follow the first option, proving that the plan for this development is too much of an encroachment on our town. Our concerns are the environment — we agree with Yuki's group — and also the overcrowding of our school.

"We found out that a piece of his land used to belong to Ariel, so we can try to claim that it should therefore go under our zoning code. Another way we can prevail is by permanently halting the clear cutting of the trees. We do have state restrictions on that. He had no right to cut down the ones that he did, and he can be fined for that."

He paused and looked at his notes. "We've also been looking into the possibility of gaining control of the Osborn land. We asked the town counsel to check the history of that acreage to see if there's any way we can take it over. If we can, then Hutchins will have to abide by our zoning code there. For all we know, that land may have also been part of our township at one time. We're putting all these plans in motion and hope to have an answer before traipsing off to court."

"Thanks, Bruce," said Sophia. "Now, let's hear from Communications. Hank?"

The young, wiry black man nodded. Hank was a website designer by trade.

"We've done as much research as we can about Hutchins in this short time. The most important thing to know about him is that, as Germaine said, he's created a number of developments like this around the country. He's made a fortune doing this. From what we've gathered during our research, he's a tough businessman.

"He's from Ohio, lives in Elyria and is pretty involved with the life of the town, politically and socially. At one point he was president of the local Kiwanis club. He seems to be a mover and shaker in his community.

"We tried to imagine how flexible he might be in his thinking. It is hard to know. We got the impression that he's fairly conservative in general, but that he is also pretty fair in his dealings with people. At least, we think so!"

He smiled at Sophia. "We've also done some research on his private life in the hope that we can get to know him better. He's married and has four children, two under the age of ten. We tried to find out if he definitely plans to settle here. Sounds like that might be true. We could appeal to him as a parent and talk to him about the benefits that have resulted from the effort we've put into creating the community we have now, like racial diversity and general openness and respect for each other. As you all know, we've worked very hard to get where we are now. We're not perfect, but we hold a vision of neighborliness, helpfulness and openness that draws us forward.

"In our conversations we mostly all agreed that we should approach him in this way first. That's pretty much it! But, we're not sure that he'll even want to listen to us if our plan cuts into his potential profits. The tough part of all this is the lack of zoning restrictions in Osborn. Since we have no jurisdiction over that land at all, we have no say there. Half of his project could end up being a bunch of boxes with no trees, and the other half could end up being zoned with a small amount of trees. What a mess!"

"Thank you, Hank. Let's take a 15-minute break. Please come back promptly everybody."

As the group milled around the room, Sophia and Will talked quietly together. When the break was over, everyone settled in their chairs. Sophia held up her hand.

"We still haven't resolved the issue of affordable housing in town. Most of you know that the state mandated that all towns plan for this. It just occurred to us that the Osborn part of the acreage could be designated for affordable housing. Because of the lack of zoning restrictions, we'd have the flexibility to create anything we want there. We've all been coming from a place of fear and assuming that this situation is all negative. My dear husband just came up with a great idea!" She grinned at him. "Tell them!"

Will, his gray eyes twinkling, said, "I've been reading about 'green housing' communities lately. Just the other night I saw a film about one that was established a few years ago in Colorado. These communities are springing up all over the country. They're using the most advanced energy technologies, and the best part is, green housing projects are affordable! If we can convince Hutchins to reserve the Osborn land for that purpose, we can be as experimental and creative as we want and solve the mandated housing issue at the same time."

Sophia commented, "It's beginning to come together. Steve! How about the Education Team?"

Steve said, "We've defined our team pretty broadly. Not only do we represent education in its literal sense, but we also represent learning on all levels and for all ages. So, in the context we're talking about now, we can facilitate learning in relation to green building if we reach that point in the negotiations. Looks like we'd better start learning about green building ourselves!

"We can also emphasize to him, if he plans to move here, how much his children can benefit by living in this community. Even if he sends his children to private schools in the area, there are many fun community events for children other then playing on the beaches and going on hikes. Our mountains have skiing, we freeze over the firehouse pavilion in the winter for skating and we have regular sports all summer in the town park. We also teach our children to respect the beauty of nature."

"Great," said Sophia. "Let's move on to Nancy's Aesthetics Team. How about it, Nancy?"

"Wait," said Steve. "Just one more thing. I propose that we include our kids to be part of the nature projects of this committee, at least starting with kids at about age 11. That's when kids often become idealistic. It's a great age, developmentally. Those kids who are interested could rotate in meetings."

"Wonderful idea," enthused Sophia. "You're absolutely right. They're our future!"

Nancy nodded. "Obviously, our Aesthetics Team totally agrees with the importance of maintaining the beauty of our town. So, we put together something for us to use when we meet Mr. Hutchins. It's pretty much what we've just talked about, that this area attracts people because of the beautiful landscape. I really can't understand how he wouldn't know that. We think that fact alone should convince him that he shouldn't cut down all the trees. We also have put together a collection of beautiful photographs to show him of different areas in the town. They will be part of our presentation to him."

"Good, Nancy," said Will. He looked around the room and saw that Rick's hand had shot up.

"Hey, Rick. Let's hear from you now."

Will waved him forward to the front of the room. "Give us a report on your research of the businesses in town."

Rick stood up, grinned at everyone and said, "Well, as far as Finance goes, Joe and I decided that less is better. I mean less people and less cars. Like you said, we don't need any more pollution than we have already. What with the summer visitors, we don't need to get any bigger. So far we're doing all right economically. It makes me think of what my dad used to say, 'Grow your crops and don't get greedy.'

"We'll talk to Hutchins about our farms and their produce and about how organically grown vegetables will appeal to his wealthier homeowners. His new housing can help our farmers financially. They will need to grow more to accommodate them. It's better to develop that aspect than to add more stores that'll bring in more traffic."

With that, he waved and returned to his seat.

"Thanks, Rick," said Will, looking around the room. "Oh, there you are, Frank. Come on up. Last but not least, Frank from the Organization Team."

"Fine!" said the elderly man who'd been listening intently to the others. His craggy lined face and piercing blue eyes showed evidence of a strong character and a sense of humor.

"Well now, we've thought a lot about 'organization' for the last couple of weeks, mostly to define our role in this process. I think our group was pretty thoughtful and came up with a fine approach. A major point is that our function is to be watchdogs over the whole process. What's happening now is something pretty unique. This town, like every other town, has been run solely by town officials! I mean, we vote them in – shucks, I was a selectman for eight years, but this is something else!"

He grinned at Sophia and Will. "You two have turned us upside down in a good way, so we can see everything from another viewpoint.

"It seems to me we're building a community of concerned citizens who will have some clout, instead of leaving it all up to the town boards. So, our group came up with the idea that our main job now is to oversee this whole project and make sure that we're all on the same page. And, looking into the future, after this project is resolved we will also deal with the next issue that comes along. I think we've really got something, not just for overseeing this project, but for creating a citizens' group that's not just political, but that can contribute to our way of life in this town."

"You mean we should make this a permanent body?" asked Yuki.

"Why not?" said Frank. "I think it's a great idea. An informed and active citizenry would add so much to this town. With this arrangement, the Town Boards and all of the rest of us can work together!"

"That's the idea," said Sophia. "It truly would be democracy in action!"

She smiled at Will, who stood up and said, "All right! This is the group that will meet with Hutchins. It's set for this coming Saturday at 10 am."

Sophia added, "One more thing! I really like the idea of appealing to his better nature. It can't hurt to try. Let's do what we talked about earlier, welcome him to the neighborhood. Show him that it's in his interest to follow our plan, that more is not necessarily better and that squeezing people together is not the answer.

"I'll be introducing you as leaders of each segment. All you need to do is represent your own perspective and offer him an option that will be profitable to him. Hopefully, he'll feel good about it because he'd be creating something that benefits people."

It rained the day of the meeting with Hutchins. Clouds had tracked across the sky, prodded by gusty winds. Change was in the air. In the Town Hall meeting room, Sophia and Will had arranged the chairs in a semi-circle. The team leaders arrived and were talking quietly. Hutchins and his attorney Joel Brown arrived promptly at 10 o'clock. Sophia and Will greeted them at the door and led them into the meeting room.

"We want to introduce you both to the leaders of the teams who comprise our citizen governance model."

"Citizen governance?" Hutchins said. "I've never heard of that."

The team leaders each greeted him as Sophia introduced them.

"Well, well, well!" he said, as he and his lawyer, Brown, sat down. "How does all this work?"

Sophia then turned her brightness on Hutchins. "First of all, we all want to welcome you to Ariel. As you know, your plan was quite a shock for us, but we are a welcoming community, and it is in this spirit that we meet you here.

"I may be the Mayor, but we feel decisions should be discussed and agreed upon in the community. When your project came up, we formed teams to examine all the aspects of the situation. That's why the team leaders are here. They represent many more people who are on their teams, and their reports are a result of those people working together."

Mr. Hutchins looked surprised, "I've never heard of anything like that before."

"We hope you'll become a part of this governance system if you plan to move here."

Hutchins' face turned pink and attorney Brown cleared his throat. Hutchins looked at him as if for support.

"Umm, so you're not going to try to block Mr. Hutchins from tree cutting?" he asked Sophia.

Hank then said to Hutchins, "As leader of the Communications Team, I'd like to tell you something about our town. We've all been talking about this project, as you may guess, for the last month. As you well know, people have moved here from all over, and they stay because of the beauty of this place. They build their houses, put down their roots, and raise their children. Very few leave. Now, we have a proposal for you that I think you'll like."

Hutchins said, "Yes? Let's hear it."

"We'd like to work with you on your plan at no charge. I guarantee you'll attract more people than honey attracts bees. Mr. Hutchins, uh, can I call you Clay?" Without waiting for a reply, he said, "We've looked at some of your other projects around the country, and if it's like any of those, it won't work here."

"Why not?" asked Hutchins, frowning.

"Because this is a different part of the country! People are attracted here because of the beauty of the area. By ripping out trees you are shooting yourself in the foot. Trust me, in this case, more is not better!"

Bruce than said, "I'm head of the Governance Team, and I'm also on the Select Board. Our research has discovered that a part of your land could still be under the jurisdiction of Ariel. Rather than go to court, we would like to suggest that you designate that land for the building of beautiful, expensive housing, each on two acres of land. We have many homes like that here, which should be an attraction to the people that can afford them."

He added, "If you do move here, we hope that you will own one of these homes and become a part of this community. I understand you have children. They'll love the sports and swimming that are part of this community. There are several naturalists here who are very knowledgeable, and they love to take the kids on nature hikes. There are also many animals here that have their habitats in our mountains and woods, which is another reason the clearing of trees is so harmful. It not only destroys the beauty that has been here for centuries, but it also harms the wild life."

Hutchins nodded.

"If you would like, the other teams will present their ideas."

"That would be fine. I'd be interested in hearing them."

After each group reported, Sophia said, "We've been looking for a place where we can provide affordable housing. It's a state mandate and something we've wanted to do anyway, but just because it's affordable doesn't mean it can't be beautiful. I'm sure you have the know how to combine the trees on the Osborn land with inexpensive housing. As a matter of fact, if you were willing, our team could take on the project and submit plans to you for your approval. It will cost far less if you don't have to clear-cut the land. We would want to use some of the green technology that's available now. Of course, it would be subject to your approval."

"This is all very interesting," said Hutchins, glancing at his attorney. "I'll have to think about it, of course."

"One more thing," said Sophia. "I'd like to clarify what we've been doing during these past few weeks. We've put together an image of what we hope will be the outcome of your project – it is a model of community living that combines the best qualities of life we are capable of, such as neighborliness, mutual support, creativity and fun. The combination of the individual reports that we've presented to you can make this vision a reality if you are open to it. We hope that you are."

Just then, the door burst open, revealing Ruel and Lillith, their eyes blazing. Hutchins glanced at them, stood up and said, "Well, it's clear that I have a lot to think about. This has been very educational. For one thing, I'll need to talk to my contractor and my designers to see what's possible, and what it would all cost. I'll be getting back to you in a few days."

"Let's go, Joel," he said to his attorney.

Ruel blocked their way and said, "You must be John Hutchins. Sorry we missed the meeting. Our car broke down. This is my wife, Lillith. We'd like a quick word with you. How about we treat you both to a coffee and pastry across the street. We have some information that you should hear before you decide anything!"

Suddenly, Sophia and Will felt that a grey pall had seeped through the windows into the meeting room.

Commentary

There is no ending to this story or to this book. We could have wrapped it up like a nice, neat package, but that would be totally unrealistic. The underlying message of this book is that the integration of the positive masculine and feminine must begin first in each of us as individuals and then spread outward into our relationships and social structures, such as organizations and communities. Ultimately it should spread into our national and international relations. If we look at the chaos that exists in our present world, we will see that the rising tides of conflict are mainly in the Middle East and in other corners of the planet where the social systems are still in the Dark Ages in terms of balancing the masculine and feminine. In this country, we surely have a long way to go, but at least over the last century we have seen movement. If we look around the world, we will see that there are pockets of integration slowly emerging.

Clearly, the evolution of humanity, which will hopefully one day lead to a futuristic world that is at peace, has a very long way to go. In this story, Sophia and Will are attempting to bring balance into their community through their model of citizen governance. If you study the diagrams in this chapter you can get a sense of the interwoven masculine and feminine processes within it. Sophia suggests that their town's new governance model could germinate and spread to other towns. If this happened, it could become the foundation of a new type of local governance, which would integrate positive masculine and feminine qualities on a societal level.

Try to imagine what the world could become once such balance was achieved. For a family, the message to girls would be of freedom and respect in those countries where women are veiled both physically and psychically, and to boys, the message would be one of equality and of respect for the feminine spirit within themselves.

We all have a choice: To pursue the path of Sophia and Will and lead an inner life that is balanced between our positive feminine and masculine sides, or to be taken over by the negative, life-sucking energy of Ruel and Lillith. We, the authors, hope that this book has opened the door for those of you who wish to embark on the journey of inspiration and outer expression.

This chapter was about how, when people start to integrate the masculine and feminine, it can go beyond personal relationships and even communities, eventually extending to countries and the whole planet.

We feel that it is up to each one of us to work on the balance within ourselves, within our relationships, and within our communities; only then can this chapter end positively.

We hope you will do the exercises in this book and come to a better understanding of your own masculine and feminine balance, and we hope that this experience will help you with your own personal growth.

Selected Books from MSI Press

CPSIA information can be obtained
at www.ICGtesting.com
Printed in the USA
FSHW010831241118
53941FS